The Faber Book of
Poems and Places

The Faber Book of
POEMS AND PLACES

Edited with an Introduction

by

GEOFFREY GRIGSON

faber and faber

First published in 1980
by Faber and Faber Limited
3 Queen Square, London WC1N 3AU
First published in Faber Paperbacks in 1983
Phototypeset by Western Printing Services Ltd, Bristol
Printed in Great Britain by
Richard Clay (The Chaucer Press) Ltd, Bungay, Suffolk
All rights reserved

British Library Cataloguing in Publication Data

The Faber book of poems and places
1. English poetry
2. Great Britain—Poetry
I. Grigson, Geoffrey
821'.008'032 41   PR1195.G/

ISBN 0-571-11647-7
ISBN 0-571-13008-9 PBK

—O quis me gelidis in vallibus ISCÆ
Sistat, et ingenti ramorum protegat umbra!

HENRY VAUGHAN, after Virgil,
Georgics 2, 488–9

Contents

	page
Content by Locality	9
The Poets	18
Introduction: On Poems and Places	31
A Prologue	35
The South	44
The South-West	64
Oxford and the Midlands	103
London	143
Cambridge and the Eastern Counties	180
Wales and the Marches	209
The Lakes and the North	244
Scotland and Ireland	271
France	306
Italy	341
Acknowledgements	371
Some Notes and References	373
Index of First Lines	381

Content by Locality

A Prologue   pages 35–43
1   The Properties of the Shires of England, Anon
2   The Rivers Come to the Hall of Proteus, Edmund Spenser
3   Rivers Arise, John Milton
4   *from* John of Gaunt's Speech, William Shakespeare
5   The Halcyon's Nest, Giles Fletcher
6   (The fresh green lap), William Shakespeare
7   Britannia, James Thomson
8   O My Mother Isle, S. T. Coleridge

The South   pages 44–63
9   Dover, the Samphire Cliff, William Shakespeare
10   Dover Beach, Matthew Arnold
11   The Old Summerhouse (on the Thames, Taplow), Walter de la
       Mare
12   Green Sussex, Alfred Tennyson
13   To Penshurst (Kent), Ben Jonson
14   Erith, on the Thames, Anon
15   Hops along the Medway, Christopher Smart
16   Twilight Time (Shoreham, Kent), Samuel Palmer
17   Above the Medway, A. J. Munby
18   Tunbridge Wells, Lord Rochester
19   In Romney Marsh, John Davidson
20   November in the Isle of Wight, Alfred Tennyson
21   A Forsaken Garden (Isle of Wight), A. C. Swinburne
22   At Farringford (Isle of Wight), Alfred Tennyson
23   The Needles' Lighthouse, Charles Tennyson Turner
24   Jersey, Victor Hugo
25   Sark, A. C. Swinburne
26   A Guernesey, Victor Hugo
27   Églogue (Procession of 'teatotallers' at Peter-Port), Victor
       Hugo

The South-West   pages 64–102

28 On the Ridgeway, Andrew Young
29 The Houseless Downs, George Ferebe
30 Stonehenge, Sir Philip Sidney
31 Stonehenge, Michael Drayton
32 Salisbury Plain and Stonehenge, William Wordsworth
33 In Love, at Stonehenge, Coventry Patmore
34 Epilogue (Wiltshire), John Meade Falkner
35 Salisbury: the Cathedral Close, Coventry Patmore
36 In a Cathedral City (Salisbury), Thomas Hardy
37 Bristol, Richard Savage
38 Weston-super-Mare, Valery Larbaud
39 Widcombe Churchyard (near Bath), Walter Savage Landor
40 Nightfall on Sedgemoor (Somerset), Andrew Young
41 Brent (Somerset), William Diaper
42 Apostrophe to the Parret (Sedgemoor), E. H. Burrington
43 The Quantocks, William Wordsworth
44 Seen from the Quantocks, S. T. Coleridge
45 Bournemouth, Paul Verlaine
46 La Mer de Bournemouth, Paul Verlaine
47 Ad Henricum Wottonem (Bere Regis, Dorset), Thomas
        Bastard
48 Domicilium (his birthplace at Higher Bockhampton,
        Dorset), Thomas Hardy
49 The Roman Road (Dorset: Puddletown Heath), Thomas
        Hardy
50 Once at Swanage, Thomas Hardy
51 Overlooking the River Stour (Dorset), Thomas Hardy
52 On Sturminster Footbridge (Dorset), Thomas Hardy
53 Wessex Heights, Thomas Hardy
54 To Dean-bourn, Robert Herrick
55 A Devonshire Walk, William Browne of Tavistock
56 The Course of the Tavy (Devonshire), William Browne of
        Tavistock
57 On Seeing a Fine Frigate off Mount Edgecumbe (Plymouth
        Sound), N. T. Carrington
58 Devonshire Scenes, Coventry Patmore
59 The Marble-Streeted Town (Plymouth), Thomas Hardy
60 Hardy's Plymouth, Geoffrey Grigson
61 The River Lynher (East Cornwall), Richard Carew
62 Green Slates (Penpethy Quarries, near Delabole), Thomas
        Hardy
63 After a Journey (North Cornwall, St Juliot), Thomas Hardy

64 The Phantom Horsewoman (North Cornwall, near Beeny
       Cliff), Thomas Hardy
65 At Carbis Bay (Cornwall), Arthur Symons
66 Back again for the Holidays (Trebetherick, North
       Cornwall), Sir John Betjeman
67 Tregardock (North Cornwall), Sir John Betjeman
68 Tresco (in the Isles of Scilly), Geoffrey Grigson

Oxford and the Midlands   pages 103–42
69 A Love Sonnet (an undergraduate outing: Oxford), George
       Wither
70 Binsey Poplars (Oxford), Gerard Manley Hopkins
71 Philomela (Oxford and Bagley Wood), John Crowe
       Ransom
72 *from* The Scholar-Gipsy (Oxford and Berkshire), Matthew
       Arnold
73 *from* Thyrsis (Oxford and Berkshire), Matthew Arnold
74 Laleham: Matthew Arnold's Grave (Berkshire), Lionel
       Johnson
75 To Oxford, Gerard Manley Hopkins
76 By Magdalen Bridge, Oxford, Gerard Manley Hopkins
77 Oxford Bells, Gerard Manley Hopkins
78 Duns Scotus's Oxford, Gerard Manley Hopkins
79 Oxford, Lionel Johnson
80 Autumn on the Upper Thames (Kelmscott), William
       Morris
81 Elegy Written in a Country Churchyard (Stoke Poges,
       Buckinghamshire), Thomas Gray
82 The Poplar-Field (Olney, Buckinghamshire), William
       Cowper
83 On Westwell Downs (the Cotswolds), William Strode
84 The High Hills (the Cotswolds), Ivor Gurney
85 Possessions (near Gloucester, on the Cotswold Scarp), Ivor
       Gurney
86 Adlestrop (the Cotswolds), Edward Thomas
87 Dawns I Have Seen (over Cotswold), Ivor Gurney
88 Song (Severn meadows), Ivor Gurney
89 Elver Fishermen on the Severn: Two Gloucester
       Fragments, Ivor Gurney
90 Bredon Hill (Worcestershire), A. E. Housman
91 Larches (Cotswold, Malvern, Bredon), Ivor Gurney
92 The Dwindling Forest of Arden (Warwickshire), Michael
       Drayton

93 At Arley (Worcestershire), Andrew Young
94 I Remember, I Remember (Coventry), Philip Larkin
95 Charnwood Forest, Michael Drayton
96 Sir Gawayn Goes to Receive His Return Blow from the
       Green Knight (Ludchurch, Staffordshire), Anon
97 An Ode written in the Peak, Michael Drayton
98 The Trent, Michael Drayton
99 The Trent Again, Michael Drayton
100 The Retirement (Dovedale, Derbyshire), Charles Cotton

London   pages 143–79
101 To the City of London, William Dunbar
102 London Lickpenny, Anon
103 Prothalamion, Edmund Spenser
104 Twicknam Garden, John Donne
105 His Tears to Thamasis, Robert Herrick
106 His Return to London, Robert Herrick
107 Of London Bridge, James Howell
108 London in 1646, Henry Vaughan
109 Solitude and Reason, Abraham Cowley
110 About in London, John Gay
111 Hampton Court, Alexander Pope
112 London Suburbs, William Cowper
113 London, William Blake
114 The Young Wordsworth's London, William Wordsworth
115 Composed upon Westminster Bridge, William Wordsworth
116 London, from Hampstead Heath, William Wordsworth
117 Lines written in Kensington Gardens, Matthew Arnold
118 London Snow, Robert Bridges
119 À Germain Nouveau, Paul Verlaine
120 Londres, Paul Verlaine
121 (L'immensité de l'humanité), Paul Verlaine
122 A Ballad of London, Richard le Gallienne
123 There, Paul Verlaine
124 Symphony in Yellow, Oscar Wilde
125 Sonnet Boiteux, Paul Verlaine
126 London Town, Lionel Johnson
127 Vœux du Poète, Valery Larbaud
128 Londres, Valery Larbaud
129 Regent's Park Terrace, Bernard Spencer
130 The Rainbow (Essex), Gerard Manley Hopkins
131 In Epping Forest, John Clare
132 London versus Epping Forest, John Clare

133 The Green Roads (Essex: Hainault Forest), Edward Thomas

Cambridge and the Eastern Counties   pages 180–208
134 Cambridge and the Cam, Phineas Fletcher
135 Residence at Cambridge, William Wordsworth
136 He Revisits Cambridge, Alfred Tennyson
137 The Old Vicarage, Grantchester, Rupert Brooke
138 Sunrise in Summer (over the Northamptonshire Fens), John
        Clare
139 Northamptonshire Fens, John Clare
140 Bedford Level (Cambridgeshire), John Dyer
141 A Lament for the Priory of Walsingham (Norfolk), Anon
142 In Suffolk, George Crabbe
143 East Anglian Fen, George Crabbe
144 Peter Grimes at Aldeburgh, George Crabbe
145 The Suffolk Shore, George Crabbe
146 Evening by the Sea (Suffolk), A. C. Swinburne
147 Where Dunwich Used To Be (Suffolk), A. C. Swinburne
148 Suffolk: by the North Sea, A. C. Swinburne
149 Horsey Gap (Norfolk), Anon
150 Lincolnshire: from the Wolds to the Fens, Ben Jonson
151 The Fen-men of Lincolnshire's Holland, Michael Drayton
152 Lincolnshire's Holland Speaks of Her Waterfowl, Michael
        Drayton
153 The High Tide on the Coast of Lincolnshire (1571), Jean
        Ingelow
154 Paysage en Lincolnshire, Paul Verlaine
155 Boston, Lincolnshire, Anon
156 Lincolnshire Shores (at Mablethorpe), Alfred Tennyson
157 Somersby, Lincolnshire: after Leaving the Rectory, Alfred
        Tennyson
158 Lincolnshire Wolds and Lincolnshire Sea, Alfred Tennyson

Wales and the Marches   pages 209–43
159 The Snowdon Sunrise, William Wordsworth
160 The Primrose, being at Montgomery Castle, John Donne
161 Upon the Priory Grove (Brecon), Henry Vaughan
162 The Shower (at Llangorse Lake, Breconshire), Henry
        Vaughan
163 The Storm (Breconshire), Henry Vaughan
164 To the River Isca (the Usk), Henry Vaughan
165 'So Have I Spent on the Banks of Ysca' (Breconshire), Thomas
        Vaughan

166   The Waterfall (Breconshire), Henry Vaughan
167   The Brecon Beacons and the Black Mountains, Henry
           Vaughan
168   Grongar Hill (Carmarthenshire), John Dyer
169   Pent-y-Wern (Denbighshire), Arthur Hugh Clough
170   Cader Idris at Sunset, Charles Tennyson Turner
171   The Artist on Penmaenmawr, Charles Tennyson Turner
172   At a Welsh Waterfall, Gerard Manley Hopkins
173   Moonrise (Denbighshire), Gerald Manley Hopkins
174   Hurrahing in Harvest (Denbighshire), Gerard Manley
           Hopkins
175   Days that Have Been (South Wales), W. H. Davies
176   Lines Composed a Few Miles above Tintern Abbey, William
           Wordsworth
177   The Hushing of the Wye, Alfred Tennyson
178   Fern Hill (Llangain, Carmarthenshire), Dylan Thomas
179   On Malverne Hilles (Colwall?), William Langland
180   Aurora Leigh Reaches Herefordshire from Italy (Colwall),
           Elizabeth Barrett Browning
181   Acton Beauchamp, Herefordshire, Anon
182   Wenlock Edge (Shropshire), A. E. Housman
183   Hughley Steeple (Shropshire), A. E. Housman
184   The Churchyard on the Sands (Cheshire: the Wirrall), Lord de
           Tabley
185   The Sands of Dee (Cheshire), Charles Kingsley
186   Braddan Vicarage (Isle of Man), T. E. Brown

           The Lakes and the North   pages 244–70
187   On the Solitary Fells around Hawkshead, William Wordsworth
188   Wordsworth Skates on Esthwaite Water, William Wordsworth
189   It was an April Morning (Easedale), William Wordsworth
190   On Windermere, William Wordsworth
191   On Ullswater, William Wordsworth
192   I Wandered Lonely as a Cloud (Ullswater), William
           Wordsworth
193   The Voice of the Derwent, William Wordsworth
194   The Fair below Helvellyn, William Wordsworth
195   A Recollection of the Stone Circle near Keswick, John
           Keats
196   Southey Looks out of the Window at Greta Hall, Robert
           Southey
197   Elegiac Stanzas Suggested by a Picture of Peele Castle
           (Lancashire), William Wordsworth

198 To the River Duddon: After-thought, William Wordsworth
199 The Youth of Nature: Wordsworth's Country, Matthew Arnold
200 Wordsworth's Grave, Matthew Arnold
201 Hayeswater, Matthew Arnold
202 After Floods on the Wharfe (Yorkshire, West Riding), Andrew Marvell
203 In Teesdale (Yorkshire, North Riding), Andrew Young
204 Haworth Churchyard (Yorkshire, West Riding), Matthew Arnold
205 Ilkla Moor (Ilkley, Yorkshire, West Riding), Anon
206 The Wensleydale Lad (a visit to Leeds), Anon
207 Inside the Cave (Chapel-le-Dale, Yorkshire, West Riding), Geoffrey Grigson
208 Ma Canny Hinny (a search in Newcastle-upon-Tyne), Anon
209 At Elsdon (Northumberland), George Chatt
210 Elsdon (Northumberland), Freda Downie
211 Tweed and Till, Anon

Scotland and Ireland   pages 271–305
212 O Caledonia!, Sir Walter Scott
213 Arran, Anon, tr. Kenneth Jackson
214 The Quiet Tide near Ardrossan (Ayrshire), Charles Tennyson Turner
215 To the Merchantis of Edinburgh, William Dunbar
216 Edinburgh from the Pentland Hills, Sir Walter Scott
217 Melrose Abbey (Roxburghshire), Sir Walter Scott
218 The Dreary Change (Selkirkshire), Sir Walter Scott
219 To S. R. Crockett (the Pentland Hills), Robert Louis Stevenson
220 Ettrick Forest in November (Selkirkshire), Sir Walter Scott
221 The Village of Balmaquhapple, James Hogg
222 Afton Water (SE. Ayrshire), Robert Burns
223 To Aberdein, William Dunbar
224 On an Aberdeen Favourite, Anon
225 My Heart's in the Highlands, Robert Burns
226 A Highland Glen near Loch Ericht (Inverness-shire), Arthur Hugh Clough
227 Inversnaid (Stirlingshire), Gerard Manley Hopkins
228 Rannoch, by Glen Coe (Argyllshire), T. S. Eliot
229 The Fair Hills of Ireland, Sir Samuel Ferguson
230 The Dead at Clonmacnois, T. W. Rolleston
231 He Hears the Bugle at Killarney, Alfred Tennyson
232 Mountown! Thou Sweet Retreat (Dublin), William King

233   At Ballyshannon, Co. Donegal, William Allingham
234   The Fairies (Co. Donegal), William Allingham
235   The Groves of Blarney (Blarney Castle, Co. Cork), R. A. Millikin
236   Castle Hyde (Fermoy, Co. Cork), Anon
237   The Attractions of a Fashionable Irish Watering-Place (Passage West, Co. Cork), Francis Sylvester Mahony
238   By the Pool at the Third Rosses (Co. Donegal), Arthur Symons
239   The Wild Swans at Coole (Coole Park, Galway), W. B. Yeats
240   The Lake Isle of Innisfree (Lough Gill, Sligo), W. B. Yeats
241   In Kerry, J. M. Synge
242   Prelude (Wicklow), J. M. Synge
243   Carrickfergus, Louis MacNeice
244   Dublin, Louis MacNeice
245   Glen Lough (Co. Donegal), Geoffrey Grigson
246   Sligo and Mayo, Louis MacNeice
247   Ireland, John Hewitt

France   pages 306–40

248   Heureux qui, comme Ulysse (Liré, Maine-et-Loire), Joachim du Bellay
249   Ode: Les Louanges de Vandomois (the Vendômois, Loir-et-Cher), Pierre de Ronsard
250   Ode à la Fontaine Bellerie (Couture, Loir-et-Cher), Pierre de Ronsard
251   Elegie sur la forêt de Gastine (the Vendômois, Loir-et-Cher), Pierre de Ronsard
252   Blois, Pierre de Ronsard
253   Gastine and the Loir (the Vendômois, Loir-et-Cher), Pierre de Ronsard
254   Ode de l'élection de son sepulcre (Couture, Loir-et-Cher), Pierre de Ronsard
255   Midsummer Day in France, Alexander Hume
256   Stances (St-Paterne-Racan, Indre-et-Loire), Honorat de Racan
257   It is a Beauteous Evening, Calm and Free (on the beach at Calais), William Wordsworth
258   To the Seine, André Chénier
259   Près d'Avranches (Manche), Victor Hugo
260   Le Retour à Tancarville (on the Seine, near Le Havre), Pierre Lebrun
261   Lettre (from Champagne), Victor Hugo

262 Un Peintre (Brittany, baie de Douarnenez), José-Maria de Heredia
263 Scenes from Carnac, Matthew Arnold
264 Au Vieux Roscoff, Tristan Corbière
265 Paris aux Réverbères, Alphonse Esquiros
266 Nocturne Parisien, Paul Verlaine
267 At Dieppe: Green and Grey, Arthur Symons
268 Châteaux de Loire, Paul Claudel
269 The Cathedral and the Plain (Notre-Dame de Chartres and the Beauce), Paul Claudel
270 Le Pont Mirabeau (Paris), Guillaume Apollinaire
271 Fishing Boats in Martigues, Roy Campbell

Italy   pages 341–69
272 Satan's Legions and the Beech Leaves of the Casentino, John Milton
273 Frater Ave atque Vale (Sirmione, Lago di Garda), Alfred Tennyson
274 Près des Bords où Venise, André Chénier
275 On the Bridge of Sighs, Lord Byron
276 Ruins of Rome, Joachim du Bellay and Edmund Spenser
277 Rome by Metella's Tomb, Lord Byron
278 The Grave of Keats, P. B. Shelley
279 At Pompeii, P. B. Shelley
280 Piano di Sorrento (between the Gulfs of Naples and Salerno), Robert Browning
281 Italy of the South, Robert Browning
282 Upon Apennine Slope, Arthur Hugh Clough
283 Aurora Leigh's Return to Italy, Elizabeth Barrett Browning
284 Up at a Villa—Down in the City, Robert Browning
285 Rome, Arthur Hugh Clough
286 The Valley and Villa of Horace, Arthur Hugh Clough
287 Cypresses (Fiesole), D. H. Lawrence
288 Bare Almond-Trees (Taormina, Sicily), D. H. Lawrence
289 Almond Blossom (Torrente Fontana Vecchia, Taormina), D. H. Lawrence
290 Peace (Taormina, below Etna), D. H. Lawrence

The Poets

William Allingham (1824–89)
233 At Ballyshannon
234 The Fairies

Anon
  1 The Properties of the Shires of England
 14 Erith
 96 Sir Gawayn Goes to Receive His Return Blow
102 London Lickpenny
141 A Lament for the Priory of Walsingham
149 Horsey Gap
155 Boston, Lincolnshire
181 Acton Beauchamp, Herefordshire
201 Winwick, Lancashire
205 Ilkla Moor
206 The Wensleydale Lad
208 Ma Canny Hinny
211 Tweed and Till
213 Arran
224 On an Aberdeen Favourite
236 Castle Hyde

Guillaume Apollinaire (1880–1918)
270 Le Pont Mirabeau

Matthew Arnold (1822–88)
 10 Dover Beach
 72 *from* The Scholar-Gipsy
 73 *from* Thyrsis
117 Lines Written in Kensington Gardens
199 The Youth of Nature
200 Wordsworth's Grave
201 Hayeswater

204   Haworth Churchyard
263   Stanzas from Carnac

Thomas Bastard (1566–1618)
 47   Ad Henricum Wottonem

Sir John Betjeman (b. 1906)
 66   Back Again for the Holidays
 67   Tregardock

William Blake (1757–1827)
113   London

Robert Bridges (1844–1930)
118   London Snow

Rupert Brooke (1887–1915)
137   The Old Vicarage, Grantchester

T. E. Brown (1830–97)
186   Braddan Vicarage

William Browne of Tavistock (1591–1643?)
 55   A Devonshire Walk
 56   The Course of the Tavy

Elizabeth Barrett Browning (1806–61)
280   Aurora Leigh Reaches Herefordshire
283   Aurora Leigh Returns to Italy

Robert Browning (1812–89)
280   Piano di Sorrento
281   Italy of the South
284   Up at a Villa—Down in the City

Robert Burns (1759–96)
222   Afton Water
225   My Heart's in the Highlands

R. H. Burrington (fl. 1830–80)
 42   Apostrophe to the Parret

Lord Byron (1788–1824)
275   On the Bridge of Sighs
277   Rome, by Metella's Tomb

Roy Campbell (1902–57)
271   Fishing Boats in Martigues

Richard Carew (1555–1620)
61   The River Lynher

N. T. Carrington (1777–1830)
57   On Seeing a Fine Frigate off Mount Edgcumbe

George Chatt (1839–90)
209   At Elsdon

André Chénier (1762–94)
258   To the Seine
274   Près des bords où Venise

John Clare (1793–1864)
131   In Epping Forest
132   London versus Epping Forest
138   Sunrise in Summer
139   Northamptonshire Fens

Paul Claudel (1873–1914)
268   Châteaux de Loire
269   The Cathedral and the Plain

Arthur Hugh Clough (1819–61)
169   Pont-y-Wern
226   A Highland Glen near Loch Ericht
282   Upon Apennine Slope
285   Rome
286   The Valley and Villa of Horace

S. T. Coleridge (1772–1834)
8   O My Mother Isle
44   Seen from the Quantocks

Tristan Corbière (1873–1914)
264   Au Vieux Roscoff

Charles Cotton (1630–87)
100   The Retirement

Abraham Cowley (1618–67)
109   Solitude and Reason

William Cowper (1731–1800)
 82   The Poplar-Field
112   London Suburbs

George Crabbe (1754–1832)
142   In Suffolk
143   East Anglian Fen
144   Peter Grimes at Aldeburgh
145   The Suffolk Shore

John Davidson (1857–1909)
 19   In Romney Marsh

W. H. Davies (1871–1940)
175   Days that Have Been

Walter de la Mare (1873–1956)
 11   The Old Summer House

Lord de Tabley (1835–95)
184   The Churchyard on the Sands

William Diaper (1686?–1717)
 41   Brent

John Donne (1573–1631)
104   Twicknam Garden
160   The Primrose, being at Montgomery Castle

Freda Downie (b. 1929)
210   Elsdon

Michael Drayton (1563–1631)
 31   Stonehenge
 92   The Dwindling Forest of Arden
 95   Charnwood Forest
 97   An Ode Written to the Peak

98   The Trent
99   The Trent Again
151   The Fen-men of Lincolnshire's Holland
152   Lincolnshire's Holland Speaks of Her Waterfowl

Joachim du Bellay (1522–60)
248   Heureux qui, comme Ulysse
276   Ruins of Rome

William Dunbar (1465?–1530?)
101   To the City of London
215   To the Merchantis of Edinburgh
223   To Aberdein

John Dyer (1694–1758)
140   Bedford Level
168   Grongar Hill

T. S. Eliot (1888–1965)
228   Rannoch by Glen Coe

Alphonse Esquiros (1812–76)
265   Paris aux Réverbères

John Meade Falkner (1858–1932)
 34   Epilogue

George Ferebe (fl. 1593–1613)
 29   The Houseless Downs

Sir Samuel Ferguson (1810–86)
229   The Fair Hills of Ireland

Giles Fletcher (1588?–1623)
  5   The Halcyon's Nest

Phineas Fletcher (1582–1650)
134   Cambridge and the Cam

John Gay (1688–1744)
110   About in London

Thomas Gray (1716–71)
 81   Elegy Written in a Country Churchyard

Geoffrey Grigson (b. 1905)
 60   Hardy's Plymouth
 68   Tresco
207   Inside the Cave
245   Glen Lough

Ivor Gurney (1890–1937)
 84   The High Hills
 85   Possessions
 87   Dawns I Have Seen
 88   Song
 89   Elver Fishermen on the Severn
 91   Larches

Thomas Hardy (1840–1928)
 36   In a Cathedral City
 48   Domicilium
 49   The Roman Road
 50   Once at Swanage
 51   Overlooking the River Stour
 52   On Sturminster Footbridge
 53   Wessex Heights
 59   The Marble-Streeted Town
 62   Green Slates
 63   After a Journey
 64   The Phantom Horsewoman

José-Maria de Heredia (1842–1905)
262   Un Peintre

Robert Herrick (1591–1674)
 54   To Dean-bourn
105   His Tears to Thamasis
106   His Return to London

John Hewitt (b. 1907)
 47   Ireland

James Hogg (1770–1835)
 21   The Village of Balmaquhapple

Gerard Manley Hopkins (1844–89)
  70 Binsey Poplars
  75 To Oxford
  76 By Magdalen Bridge
  77 Oxford Bells
  78 Duns Scotus's Oxford
 130 The Rainbow
 172 At a Welsh Waterfall
 173 Moonrise
 174 Hurrahing in Harvest
 227 Inversnaid

A. E. Housman (1859–1936)
  90 Bredon Hill
 182 Wenlock Edge, Shropshire
 183 Hughley Steeple

James Howell (1594?–1666)
 107 Of London Bridge

Victor Hugo (1802–85)
  24 Jersey
  26 A Guernesey
  27 Églogue
 259 Près d'Avranches
 261 Lettre

Alexander Hume (1557?–1609)
 255 Midsummer Day in France

Jean Ingelow (1820–97)
 153 The High Tide on the Coast of Lincolnshire (1571)

Lionel Johnson (1867–1902)
  74 Laleham
  79 Oxford
 126 London Town

Ben Jonson (1573?–1637)
  13 Penshurst
 150 Lincolnshire: from the Wolds to the Fens

John Keats (1795–1821)
195   A Recollection of the Stone Circle near Keswick

William King (1663–1712)
232   Mountown! Thou Sweet Retreat

Charles Kingsley (1819–75)
185   The Sands of Dee

Walter Savage Landor (1775–1864)
 39   In Widcombe Churchyard

William Langland (c. 1330–88)
179   On Malverne Hilles

Valery Larbaud (1881–1957)
 38   Weston-super-Mare
127   Vœux de Poète
128   Londres

Philip Larkin (b. 1922)
 94   I Remember, I Remember

D. H. Lawrence (1885–1930)
287   Cypresses
288   Bare Almond-Trees
289   Almond Blossom
290   Peace

Pierre Lebrun (1785–1873)
260   Le Retour à Tancarville

Richard le Gallienne (1866–1947)
122   A Ballad of London

Louis MacNeice (1907–63)
243   Carrickfergus
244   Dublin
246   Sligo and Mayo

Francis Sylvester Mahony (1804–66)
237   The Attractions of a Fashionable Irish Watering-Place

Andrew Marvell (1621–78)
202   After Floods on the Wharfe

Richard Alfred Millikin (1767–1815)
235   The Groves of Blarney

John Milton (1608–74)
3   Rivers Arise
272   Satan's Legions and the Beech Leaves of the Casentino

William Morris (1834–96)
80   Autumn on the Upper Thames

A. J. Munby (1828–1910)
17   Above the Medway

Samuel Palmer (1805–81)
16   Twilight Time

Coventry Patmore (1823–96)
33   In Love at Stonehenge
35   Salisbury
58   Devonshire Scenes

Honorat de Racan (1589–1670)
256   Stances

John Crowe Ransom (b. 1888)
71   Philomela

Lord Rochester (1647–80)
19   Tunbridge Wells

Thomas William Rolleston (1837–1910)
230   Clonmacnoise

Pierre de Ronsard (1524–85)
249   Ode: Les Louanges de Vandomois
250   Ode à la Fontaine Bellerie
251   Elégie sur la forêt de Gastine
252   Blois
253   Gastine and the Loir
254   Ode de l'élection de son sepulcre

Richard Savage (1697?–1742)
  27   Bristol

Sir Walter Scott (1771–1832)
212   O Caledonia!
216   Edinburgh from the Pentland Hills
217   Melrose Abbey
218   The Dreary Change
220   Ettrick Forest

William Shakespeare (1564–1616)
   4   *from* John of Gaunt's Speech
   6   The fresh green lap
   9   Dover, the Samphire Cliff

P. B. Shelley (1792–1822)
278   The Grave of Keats
279   At Pompeii

Sir Philip Sidney (1554–86)
  30   Stonehenge

Christopher Smart (1722–71)
  15   Hops along the Medway

Robert Southey (1774–1843)
196   Southey Looks out of the Window at Greta Hall

Bernard Spencer (1909–62)
129   Regent's Park Terrace

Edmund Spenser (1562?–99)
   2   The Rivers Come to the Hall of Proteus
103   Prothalamion
276   Ruins of Rome

Robert Louis Stevenson (1850–94)
219   To S. R. Crockett

William Strode (1600–45)
  83   On Westwell Downs

A. C. Swinburne (1837–1909)
 21   A Forsaken Garden
 25   Sark
146   Evening by the Sea
147   Where Dunwich Used To Be
148   Suffolk: by the North Sea

Arthur Symons (1865–1945)
 65   Carbis Bay
238   By the Pool at the Third Rosses
267   At Dieppe: Green and Grey

J. M. Synge (1871–1909)
241   In Kerry
242   Prelude

Alfred Tennyson (1809–92)
 12   Green Sussex
 20   November in the Isle of Wight
 22   At Farringford
136   He Revisits Cambridge
156   Lincolnshire Shores (at Mablethorpe)
157   Somersby, Lincolnshire: After Leaving the Rectory
158   Lincolnshire Wolds and Lincolnshire Sea
174   The Hushing of the Wye
231   He Hears the Bugle at Killarney
273   Frater Ave atque Vale

Dylan Thomas (1914–53)
178   Fern Hill

Edward Thomas (1878–1917)
 86   Adlestrop
133   The Green Roads

James Thomson (1700–48)
  7   Britannia

Charles Tennyson Turner (1808–79)
 23   The Needles' Lighthouse
170   Cader Idris at Sunset
171   The Artist on Penmaenmawr
214   The Quiet Tide near Ardrossan

Henry Vaughan (1622–95)
108   London in 1646
161   Upon the Priory Groves, His Usual Retirement
162   The Shower
163   The Storm
164   To the River Isca
166   The Waterfall
167   The Brecon Beacons and the Black Mountains

Thomas Vaughan (1622–66)
165   'So Have I Spent on the Banks of Ysca'

Paul Verlaine (1844–96)
 45   Bournemouth
 46   La Mer de Bournemouth
119   À Germain Nouveau
120   Londres
121   L'immensité de l'humanité
123   There
125   Sonnet Boiteux
154   Paysage en Lincolnshire
266   Nocturne Parisien

Oscar Wilde (1854–1900)
124   Symphony in Yellow

George Wither (1588–1667)
 69   A Love Sonnet

William Wordsworth (1770–1856)
 32   Salisbury Plain and Stonehenge
 43   The Quantocks
114   Young Wordsworth's London
115   Composed upon Westminster Bridge
116   London, from Hampstead Heath
135   Residence at Cambridge
159   The Snowdon Sunrise
 76   Lines Composed above Tintern Abbey
 87   On the Solitary Fells around Hawkshead
 88   Wordsworth Skates on Esthwaite Water
 89   It was an April Morning
 90   On Windermere
 91   On Ullswater

192   I Wandered Lonely as a Cloud
193   The Voice of the Derwent
194   The Fair below Helvellyn
197   Elegiac Stanzas Suggested by a Picture of Peele Castle
198   To the River Duddon
257   It is a Beauteous Evening, Calm and Free

W. B. Yeats (1865–1939)
239   The Wild Swans at Coole
240   The Lake Isle of Innisfree

Andrew Young (1885–1971)
 28   On the Ridgeway
 40   Nightfall on Sedgemoor
 93   At Arley
203   In Teesdale

Introduction: On Poems and Places

Places enter poems, sometimes incidentally, sometimes penetrating the poems as if place were their whole substance. It is not surprising. After all in places we grow up. Place is our external condition; place is garden, field, landscape, woods, fells, springs, rivers, estuaries, beaches, valleys, villages, towns, streets. Place is sunshine, rain, snow, ice. It is west, east, north and south. It is where the seasons change. Our feeling flows into places, and an accumulation of feeling, historical, cultural and personal, flows back from places into our consciousness: 'O fons Bandusiae, O venusta Sirmio'. So there should be more than a vague pastoralism to be experienced from a choice of poems in which place is prominent, either pleasurably or with that sensation which the particular skills of poetry can give to being inevitably sad or (possibly) resigned.

It does not surprise me, and it cannot be smartly dismissed as 'romanticism', or anything other than human, that Tennyson should have written to his fiancée Emily Sellwood, when the Tennysons had to leave the parsonage at Somersby, about the essential friendliness of familiar landscape. He declared: 'A known landscape is to me an old friend that continually talks to me of my own youth and half-forgotten things.' It does not surprise me that the philosophically minded Coleridge at Nether Stowey should have thought of writing a long poem about a stream, 'traced from its source in the hills among the yellow-red moss and conical glass-shaped tufts of bent to the first break or fall, where its drops become audible . . . to the sheep-fold; to the first cultivated plot of ground; to the lonely cottage and its bleak garden won from the heath; to the hamlet, the villages, the market-town, the manufactures, and the sea-port'.

Coleridge never wrote that poem, which would freely have allowed him room for incident and description and for 'impassioned reflections on men, nature and society'. But he says that in preparation for it he walked day by day on Quantock and among its combes, making studies and composing lines 'with the objects and imagery immediately before my senses'.

Earlier in our literature few poets felt landscape more powerfully and with a completer consciousness than Henry Vaughan, living in Breconshire above the Usk, and between the Brecon Beacons and the Black Mountains. It was where he was born, it was the country he returned to from Oxford and London, as a local doctor. He names the Usk frequently, and in poem after poem in which no place is named, we can be fairly sure which actual place was at the front and the back of his mind.

Vaughan's twin brother Thomas, alchemist and clergyman in the same parish, wrote aptly about poems and places, or poems and nature. 'There is in nature a certain chain or subordinate propinquity of complexions between visibles and invisibles.' He told readers they should learn 'to refer all naturals to their spirituals by the way of secret analogy'. In summer we should translate ourselves 'to the fields, where all are green with the breath of God and fresh with the powers of heaven'. Sometimes we should 'walk in groves, which being full of majesty will much advance the soul; sometimes by clear active waters, for by such—say the mystic poets—Apollo contemplated'; and for him too the clearest of active waters were of course those of the Usk winding through his parish.

If 'spirituals' for Thomas Vaughan or Henry Vaughan were Christian ones—'for Nature is the voice of God'—for us three centuries later they must be what each one of us contrives to be vis-à-vis life. In place-poems, in place-passages out of poems, in place-images in poems, even in lines which earn the sneer of being only 'descriptive', a reference is being made of naturals into whatever word you may prefer to Thomas Vaughan's spirituals and invisibles. The greatest poetry, as well as minor poetry, confirms this; it confirms that spirituals without naturals (as in too much of Shelley's verse, let' say) become vapid.

And then, after all, as readers we each have our affairs of heart and mind with particular places and with particular poets. Sirmione, in Lago di Garda, is our peninsula still, and Catullus may still be our poet; and then Tennyson—'all-but-island, olive-silvery Sirmio'—as well. Affections meet, for place and poet, in each particular poem. Is it possible, if we know Piers Plowman—or know only the opening lines of Piers Plowman—to contemplate the world of men from the ledge of the Malverns without having thoughts about Langland; or possible, if we know Piers Plowman, not to think of that extraordinary perch above the counties? And then what about Snowdon and Wordsworth, each to each, each with each; or the primroses of Montgomery Castle and John Donne; or Italy and Browning—Browning seeing the wild tulip up on the hills above Florence

'Mid the sharp short emerald wheat, scarce risen three fingers well,
The wild red tulip, at the end of its tube, blows out its great red bell
Like a thin clear bubble of blood

(lines which first converted me at all to Browning)?

In this anthology I have chosen verse about places in England, ⌐ales, Scotland and Ireland, and the Channel Islands, into all of ⌐hich our emotion flows outward, to be returned to us gladly or ⌐flectively as well.

Across the Channel, up to the present (but how will it be later?) ⌐ır general emotions have flowed with most willingness and famil-⌐ʒity into France and Italy (as in that poem of Browning's which I ⌐ıve quoted). So I add a section for each country. Also it seems to me ⌐gitimately entertaining to discover what at any rate a few French ⌐ets have made in their own lines and stanzas, not only about places ⌐ their country, but about places in our country too; Verlaine, for ⌐stance, 'about'—how 'about' requires the extension of those ⌐verted commas—'about' the fen village in Lincolnshire where he ⌐as so happy, and 'about' London and Bournemouth; or Valery ⌐ırbaud 'about' a wet day in Weston-super-Mare. (I know little of ⌐omparable Italian poetry, though readers may like to be referred to ⌐ıgenio Montale's poem about, or decidedly *'about'*, Eastbourne on ⌐ınk Holiday:

> *'Dio salvi il Re' intonano le trombe*
> *da un padiglione erto su palafitte*
> *che aprono il varco al mare quando sale*
> *a distruggere peste*
> *umide di cavalli nella sabbia*
> *del litorale.*
>
> *Freddo un vento m'investe . . .)*

Translations, by the way, I have eschewed (allowing only a few of ⌐ºenser's translations from du Bellay, one translation from the Irish, ⌐d a stanza or two from the Middle English of *Sir Gawain and the* ⌐⌐een Knight to direct attention to Ludchurch as the place which the ⌐ºet thought of for the site of the Green Chapel and the Green ⌐ʒight's sharpening of his great Danish axe). Translations which are ⌐ºo poems are too uncommon, and just now the thin prosiness of ⌐ntemporary verse translation, on the after-track of Ezra Pound, is ⌐ʒing damage enough to the good name of verse.

GEOFFREY GRIGSON

Note

As a rule, titles have been given to extracts from poems. In every
such case the proper title of the whole poem, the poet's own title, that
is to say, or the title given in standard editions of his work, will be
found in the notes.

1 A Prologue

1 The Properties of the Shires of England

The properte of every shire
I shall you tell, and ye will hear.
  Herefordshire shield and spear:
  Worsetshire wring pear.
  Gloucetershire shoe and nail:
  Bristowe ship and sail.
  Oxenfordshire gird the mare:
  Warwykshire bind bere.
  London resortere:
  Sowtherey great bragere.
  Esex full of good hoswifes:
  Middlesex full of strives.
  Kentshire hot as fire:
  Sowseke full of dirt and mire.
  Hertfordshire full of wood:
  Huntingdonshire corn full good.
  Bedfordshire is nought to lack:
  Bokinghamshire is his make.
  Northamptonshire full of love
Beneath the girdle and not above.
  Lancastreshire fair archere:
  Chestreshire thwakkere.
  Northumbreland hasty and hot:
  Westmorland [tot for sote!]
  Yorkshire full of knights:
  Lincolnshire men full of mightes.
  Cambridgeshire full of pikes:
  Holond full of great dykes.
  Norfolk full of wiles:
  Southfolk full of stiles.
  I am of *Shropshire* my shins be sharp:

Lay wood to the fire, and dress me my harp.
Notinghamshire full of hogs:
Derbyshire full of dogs.
Leicetershire full of beans:
Staffordshire full of queans.
Wiltshire fair and plain:
Barkshire fill the wain.
Hampshire dry and wete.
Somersetshire good for wheat.
Devenshire mighty and strong:
Dorseteshire will have no wrong.
Pinnokshire is not to praise:
A man may go it in two days.
Cornewaile full of tin:
Walis full of goote and kene.
That Lord that for us all did die
Save all these shires. *Amen* say I.

And

2   The Rivers Come to the Hall of Proteus for the Marriage of
the Thames and the Medway

Then was there heard a most celestial sound,
  Of dainty music, which did next ensue
  Before the spouse: that was Arion crowned,
  Who playing on his harp, unto him drew
  The ears and hearts of all that goodly crew,
  That even yet the dolphin, which him bore
  Through the Aegean seas from pirates' view,
  Stood still by him astonished at his lore,
And all the raging seas for joy forgot to roar.

So went he playing on the watery plain,
  Soon after whom the lovely bridegroom came,
  The noble Thames, with all his goodly train.
  But him before there went, as best became,
  His ancient parents, namely th'ancient Thame.
  But much more aged was his wife than he,
  The Ouze, whom men do Isis rightly name;
  Full weak and crooked creature seemed she,
And almost blind through eld, that scarce her way could see.

Therefore on either side she was sustained
  Of two small grooms, which by their names were hight
  The Churne, and Charwell, two small streams, which pained
  Themselves her footing to direct aright,
  Which failed oft through faint and feeble plight:
  But Thame was stronger, and of better stay;
  Yet seemed full ancient by his outward sight,
  With head all hoary, and his beard all gray,
Dewed with silver drops, that trickled down alway.

And eke he somewhat seemed to stoop afore
  With bowed back by reason of the load,
  And ancient heavy burden, which he bore
  Of that fair City, wherein make abode
  So many learned impes, that shoot abrode,
  And with their branches spread all Britany,
  No less than do her elder sister's brood.
  Joy to you both, ye double nursery
Of arts, but Oxford thine doth Thame most glorify.

But he their son full fresh and jolly was,
  All decked in a robe of watchet hue,
  Of which the waves, glittering like crystal glass,
  So cunningly enwoven were, that few
  Could weenen, whether they were false or true.
  And on his head like to a coronet
  He wore, that seemed strange to common view,
  In which were many towers and castles set,
That it encompassed round as with a golden fret.

Like as the mother of the Gods, they say,
  In her great iron charet wonts to ride,
  When to Jove's palace she doth take her way:
  Old Cybele, arrayed with pompous pride,
  Wearing a diadem embattled wide
  With hundred turrets, like a turribant,
  With such an one was Thamis beautified;
  That was to weet the famous Troynovant,
  which her kingdom's throne is chiefly resiant.

impes: scions, shoots	turribant: turban
Britany: Britain	Troynovant: London (New Troy)
her sister: Cambridge	resiant: resident
watchet: light blue	

And round about him many a pretty page
   Attended duly, ready to obey;
   All little rivers, which owe vassalage
   To him, as to their lord, and tribute pay:
   The chalky Kenet, and the Thetis gray,
   The moorish Cole, and the soft sliding Breane,
   The wanton Lee, that oft doth lose his way,
   And the still Darent, in whose waters clean
Ten thousand fishes play, and deck his pleasant stream.

Then came his neighbour floods, which nigh him dwell,
   And water all the English soil throughout;
   They all on him this day attended well;
   And with meet service waited him about;
   Ne none disdained low to him to lout:
   No not the stately Severne grudged at all,
   Ne storming Humber, though he looked stout;
   But both him honoured as their principal
And let their swelling waters low before him fall.

There was the speedy Tamar, which divides
   The Cornish and the Devonish confines;
   Through both whose borders swiftly down it glides,
   And meeting Plim, to Plimmouth thence declines:
   And Dart, nigh choked with sands of tinny mines.
   But Avon marched in more stately path,
   Proud of his adamants, with which he shines
   And glisters wide, as als' of wondrous Bath,
And Bristow fair, which on his waves he builded hath.

And there came Stoure with terrible aspect,
   Bearing his six deformed heads on high,
   That does his course through Blandford plains
     direct,
   And washeth Winborne meads in season dry.
   Next him went Wylibourne with passage sly,
   That of his wiliness his name doth take,
   And of himself doth name the shire thereby:
   And Mole, that like a nuzzling mole doth make
His way still underground, till Thamis he overtake.

adamants: Bristol diamonds
six deformed heads on high: six springs at Stourhead in Wiltshire

Then came the Rother, decked all with woods
  Like a wood god, and flowing fast to Rhy:
  And Sture, that parteth with his pleasant floods
  The Eastern Saxons from the Southern nigh,
  And Clare, and Harwich both doth beautify:
  Him followed Yare, soft washing Norwitch wall,
  And with him brought a present joyfully
  Of his own fish unto their festival,
Whose like none else could show, the which they
    ruffins call.

Next these the plenteous Ouse came far from land,
  By many a city, and by many a town,
  And many rivers taking under hand
  Into his waters, as he passeth down,
  The Cle, the Were, the Grant, the Sture, the Rowne.
  Thence doth by Huntingdon and Cambridge flit,
  My mother Cambridge, whom as with a crown
  He doth adorn, and is adorned of it
With many a gentle Muse, and many a learned wit.

And after him the fatal Welland went,
  That if old saws prove true (which God forbid)
  Shall drown all Holland with his excrement,
  And shall see Stamford, though now homely hid,
  Then shine in learning, more than ever did
  Cambridge or Oxford, England's goodly beams.
  And next to him the Nene down softly slid;
  And bounteous Trent, that in himself enseams
Both thirty sorts of fish, and thirty sundry streams.

Next these came Tyne, along whose stony bank
  That Roman monarch built a brazen wall,
  Which mote the feebled Britons strongly flank
  Against the Picts, that swarmed over all,
  Which yet thereof Gualsever they do call:
  And Twede the limit betwixt Logris land
  And Albany: And Eden, though but amall,
  Yet often stained with blood of many a band
Of Scots and English both, that tined on his strand.

ffins: ruffs, small perch-like fish   Albany: Scotland
alsever: Severus's Wall   tined: perished
gris land: England

Then came those six sad brethren, like forlorn,
   That whilom were (as antique fathers tell)
   Six valiant knights, of one fair nymph yborn,
   Which did in noble deeds of arms excel,
   And wonned there, where now Yorke people dwell;
   Still Ure, swift Werfe, and Oze the most of might,
   High Swale, unquiet Nide, and troublous Skell;
   All whom a Scythian king, that Humber hight,
Slew cruelly, and in the river drowned quite.

But passed not long, ere Brutus' warlike son
   Locrinus them avenged, and the same date,
   Which the proud Humber unto them had done,
   By equal doom repaid on his own pate:
   For in the selfsame river, where he late
   Had drenched them, he drowned him again;
   And named the river of his wretched fate;
   Whose bad condition yet it doth retain,
Oft tossed with his storms, which therein still remain.

These after, came the stony shallow Lone,
   That to old Loncaster his name doth lend;
   And following Dee, which Britons long ygone
   Did call divine, that doth by Chester tend;
   And Conway which out of his stream doth send
   Plenty of pearls to deck his dames withal,
   And Lindus that his pikes doth most commend,
   Of which the ancient Lincolne men do call;
All these together marched toward Proteus hall.

                                        Edmund Spen

six sad brethren: the six rivers named which all flow into the Yorkshire Ouse
wonned: dwelt

3   Rivers Arise

Rivers arise; whether thou be the son
Of utmost Tweed, or Oose, or gulphie Dun,
Or Trent, who like some earth-born giant spreads
His thirty arms among the indented meads,
Or sullen Mole that runneth underneath,
Or Severn swift, guilty of maiden's death,
Or rockie Avon, or of sedgie Lee,
Or coaly Tine, or antient hallowed Dee,
Or Humber loud that keeps the Scythian's name,
Or Medway smooth, or royal towred Thame.

                                        John Milton

4   *from* John of Gaunt's Speech

This royal throne of kings, this sceptered isle,
This earth of majesty, this seat of Mars,
This other Eden, demi-paradise;
This fortress built by Nature for herself
Against infection and the hand of war;
This happy breed of men, this little world;
This precious stone set in the silver sea,
Which serves it in the office of a wall,
Or as a moat defensive to a house,
Against the envy of less happier lands;
This blessed plot, this earth, this realm, this England,
This nurse, this teeming womb of royal kings

                                  William Shakespeare

5   The Halcyon's Nest

So, in the midst of Neptune's angry tide,
Our Britan Island, like the weedy nest
Of true halcyon, on the waves doth ride,
And softly sailing, scorns the waters' pride:
  While all the rest, drowned on the continent,
    And tossed in bloody waves, their wounds lament,
And stand, to see our peace, as struck with wonderment.

The Ship of France religious waves do toss,
And Greece itself is now grown barbarous,
Spain's children hardly dare the ocean cross,
And Belges' field lies waste, and ruinous,
That unto those, the heav'ns are envious,
   And unto them, themselves are strangers grown,
   And unto these, the seas are faithless known,
And unto her, alas, her own is not her own.

Here only shut we Janus' iron gates,
And call the welcome Muses to our springs,
And are but pilgrims from our heav'nly states,
The while the trusty Earth sure plenty brings,
And ships through Neptune safely spread their wings.
   Go, blessed Island, wander where thou please,
   Unto thy God, or men, heav'n, lands, or seas,
Thou canst not lose thy way, thy king with all hath peace.

Giles Fletcher

envious: inimical

6

The fresh green lap of fair King Richard's land

William Shakespeare

7   Britannia

Heavens! what a goodly prospect spreads around,
Of hills, and dales, and woods, and lawns, and spires,
And glittering towns, and gilded streams, till all
The stretching landscape into smoke decays!
Happy Britannia! where, the Queen of Arts
Inspiring vigour, liberty abroad
Walks, unconfined, e'en to thy farthest cots,
And scatters plenty with unsparing hand.
  Rich is thy soil, and merciful thy clime;
Thy streams unfailing in the summer's drought;
Unmatched thy guardian oaks; thy valleys float
With golden waves: and, on thy mountains flocks
Bleat numberless; while, roving round their sides,
Bellow the blackening herds in lusty droves.
Beneath, thy meadows glow, and rise unquelled

Against the mower's scythe. On every hand
Thy villas shine. Thy country teems with wealth;
And property assures it to the swain,
Pleased and unwearied, in his guarded toil.

James Thomson

8   O My Mother Isle!
(i)

Not yet enslaved, not wholly vile,
O Albion! O my mother Isle!
Thy vallies, fair as Eden's bowers,
Glitter green with sunny showers.

1796

(ii)

O native Britain! O my Mother Isle!
How shouldst thou prove aught else but dear and holy
To me, who from thy lakes and mountain-hills,
Thy clouds, thy quiet dales, thy rocks and seas,
Have drunk in all my intellectual life,
All sweet sensations, all ennobling thoughts,
All adoration of the God in nature,
All lovely and all honourable things,
Whatever makes this mortal spirit feel
The joy and greatness of its future being?

1798

S. T. Coleridge

2   The South

9   Dover, the Samphire Cliff

Come on, sir; here's the place. Stand still. How fearful
And dizzy 'tis to cast one's eyes so low!
The crows and choughs that wing the midway air
Show scarce so gross as beetles. Halfway down
Hangs one that gathers sampire: dreadful trade;
Methinks he seems no bigger than his head.
The fishermen that walk upon the beach
Appear like mice; and yond tall anchoring bark,
Diminished to her cock; her cock, a buoy
Almost too small for sight. The murmuring surge
That on th' unnumb'red idle pebble chafes
Cannot be heard so high. I'll look no more,
Lest my brain turn, and the deficient sight
Topple down headlong.

                                                        William Shakespear

10   Dover Beach

The sea is calm to-night.
The tide is full, the moon lies fair
Upon the straits;—on the French coast the light
Gleams and is gone; the cliffs of England stand,
Glimmering and vast, out in the tranquil bay.
Come to the window, sweet is the night-air!
Only, from the long line of spray
Where the sea meets the moon-blanched land,
Listen! you hear the grating roar
Of pebbles which the waves draw back, and fling,
At their return, up the high strand,
Begin, and cease, and then again begin,
With tremulous cadence slow, and bring
The eternal note of sadness in.

Sophocles long ago
Heard it on the Ægæan, and it brought
Into his mind the turbid ebb and flow
Of human misery; we
Find also in the sound a thought,
Hearing it by this distant northern sea.

The Sea of Faith
Was once, too, at the full, and round earth's shore
Lay like the folds of a bright girdle furled.
But now I only hear
Its melancholy, long, withdrawing roar,
Retreating, to the breath
Of the night-wind, down the vast edges drear
And naked shingles of the world.

Ah, love, let us be true
To one another! for the world, which seems
To lie before us like a land of dreams,
So various, so beautiful, so new,
Hath really neither joy, nor love, nor light,
Nor certitude, nor peace, nor help for pain;
And we are here as on a darkling plain
Swept with confused alarms of struggle and flight,
Where ignorant armies clash by night.

Matthew Arnold

11   The Old Summerhouse
(on the Thames, Taplow)

This blue-washed, old, thatched summerhouse—
Paint scaling, and fading from its walls—
How often from its hingeless door
I have watched—dead leaf, like the ghost of a mouse,
Rasping the worn brick floor—
The snows of the weir descending below,
And their thunderous waterfall.

Fall—fall: dark, garrulous rumour,
Until I could listen no more.
Could listen no more—for beauty with sorrow

Is a burden hard to be borne:
The evening light on the foam, and the swans, there;
That music, remote, forlorn.

                                   Walter de la Mar

12   Green Sussex

You came, and looked and loved the view
     Long-known and loved by me,
Green Sussex fading into blue
     With one gray glimpse of sea.

                                   Alfred Tennyso

13   To Penshurst
     (Kent)

Thou art not, Penshurst, built to envious show
     Of touch or marble, nor canst boast a row
Of polished pillars, or a roof of gold;
     Thou hast no lantern whereof tales are told,
Or stair, or courts; but stand'st an ancient pile,
     And these grudged at, art reverenced the while.
Thou joy'st in better marks, of soil, of air,
     Of wood, of water; therein thou art fair.
Thou hast thy walks for health as well as sport:
     Thy Mount, to which the dryads do resort,
Where Pan and Bacchus their high feasts have made,
     Beneath the broad beech and the chestnut shade;
That taller tree, which of a nut was set
     At his great birth, where all the muses met.
There, in the writhed bark, are cut the names
     Of many a sylvan taken with his flames;
And thence the ruddy satyrs oft provoke
     The lighter fauns to reach thy lady's oak.
Thy copse, too, named of Gamage, thou hast there,
     That never fails to serve thee seasoned deer
When thou wouldst feast or exercise thy friends.
     The lower land, that to the river bends,
Thy sheep, thy bullocks, kine and calves do feed;
     The middle grounds thy mares and horses breed.
Each bank doth yield thee conies, and the tops,
     Fertile of wood, Ashour and Sidney's copse,
To crown thy open table, doth provide

The purpled pheasant with the speckled side;
The painted partridge lies in every field,
  And for thy mess is willing to be killed.
And if the high-swoll'n Medway fail thy dish,
  Thou hast thy ponds that pay thee tribute fish:
Fat, aged carps, that run into thy net;
  And pikes, now weary their own kind to eat,
As loath the second draught or cast to stay,
  Officiously, at first, themselves betray.
Bright eels, that emulate them, and leap on land
  Before the fisher, or into his hand.
Then hath thy orchard fruit, thy garden flowers,
  Fresh as the air and new as are the hours:
The early cherry, with the later plum,
  Fig, grape and quince, each in his time doth come;
The blushing apricot and woolly peach
  Hang on thy walls, that every child may reach.
And though thy walls be of the country stone,
  They're reared with no man's ruin, no man's groan;
There's none that dwell about them wish them down,
  But all come in, the farmer and the clown,
And no one empty-handed, to salute
  Thy lord and lady, though they have no suit.
Some bring a capon, some a rural cake,
  Some nuts, some apples; some that think they make
The better cheeses, bring 'em; or else send
  By their ripe daughters, whom they would commend
This way to husbands; and whose baskets bear
  An emblem of themselves, in plum or pear.
But what can this (more than express their love)
  Add to thy free provisions, far above
The need of such? whose liberal board doth flow
  With all that hospitality doth know!
Where comes no guest but is allowed to eat
  Without his fear, and of thy lord's own meat;
Where the same beer and bread and self-same wine
  That is his lordship's shall be also mine;
And I not fain to sit, as some this day
  At great men's tables, and yet dine away.
Here no man tells my cups, nor, standing by,
  A waiter, doth my gluttony envy,
But gives me what I call, and lets me eat;
  He knows below he shall find plenty of meat,

Thy tables hoard not up for the next day.
  Nor, when I take my lodging, need I pray
For fire or lights or livery: all is there,
  As if thou then wert mine, or I reigned here;
There's nothing I can wish, for which I stay.
  That found King James, when, hunting late this way
With his brave son, the Prince, they saw thy fires
  Shine bright on every hearth as the desires
Of thy Penates had been set on flame
  To entertain them; or the country came
With all their zeal to warm their welcome here.
  What (great, I will not say, but) sudden cheer
Didst thou then make 'em! and what praise was heaped
  On thy good lady then! who therein reaped
The just reward of her high housewifery:
  To have her linen, plate, and all things nigh
When she was far; and not a room but dressed
  As if it had expected such a guest!
These, Penshurst, are thy praise, and yet not all.
  Thy lady's noble, fruitful, chaste withal;
His children thy great lord may call his own,
  A fortune in this age but rarely known.
They are and have been taught religion; thence
  Their gentler spirits have sucked innocence.
Each morn and even they are taught to pray
  With the whole household, and may every day
Read in their virtuous parents' noble parts
  The mysteries of manners, arms and arts.
Now, Penshurst, they that will proportion thee
  With other edifices, when they see
Those proud, ambitious heaps, and nothing else,
  May say, their lords have built, but thy lord dwells.

Ben Jonson

14   Erith, on the Thames

There are men in the village of Erith
Whom nobody seeth or heareth,
  And there looms, on the marge
  Of the river a barge
That nobody roweth or steereth.

Anon

15   Hops along the Medway

Now are our labours crowned with their reward,
Now bloom the florid hops, and in the stream
Shine in their floating silver, while above
T' embow'ring branches culminate, and form
A walk impervious to the sun; the poles
In comely order stand; and while you cleave
With the small skiff the Medway's lucid wave,
In comely order still their ranks preserve,
And seem to march along th' extensive plain.

                                   Christopher Smart

16   Twilight Time
(Shoreham, Kent)

And now the trembling light
Glimmers behind the little hills, and corn,
Ling'ring as loth to part: yet part thou must
And though than open day far pleasing more
(Ere yet the fields, and pearled cups of flowers
      Twinkle in the parting light;)
Thee night shall hide, sweet visionary gleam
That softly lookest through the rising dew;
      Till all like silver bright,
      The Faithful Witness, pure, and white,
      Shall look o'er yonder grassy hill,
      At this village, safe and still.
All is safe and all is still
Save what noise the watch-dog makes
Or the shrill cock the silence breaks
            Now and then—
            And now and then—
            Hark!—Once again,
            The wether's bell
            To us doth tell
Some little stirring in the fold.

      Me thinks the ling'ring dying ray
         Of twilight time doth seem more fair
      And lights the soul up more than day,
         When wide-spread sultry sunshines are.

Yet all is right, and all most fair,
   For Thou, dear God, hast formed all;
Thou deckest ev'ry little flower,
   Thou girdest ev'ry planet ball—
      And mark'st when sparrows fall.
Thou pourest out the golden day
On corn-fields rip'ning in the sun
Up the side of some great hill
   Ere the sickle has begun.

Samuel Palmer

17   Above the Medway

Hark! from yon high grey Downs the tremulous musical
      sheep-bells
Call us to come and behold all that our shepherds can show;
Who with their low-wheel'd huts abide in the field for the
      lambing,
Watching night and day over the weak of the fold.
Ah! from those high grey Downs, what a height, what a
      scope, of enjoyment!
Songs of the mating birds heard in the hollows afar—
Songs of the lark in air, or the clamorous chirp of the
      starlings,
Seated aloft in crowds, talking together at eve.

You who would know what it is to rejoice in the beauty of
      England,
Come to these high grey Downs; come in an evening of
      Spring—
Come in the Autumn noons, or come in a sweet Summer
      morning—
Stand upon Darland Heights, gaze on the glories around!
Look to the east, far down, where the broad white Roman
      highway
Scores the green flank of the hills, stately and sound as of old:
Look to the east, far down, where Medway sweeps to the
      ocean,
Meeting the broader Thames, surging away to the Nore.
There, by the tall sea banks, by the low rich pastures of Essex,
There go the ships, far off, bearing the wealth of the world;
Bearing it on the tide, to the port and harbour of London,
Bearing it thence in turn out to the ocean again.

Near, o'er the Medway stream, look down on an humbler
    traffic—
Fishermen's craft alone, barges and boats of the shore:
Yes, and yon giant hulks, where soldiers live as in barracks,
Learning their terrible trade, disciplined daily to war.
Ah, look away from them, look away from the forts in the
    channel
(Needed and wanting once, soon to be needed again),
Look to the smiling shores, to the villages set in the
    woodland,
Orchards and red-roof'd farms, churches and castles and all.
Then to the west turn round, and see right on to the
    landward,
Fold upon fold, the hills rising like waves of the sea:
But at your feet, low down, lies the silent valley of Darland,
Winding in many a curve up to the highlands afar;
Steep are its purple sides, where folded flocks are a-slumber,
And on the further slope, warm in the depth of the vale,
Cluster'd hop-poles stand, like the tents of an army
    encamping,
Soon to be sever'd and ranged, soon to be leafy and green.
Over against us here, on the opposite height, on the summit,
Hempstead stands alone, grey with its gables and barns;
And from Hempstead farm, right on to the western horizon,
Fold upon fold, our hills rise like the waves of the sea;
Crested with high dim lawns, and tufted with copses and
    timber,
Till on the lucid sky loftier ridges appear.

A. J. Munby

18   Tunbridge Wells

At five this morn, when Phoebus raised his head
From Thetis' lap, I raised myself from bed,
And mounting steed, I trotted to the waters,
The rendezvous of fools, buffoons, and praters,
Cuckolds, whores, citizens, their wives and daughters.
    My squeamish stomach I with wine had bribed
To undertake the dose that was prescribed;
But turning head, a sudden cursed view
That innocent provision overthrew,
And without drinking, made me purge and spew.
From coach and six a thing unwieldy rolled,

Whose lumber, cart more decently would hold.
As wise as calf it looked, as big as bully,
But handled, proves a mere Sir Nicholas Cully;
A bawling fop, a natural Nokes, and yet
He dares to censure as if he had wit.
To make him more ridiculous, in spite
Nature contrived the fool should be a knight.
Though he alone were dismal sight enough,
His train contributed to set him off,
All of his shape, all of the selfsame stuff.
No spleen or malice need on them be thrown:
Nature has done the business of lampoon,
And in their looks their characters has shown.
  Endeavoring this irksome sight to balk,
And a more irksome noise, their silly talk,
I silently slunk down t' th' Lower Walk.
But often when one would Charybdis shun,
Down upon Scylla 'tis one's fate to run,
For here it was my cursed luck to find
As great a fop, though of another kind,
A tall stiff fool that walked in Spanish guise:
The buckram puppet never stirred its eyes,
But grave as owl it looked, as woodcock wise.
He scorns the empty talking of this mad age,
And speaks all proverbs, sentences, and adage;
Can with as much solemnity buy eggs
As a cabal can talk of their intrigues;
Master o' th' Ceremonies, yet can dispense
With the formality of talking sense.
  From hence unto the upper end I ran,
Where a new scene of foppery began.
A tribe of curates, priests, canonical elves,
Fit company for none besides themselves,
Were got together. Each his distemper told,
Scurvy, stone, strangury; some were so bold
To charge the spleen to be their misery,
And on that wise disease brought infamy.
But none had modesty enough t' complain
Their want of learning, honesty, and brain,
The general diseases of that train.
These call themselves ambassadors of heaven,

Sir Nicholas Cully: foolish character in *The Comical Revenge* by Etherege, a part m[a]
famous by the actor James Nokes

And saucily pretend commissions given;
But should an Indian king, whose small command
Seldom extends beyond ten miles of land,
Send forth such wretched tools in an embassage,
He'd find but small effects of such a message.
Listening, I found the cob of all this rabble
Pert Bayes, with his importance comfortable.
He, being raised to an archdeaconry
By trampling on religion, liberty,
Was grown too great, and looked too fat and jolly,
To be disturbed with care and melancholy,
Though Marvell has enough exposed his folly.
He drank to carry off some old remains
His lazy dull distemper left in 's veins.
Let him drink on, but 'tis not a whole flood
Can give sufficient sweetness to his blood
To make his nature or his manners good.

   Next after these, a fulsome Irish crew
Of silly Macs were offered to my view.
The things did talk, but th' hearing what they said
I did myself the kindness to evade.
Nature has placed these wretches beneath scorn:
They can't be called so vile as they are born.

   Amidst the crowd next I myself conveyed,
For now were come, whitewash and paint being laid,
Mother and daughter, mistress and the maid,
And squire with wig and pantaloon displayed.
But ne'er could conventicle, play, or fair
For a true medley, with this herd compare.
Here lords, knights, squires, ladies and countesses,
Chandlers, mum-bacon women, sempstresses
Were mixed together, nor did they agree
More in their humours than their quality.

   Here waiting for gallant, young damsel stood,
Leaning on cane, and muffled up in hood.
The would-be wit, whose business was to woo,
With hat removed and solemn scrape of shoe
Advanceth bowing, then genteelly shrugs,
And ruffled foretop into order tugs,
And thus accosts her: 'Madam, methinks the weather

yes: Samuel Parker, Archdeacon of Oxford. Marvell satirized him as Bayes in *The*
?earsal Transprosed for his writings on the subservience of Church to State
?m-bacon: ? bacon-chewing

Is grown much more serene since you came hither.
You influence the heavens; but should the sun
Withdraw himself to see his rays outdone
By your bright eyes, they would supply the morn,
And make a day before the day be born.'
With mouth screwed up, conceited winking eyes,
And breasts thrust forward, 'Lord, sir!' she replies.
'It is your goodness, and not my deserts,
Which makes you show this learning, wit, and parts.'
He, puzzled, bites his nail, both to display
The sparkling ring, and think what next to say,
And thus breaks forth afresh: 'Madam, egad!
Your luck at cards last night was very bad:
At cribbage fifty-nine, and the next show
To make the game, and yet to want those two.
God damn me, madam, I'm the son of a whore
If in my life I saw the like before!'
To peddler's stall he drags her, and her breast
With hearts and such-like foolish toys he dressed;
And then, more smartly to expound the riddle
Of all his prattle, gives her a Scotch fiddle.
    Tired with this dismal stuff, away I ran
Where were two wives, with girl just fit for man—
Short-breathed, with pallid lips and visage wan.
Some curtsies past, and the old compliment
Of being glad to see each other, spent,
With hand in hand they lovingly did walk,
And one began thus to renew the talk:
'I pray, good madam, if it may be thought
No rudeness, what cause was it hither brought
Your ladyship?' She soon replying, smiled,
'We have a good estate, but have no child,
And I'm informed these wells will make a barren
Woman as fruitful as a cony warren.'
The first returned, 'For this cause I am come,
For I can have no quietness at home.
My husband grumbles though we have got one,
This poor young girl, and mutters for a son.
And this is grieved with headache, pangs, and throes;
Is full sixteen, and never yet had *those*.'
She soon replied, 'Get her a husband, madam:
I married at that age, and ne'er had had 'em;

Scotch fiddle: indecent invitatory sign with the finger

Was just like her. Steel waters let alone:
A back of steel will bring 'em better down.'
And ten to one but they themselves will try
The same means to increase their family.
Poor foolish fribble, who by subtlety
Of midwife, truest friend to lechery,
Persuaded art to be at pains and charge
To give thy wife occasion to enlarge
Thy silly head! For here walk Cuff and Kick,
With brawny back and legs and potent prick,
Who more substantially will cure thy wife,
And on her half-dead womb bestow new life.
From these the waters got the reputation
Of good assistants unto generation.

   Some warlike men were now got into th' throng,
With hair tied back, singing a bawdy song.
Not much afraid, I got a nearer view,
And 'twas my chance to know the dreadful crew.
They were cadets, that seldom can appear:
Damned to the stint of thirty pounds a year.
With hawk on fist, or greyhound led in hand,
The dogs and footboys sometimes they command.
But now, having trimmed a cast-off spavined horse,
With three hard-pinched-for guineas in their purse,
Two rusty pistols, scarf about the arse,
Coat lined with red, they here presume to swell:
This goes for captain, that for colonel.
So the Bear Garden ape, on his steed mounted,
No longer is a jackanapes accounted,
But is, by virtue of his trumpery, then
Called by the name of 'the young gentleman.'

   Bless me! thought I, what thing is man, that thus
In all his shapes, he is ridiculous?
Ourselves with noise of reason we do please
In vain: humanity's our worst disease.
Thrice happy beasts are, who, because they be
Of reason void, are so of foppery.
Faith, I was so ashamed that with remorse
I used the insolence to mount my horse;
For he, doing only things fit for his nature,
Did seem to me by much the wiser creature.

                         John Wilmot, Earl of Rochester

el waters: Tunbridge waters are chalybeate

19   In Romney Marsh

As I went down to Dymchurch Wall,
   I heard the South sing o'er the land;
I saw the yellow sunlight fall
   On knolls where Norman churches stand.

And ringing shrilly, taut and lithe,
   Within the wind a core of sound,
The wire from Romney town to Hythe
   Alone its airy journey wound.

A veil of purple vapour flowed
   And trailed its fringe along the Straits;
The upper air like sapphire glowed;
   And roses filled Heaven's central gates.

Masts in the offing wagged their tops;
   The swinging waves pealed on the shore;
The saffron beach, all diamond drops
   And beads of surge, prolonged the roar.

As I came up from Dymchurch Wall,
   I saw above the Downs' low crest
The crimson brands of sunset fall,
   Flicker and fade from out the west.

Night sank: like flakes of silver fire
   The stars in one great shower came down;
Shrill blew the wind; and shrill the wire
   Rang out from Hythe to Romney town.

The darkly shining salt sea drops
   Streamed as the waves clashed on the shore;
The beach, with all its organ stops
   Pealing again, prolonged the roar.

                                         John Davids⟨

20   November in the Isle of Wight

November dawns and dewy-glooming downs,
The gentle shower, the smell of dying leaves,
And the low moan of leaden-colour'd seas.

                                         Alfred Tennys⟨

21   A Forsaken Garden
(Isle of Wight)

In a coign of the cliff between lowland and highland,
    At the sea-down's edge between windward and lee,
Walled round with rocks as an inland island,
    The ghost of a garden fronts the sea.
A girdle of brushwood and thorn encloses
    The steep square slope of the blossomless bed
Where the weeds that grew green from the graves of its
        roses
            Now lie dead.

The fields fall southward, abrupt and broken,
    To the low last edge of the long lone land.
If a step should sound or a word be spoken,
    Would a ghost not rise at the strange guest's hand?
So long have the grey bare walks lain guestless,
    Through branches and briars if a man make way,
He shall find no life but the sea-wind's, restless
        Night and day.

The dense hard passage is blind and stifled
    That crawls by a track none turn to climb
To the strait waste place that the years have rifled
    Of all but the thorns that are touched not of time.
The thorns he spares when the rose is taken;
    The rocks are left when he wastes the plain.
The wind that wanders, the weeds wind-shaken,
        These remain.

Not a flower to be pressed of the foot that falls not;
    As the heart of a dead man the seed-plots are dry;
From the thicket of thorns whence the nightingale calls
        not,
    Could she call, there were never a rose to reply.
Over the meadows that blossom and wither
    Rings but the note of a sea-bird's song;
Only the sun and the rain come hither
        All year long.

The sun burns sere and the rain dishevels
    One gaunt bleak blossom of scentless breath.
Only the wind here hovers and revels
    In a round where life seems barren as death.
Here there was laughing of old, there was weeping,
    Haply, of lovers none ever will know,
Whose eyes went seaward a hundred sleeping
        Years ago.

Heart handfast in heart as they stood, 'Look thither,'
    Did he whisper? 'look forth from the flowers to the
        sea;
For the foam-flowers endure when the rose-blossoms
        wither,
    And men that love lightly may die—but we?'
And the same wind sang and the same waves whitened,
    And or ever the garden's last petals were shed,
In the lips that had whispered, the eyes that had
        lightened,
        Love was dead.

Or they loved their life through, and then went
        whither?
    And were one to the end—but what end who knows?
Love deep as the sea as a rose must wither,
    As the rose-red seaweed that mocks the rose.
Shall the dead take thought for the dead to love them?
    What love was ever as deep as a grave?
They are loveless now as the grass above them
        Or the wave.

All are at one now, roses and lovers,
    Not known of the cliffs and the fields and the sea.
Not a breath of the time that has been hovers
    In the air now soft with a summer to be.
Not a breath shall there sweeten the seasons hereafter
    Of the flowers or the lovers that laugh now or weep,
When as they that are free now of weeping and laughter
        We shall sleep.

Here death may deal not again for ever;
　Here change may come not till all change end.
From the graves they have made they shall rise up
　　　never,
　Who have left nought living to ravage and rend.
Earth, stones, and thorns of the wild ground growing,
　While the sun and the rain live, these shall be;
Till a last wind's breath upon all these blowing
　　　Roll the sea.

Till the slow sea rise and the sheer cliff crumble,
　Till terrace and meadow the deep gulfs drink,
Till the strength of the waves of the high tides humble
　The fields that lessen, the rocks that shrink,
Here now in his triumph where all things falter,
　Stretched out on the spoils that his own hand spread,
As a god self-slain on his own strange altar,
　　　Death lies dead.

A. C. Swinburne

22　At Farringford
(Isle of Wight)

Should all our churchmen foam in spite
At you, so careful of the right,
　Yet one lay-hearth would give you welcome
(Take it and come) to the Isle of Wight;

Where, far from noise and smoke of town,
I watch the twilight falling brown
　All round a careless-ordered garden
Close to the ridge of a noble down.

You'll have no scandal while you dine,
But honest talk and wholesome wine,
　And only hear the magpie gossip
Garrulous under a roof of pine:

For groves of pine on either hand,
To break the blast of winter, stand;
　And further on, the hoary Channel
Tumbles a billow on chalk and sand;

Where, if below the milky steep
Some ship of battle slowly creep,
   And on through zones of light and shadow
Glimmer away to the lonely deep,

We might discuss the Northern sin
Which made a selfish war begin;
   Dispute the claims, arrange the chances;
Emperor, Ottoman, which shall win.

Alfred Tennyso

23   The Needles' Lighthouse from Keyhaven, Hampshire

The downs and tender-tinted cliffs are lost,
And nothing but the guardian fire remains—
That crimson-headed tower on the rough coast,
Whose steady lustre ceases not, nor wanes,
Till sunrise from the east reveals to us
The mighty Vectian wold, and tawny tract
Of shingle, seen through bowers of arbutus,
Like some fair corn-field, mellow and compact.
How that deep glow the deepening gloom attests!
How much is by that noble lighthouse taught!
Mine eye rests on it, as the spirit rests
In sorrow, on some holy, ardent thought,
The sole beam in our darkness! Those who dwell
Near these great beacons are instructed well.

Charles Tennyson Turn

24   Jersey

Jersey dort dans les flots, ces éternels grondeurs;
Et dans sa petitesse elle a les deux grandeurs;
Île, elle a l'océan; roche, elle est la montagne.
Par le sud Normandie et par le nord Bretagne,
Elle est pour nous la France, et, dans son lit de fleurs,
Elle en a le sourire et quelquefois les pleurs.

Pour la troisième fois j'y vois les pommes mûres.
Terre d'exil, que mord la vague aux sourds murmures,
Sois bénie, île verte, amour du flot profond!
Ce coin de terre, où l'âme à l'infini se fond,
S'il était mon pays, serait ce que j'envie.
Là, le lutteur serein, naufragé de la vie,
Pense, et, sous l'œil de Dieu, sur cet écueil vermeil,
Laisse blanchir son âme ainsi que le soleil
Blanchit sur le gazon les linges des laveuses.

Les rocs semblent frappés d'attitudes rêveuses;
Dans leurs antres, ainsi qu'aux fentes d'un pressoir,
L'écume à flots bouillonne et luit; quand vient le soir,
La forêt jette au vent des notes sibyllines;
Le dolmen monstrueux songe sur les collines;
L'obscure nuit l'ébauche en spectre; et dans le bloc
La lune blême fait apparaître Moloch.

A cause du vent d'ouest, tout le long de la plage,
Dans tous les coins de roche où se groupe un village,
Sur les vieux toits tremblants des pêcheurs riverains,
Le chaume est retenu par des câbles marins
Pendant le long des murs avec de grosses pierres;
La nourrice au sein nu qui baisse les paupières
Chante à l'enfant qui tette un chant de matelot;
Le bateau dès qu'il rentre est tiré hors du flot;
Et les prés sont charmants.

                    Salut, terre sacrée!
Le seuil des maisons rit comme une aube dorée.
Phares, salut! amis que le péril connaît!
Salut, clochers où vient nicher le martinet;
Pauvres autels sculptés par des sculpteurs de proues;
Chemins que dans les bois emplit le bruit des roues;
Jardins de laurier rose et d'hortensia bleu;
Étangs près de la mer, sagesses près de Dieu!
Salut!

        A l'horizon s'envole la frégate;
Le flux mêle aux galets, polis comme l'agate,
Les goëmons, toison du troupeau des récifs;
Et Vénus éblouit les vieux rochers pensifs,
Dans l'ombre, au point du jour, quand, au chant de la grive,
Tenant l'enfant matin par la main, elle arrive.

O bruyères! Plémont qu'évite le steamer!
Vieux palais de Cybèle écroulé dans la mer!
Mont qu'étreint l'océan de ses liquides marbres!
Mugissement des bœufs! doux sommeils sous les arbres!
L'île semble prier comme un religieux;
Tout à l'entour, chantant leur chant prodigieux,
L'abîme et l'océan font leur immense fête;
La nue en passant pleure; et l'écueil, sur son faîte,
Pendant que la mer brise à ses pieds le vaisseau,
Garde un peu d'eau du ciel pour le petit oiseau.

                                        Victor Hugo

25   Sark

O flower of all wind-flowers and sea-flowers,
    Made lovelier by love of the sea
Than thy golden own field-flowers, or tree-flowers
    Like foam of the sea-facing tree!
No foot but the seamew's there settles
    On the spikes of thine anthers like horns,
With snow-coloured spray for thy petals,
    Black rocks for thy thorns.

                                        A. C. Swinburne

26   A Guernesey

Ces rocs de l'océan ont tout, terreur et grâce,
Cieux, mers, escarpement devant tout ce qui passe,
Bruit sombre qui parfois semble un hymne béni,
Patience à porter le poids de l'infini;
Et dans ces fiers déserts qu'un ordre effrayant règle,
On se sent croître une aile, et l'âme devient aigle.

                                        Victor Hugo

27   Églogue
(procession of 'teatotallers' at Peter-Port)

—Un journal! Donnez-moi du papier, que j'écrive
Une lettre, et voyez si le facteur arrive.
Il semble que la poste aujourd'hui tarde un peu.
Vent, brouillard, pluie. On est en juin. Faites du feu.—
Comme ces champs ont l'air bougon et réfractaire!
Un gros nuage noir est tout près de la terre;
Le jour a le front bas, et les cieux sont étroits;
Et l'on voit dans la rue, en file, trois par trois,
Serrés dans leurs boutons et droits dans leurs agrafes,
Passer des titotleurss* grisés par des carafes.
Ils sont jeunes, plusieurs ont vingt ans; et, pendant
Que, regardant la vie avec un œil pédant,
Ils laissent se transir Betsy, Goton et Lise,
L'eau qu'ils boivent leur sort du nez en chants d'église.

Jadis c'était le temps du beau printemps divin;
Silène était dans l'antre et ronflait plein de vin:
Mai frissonnait d'aurore, et des flûtes magiques
Se répondaient dans l'ombre au fond des géorgiques;
L'eau courait, l'air jouait; de son râle étranglé
La couleuvre amoureuse épouvantait Églé;
Les paons dans la lumière ouvraient leurs larges queues;
Et, lueurs dans l'azur, les neuf déesses bleues
Flottaient entre la terre et le ciel dans le soir
Et chantaient, et, laissant à travers elles voir
Les étoiles, ces yeux du vague crépuscule,
Elles mêlaient Virgile assis au Janicule,
Moschus dans Syracuse, et les sources en pleurs,
Les troupeaux, les sommeils sous les arbres, les fleurs,
Les bois, Amaryllis, Mnasyle et Phyllodoce,
A leur mystérieux et sombre sacerdoce.

Guernesey, 29 mai 1856   Victor Hugo

Teatotallers, buveurs de thé. Prononcer: titotleurss.

3   The South-West

28   On the Ridgeway

Thinking of those who walked here long ago
On this greenway in summer and in snow
She said, 'This is the oldest road we tread,
The oldest in the world?' 'Yes, love,' I said.

Andrew Young

29   The Houseless Downs
(*from the Shepherds' Song, Sung before Queen Anne, on the Wiltshire Downs, 11 June 1613*)

Shine, O thou sacred Shepherds' Star,
   on silly shepherd swaines,
Greeting with joy thy blessedness
   along these champian plains.

What! dost thou stay thy motion here?
   and does thy Grace thus grace us?
This honour we esteem next that,
   when God in Heaven shall place us.

From fair Aurora's first arise,
   till silent night begins,
The day-guide Phoebus, with his beams,
   doth scorch our tawny skins,

And Boreas' rough tempestuous blasts,
   with winter frosts and storms,
Have chang'd our habit, and our hue,
   into these ugly forms.

champian: open country, champaign

How dare we then (base Corydons)
   in every part unsightly,
Salute an Empress all renown'd
   with rhymes compos'd so lightly?

Our comfort is, thy Greatness knows
   swarth faces, coarse cloth gowns,
Are ornaments that well become
   the wide, wild, houseless downs.

George Ferebe

30   Stonehenge

Near Wilton sweet huge heaps of stone are found,
   But so confused that neither any eye
   Can count them just, nor reason reason try,
   What force brought them to so unlikely ground.

To stranger weights my mind's waste soil is bound,
   Of passion's hills reaching to reason's sky,
   From fancy's earth passing all numbers' bound,
   Passing all guess, whence into me should fly
   So mazed a mass, or if in me it grows,
A simple soul should breed so mixed woes.

Sir Philip Sidney

31   Stonehenge

(*Vansdyke addresses a reproof to Stonehenge*)

Dull heap, that thus thy head above the rest dost rear,
Precisely yet not known who first did place thee there,
But traitor basely turned to Merlin's skill dost fly,
And with his magic dost thy makers' truth belie:
Conspirator with Time, now grown so mean and poor,
Comparing these his spirits with those that went before;
But rather art content thy builders' praise to lose
Than passed greatness should thy present wants disclose.
So did those mighty men to trust thee with their story,
That hast forgot their names, who reared thee for their glory:
For all their wondrous cost, thou that hast served them so,
What 'tis to trust to tombs by thee we easily know.

Michael Drayton

32   Salisbury Plain and Stonehenge
(i)

A traveller on the skirt of Sarum's Plain
Pursued his vagrant way, with feet half bare;
Stooping his gait, but not as if to gain
Help from the staff he bore; for mien and air
Were hardy, though his cheek seemed worn with care
Both of the time to come, and time long fled:
Down fell in straggling locks his thin grey hair;
A coat he wore of military red
But faded, and stuck o'er with many a patch and shred.

While thus he journeyed, step by step led on,
He saw and passed a stately inn, full sure
That welcome in such house for him was none.
No board inscribed the needy to allure
Hung there, no bush proclaimed to old and poor
And desolate, 'Here you will find a friend!'
The pendent grapes glittered above the door;—
On he must pace, perchance 'till night descend,
Where'er the dreary roads their bare white lines extend.

The gathering cloud grew red with stormy fire,
In streaks diverging wide and mounting high;
That inn he long had passed; the distant spire,
Which oft as he looked back had fixed his eye,
Was lost, though still he looked, in the blank sky.
Perplexed and comfortless he gazed around,
And scarce could any trace of man descry,
Save cornfields stretched and stretching without bound;
But where the sower dwelt was nowhere to be found.

No tree was there, no meadow's pleasant green,
No brook to wet his lip or soothe his ear;
Long files of corn-stacks here and there were seen,
But not one dwelling-place his heart to cheer.
Some labourer, thought he, may perchance be near;
And so he sent a feeble shout—in vain;
No voice made answer, he could only hear
Winds rustling over plots of unripe grain,
Or whistling thro' thin grass along the unfurrowed plain.

Long had he fancied each successive slope
Concealed some cottage, whither he might turn
And rest; but now along heaven's darkening cope
The crows rushed by in eddies, homeward borne.
Thus warned he sought some shepherd's spreading thorn
Or hovel from the storm to shield his head,
But sought in vain; for now, all wild, forlorn,
And vacant, a huge waste around him spread;
The wet cold ground, he feared, must be his only bed.

(ii)

Hurtle the clouds in deeper darkness piled,
Gone is the raven timely rest to seek;
He seemed the only creature in the wild
On whom the elements their rage might wreak;
Save that the bustard, of those regions bleak
Shy tenant, seeing by the uncertain light
A man there wandering, gave a mournful shriek,
And half upon the ground, with strange affright,
Forced hard against the wind a thick unwieldy flight.

All, all was cheerless to the horizon's bound;
The weary eye—which, wheresoe'er it strays,
Marks nothing but the red sun's setting round,
Or on the earth strange lines, in former days
Left by gigantic arms—at length surveys
What seems an antique castle spreading wide;
Hoary and naked are its walls, and raise
Their brow sublime: in shelter there to bide
He turned, while rain poured down, smoking on every side.

Pile of Stone-henge! so proud to hint yet keep
Thy secrets, thou that lov'st to stand and hear
The Plain resounding to the whirlwind's sweep,
Inmate of lonesome Nature's endless year;
Even if thou saw'st the giant wicker rear
For sacrifice its throngs of living men,
Before thy face did ever wretch appear,
Who in his heart had groaned with deadlier pain
Than he who, tempest-driven, thy shelter now would gain?

Within that fabric of mysterious form
Winds met in conflict, each by turns supreme;
And, from the perilous ground dislodged, through storm
And rain, he wildered on, no moon to stream
From gulf of parting clouds one friendly beam,
Nor any friendly sound his footsteps led;
Once did the lightning's faint disastrous gleam
Disclose a naked guide-post's double head,
Sight which, tho' lost at once, a gleam of pleasure shed.

No swinging sign-board creaked from cottage elm
To stay his steps with faintness overcome;
'Twas dark and void as ocean's watery realm
Roaring with storms beneath night's starless gloom;
No gipsy cowered o'er fire of furze or broom;
No labourer watched his red kiln glaring bright,
Nor taper glimmered dim from sick man's room;
Along the waste no line of mournful light
From lamp of lonely toll-gate streamed athwart the night.

                                        William Wordswor

33   In Love, at Stonehenge

By the great stones we chose our ground
    For shade; and there, in converse sweet,
Took luncheon.   On a little mound
    Sat the three ladies; at their feet
I sat; and smelt the heathy smell,
    Pluck'd harebells, turn'd the telescope
To the country round.   My life went well,
    For once, without the wheels of hope;
And I despised the Druid rocks
    That scowl'd their chill gloom from above,
Like churls whose stolid wisdom mocks
    The lightness of immortal love.
And, as we talk'd, my spirit quaff'd
    The sparkling winds; the candid skies
At our untruthful strangeness laugh'd;
    I kiss'd with mine her smiling eyes;
And sweet familiarness and awe
    Prevail'd that hour on either part,
And in the eternal light I saw
    That she was mine; though yet my heart

Could not conceive, nor would confess
  Such contentation; and there grew
More form and more fair stateliness
  Than heretofore between us two.

Coventry Patmore

34   Epilogue
(Wiltshire)

The painted autumn overwhelms
  The Summer's routed last array,
The citron patches on the elms
  Bring sunshine to the sunless day.

The dahlias and chrysanthemums
  Droop in the dripping garden lane,
A drowsy insect hums and drums
  Across the imprisoning window-pane.

The creeper's hatchment red and brown
  Falls gently on the garden bed,
The lurid snow-cloud on the down
  Can scarcely hide the winter's head.

John Meade Falkner

35   Salisbury: the Cathedral Close

Once more I came to Sarum Close,
  With joy half memory, half desire,
And breathed the sunny wind that rose
  And blew the shadows o'er the Spire,
And toss'd the lilac's scented plumes,
  And sway'd the chestnut's thousand cones,
And fill'd my nostrils with perfumes,
  And shaped the clouds in waifs and zones,
And wafted down the serious strain
  Of Sarum bells, when, true to time,
I reach'd the Dean's, with heart and brain
  That trembled to the trembling chime.

'Twas half my home, six years ago.
   The six years had not alter'd it:
Red-brick and ashlar, long and low,
   With dormers and with oriels lit.
Geranium, lychnis, rose array'd
   The windows, all wide open thrown;
And some one in the Study play'd
   The Wedding-March of Mendelssohn.

Coventry Patmo

36   In a Cathedral City
(Salisbury)

These people have not heard your name;
No loungers in this placid place
Have helped to bruit your beauty's fame.

The grey Cathedral, towards whose face
Bend eyes untold, has met not yours;
Your shade has never swept its base,

Your form has never darked its doors,
Nor have your faultless feet once thrown
A pensive pit-pat on its floors.

Along the street to maids well known
Blithe lovers hum their tender airs,
But in your praise voice not a tone....

—Since nought bespeaks you here, or bears,
As I, your imprint through and through,
Here might I rest, till my heart shares
The spot's unconsciousness of you!

Thomas Har

37   Bristol

What friendship can'st thou boast? what honours claim?
To thee each stranger owes an injured name.
What smiles thy sons must in their foes excite—
Thy sons to whom all discord is delight;
From whom eternal mutual railing flows;
Who in each other's crimes, their own expose;
Thy sons, though crafty, deaf to wisdom's call;
Despising all men and despised by all;
Sons, while thy cliffs a ditch-like river laves,
Rude as thy rocks, and muddy as thy waves;
Of thoughts as narrow as of words immense;
As full of turbulence as void of sense.

                                        Richard Savage

38   Weston-super-Mare
Midi

La pluie tombera tout le jour
Sur les terrasses qui se dressent
Entre le ciel en mouvement
Et les régions solennelles
De l'Empire du Soleil Blanc.

La Montagne-Inconnue se voile,
Et les gardiens de l'estuaire,
Les deux éléphants échoués,
Plongent dans l'immense brouillard
Et partent pour l'île d'argent.

Mais dans le jardin triste et bleu
Méditant sur ce midi sombre,
Où les capucines froissées
S'affalent et mêlent, pressées,
Leur robe jaune-orange et rouge;
On découvre, au bout d'un moment,
Quand on se croyait le plus seul,
Le nid, sous le porche abrité,
Où beaucoup d'yeux clairs et tranquilles
Regardent le jardin fumer.

Oh! comme la pluie les rend sages,
Et comme elles se taisent bien!
Et comme elles sont attentives
A tous ces regards blancs qui bougent
Dans les buis et les lauriers noirs!

Est-ce bien là Maisie-la-Folle,
Et Gladys qui rit tout le temps;
Violette aux genoux écorchés,
Et Gwenny qui lance toujours
Son volant par-dessus le mur?

Valery Larbaud

39   Widcombe Churchyard
(near Bath)

The place where soon I think to lie,
In its old creviced wall hard-by
   Rears many a weed.
Whoever leads you there, will you
Drop slily in a grain or two
   Of wall-flower seed?

I shall not see it, and (too sure)
I shall not ever know that your
   Dear hand was there;
But the rich odor some fine day
Shall (what I can not do) repay
   That little care.

Walter Savage Landor

40   Nightfall on Sedgemoor
(Somerset)

The darkness like a guillotine
   Descends on the flat earth;
The flocks look white across the rhine
   All but one lamb, a negro from its birth.

The pollards hold up in the gloom
   Knobbed heads with long stiff hair
That the wind tries to make a broom
   To sweep the moon's faint feather from the air

What makes the darkness fall so soon
   Is not the short March day
Nor the white sheep nor brightening moon,
    But long June evenings when I came this way.

               Andrew Young

41 Brent
(Somerset)

Happy are you, whom Quantock over looks,
Blest with keen healthy air, and crystal brooks;
While wretched we the baneful influence mourn
Of cold Aquarius, and his weeping urn.
Eternal mists their dropping curse distil
And drizzly vapours all the ditches fill:
The swampy land's a bog, the fields are seas
And too much moisture is the grand disease.
Here every eye with brackish rheum o'erflows
And a fresh drop still hangs at every nose.
Here the winds rule with uncontested right,
The wanton Gods at pleasure take their flight;
No sheltering hedge, no tree, or spreading bough
Obstruct their course, but unconfined they blow;
With dewy wings they sweep the wat'ry meads
And proudly trample o'er the bending reeds.
We are to north, and southern blasts exposed,
Still drowned by one, or by the other frozed.
Though Venice boast, Brent is as famed a seat,
For here we live in seas, and sail through every street;
And this great privilege we farther gain,
We never are obliged to pray for rain.
And 'tis as fond to wish for sunny days,
For though the God of light condense his rays
And try his power, we must in water lie;
The marsh will still be such, and Brent will ne'er be dry.

Sure this is nature's gaol for rogues designed;
Whoever lives in Brent, must live confined.
Moated around, the water is our fence;
None comes to us, and none can go from hence:
But should a milder day invite abroad
To wade through mire, and wallow in the mud,
Some envious rine will quickly thwart the road;
And then a small round twig is all your hopes,
You pass not bridges, but you dance on ropes.

All dogs here take the water, and we find
No creature but of an amphibious kind:
Rabbits with ducks, and geese here sail with hens,
And all for food must paddle in the fens;
Nay when provision fails, the hungry mouse
Will fear no pool to reach a neighb'ring house.
The good old hen clucks boldly through the stream
And chicken newly hatched essay to swim.
All have a moorish taste, cow, sheep, and swine,
Eat all like frog, and savour of the rine.
Bread is our only sauce, a barley cake
Hard as your cheese, and as your trencher black.
Our choicest drink (and that's the greatest curse)
Is but bad water made by brewing worse;
Better to taste the ditch pure, and unmixed,
Than when to more unwholesome ale bewitched.

To him that hath is alway given more
And a new stock supplies the rising store.
Not only rain from bounteous heaven descends,
But th'Ocean with an after-flood befriends;
For nature this as a relief designs
To salt the stinking water of the rines;
As when of late enraged Neptune sware
Brent was his own, part of his lawful share;
He said, and held his trident o'er the plain,
And soon the waves assert their ancient claim,
They scorn the shore, and o'er the marshes sound,
And mudwall cotts are levelled with the ground;
Though the coarse buildings are so humbly low
That when the house is fall'n, you hardly know.
Buried we are alive; the spacious dome
Has like the grave but one poor scanty room,
Neither so large, or lofty as a tomb.
Thus, as in th'Ark, here in one common sty
Men and their fellow-brutes with equal honour lie.

No joyous birds here stretch their tuneful throats
And pierce the yielding air with thrilling notes,
But the hoarse seapies with an odious cry
Skim o'er the marsh, and tell that storms are nigh.
The curst night-raven, and the hooping owl,

Disturb our rest, and scare the guilty soul.
The beasts are of no better kind, that fill
The brakes, and caverns of the neighbouring hill,
But are all digging moles, or prowling brocks,
The lurking serpent, and the crafty fox.
Serpents innumerous o'er the mountain roam;
Man's greatest foe thought this his safest home,
Nor could expect an hated place to find
More likely to be void of human kind;
And yet if dust be doomed the serpents' meat,
'Tis wond'rous strange, if here they ever eat.

Agues, and coughs with us as constant reign,
As th'itch in Scotland, or the flux in Spain.
Under the bending Nowl's declining brow,
Where toadstools only to perfection grow,
A cave there is, I thought by nature made,
For want of trees a necessary shade.
Hither I came, and void of fear or thought
Drew near the entrance of the pensive grot.
But ah!—This was the place, the dismal cell,
Where spitting colds, and shivering agues dwell,
The constant home of that malicious fiend
That with her third-day visit plagues mankind;
Here a small fire glowed in a smoky grate,
And hovering o'er the flames old Febris sate;
A thick coarse mantle on her shoulders hung,
She gnashed her teeth through cold, and her lean fingers wrung.
A stinking lake her craving thirst supplied,
From which a muddy stream did silent glide;
Greedy she drank of the unwholesome brook,
But still the more she drank, the more she shook.
When me the Fury saw, she raised her head,
And anger to her paleness gave a red.
Lost I had been, undone! Had I not brought
Of Indian Cortex an enchanted pot;
Thus armed with sacred spells, I forward pass
And with the magic bark besmeared her haggard face.
Dreadful she shrieked, and with one mighty shake
The hag down sunk into the neighbouring lake.
The unhappy frogs perceived the fiend was come,
And all the croaking tribes forsake their home;

And from the pool to milder banks repair,
The deadly chilling cold they could not bear,
And their pale quivering lips confessed an ague there.
With equal haste I quit the fatal grot,
And safe retire, thanks to my sov'reign pot.

Had mournful Ovid been to Brent condemned,
His *Tristibus* he would more movingly have penned.
Gladly he would have changed this miry slough
For colder Pontus, and the Scythian snow.
The Getes were not so barbarous a race,
As the grim natives of this motley place,
Of reason void, and thought, whom instinct rules,
Yet will be rogues though nature meant 'em fools,
A strange half-human, and ungainly brood,
Their speech uncouth, as are their manners rude;
When they would seem to speak the mortals roar
As loud as waves contending with the shore;
Their widened mouths into a circle grow,
For all their vowels are but A and O.
The beasts have the same language, and the cow
After her owner's voice is taught to low;
The lamb to baw, as doth her keeper, tries,
And puppies learn to howl from children's cries.

Some think us honest, but through this belief,
That where all steal, there no one is a thief.
Rogues of all kinds you may at leisure choose;
One finds a horse, another fears the noose
And humbly is content to take the shoes.

It never yet could be exactly stated
What time of th'year this ball was first created.
Some plead for summer, but the wise bethought 'em
That th'earth like other fruits was ripe in autumn;
While gayer wits the vernal bloom prefer,
And think the smiling world did first appear
In th'youthful glory of the budding year.
But the bleak Noul, and all the marshes round
(A sort of chaos, and unfinished ground)
Were made in winter, one may safely swear,
For winter is the only season there.

Of four prime Elements all things below
By various mixtures were composed, but now
(At least with us) they are reduced to two.
The daily want of fire our chimneys mourn,
Cowdung, and turf may smoke, but never burn.
Water and earth are all that Brent can boast,
The air in mists and dewy steams is lost;
We live on fogs, and in this moory sink
When we are thought to breath, we rather drink.
   It's said the world at length in flames must die
And thus interred in its own ashes lie.
If any part shall then remain entire
And be excepted from that common fire,
Sure 'twas this wat'ry spot that nature meant,
For though the world be burned, this never will be Brent*.

William Diaper

An old word for burnt.

42   Apostrophe to the Parret
(Sedgemoor)

Upon the soft brown pillow of thy shore
No shells lie scattered, such as childish hands
Delight to gather, yet thy sandy shore
Is richer than the gems of Cashmere's lands,
So prettily described by Thomas Moore.
Parret, though thou art Old Ocean's lawful daughter,
And to his breast thou rushest down with glee,
I cannot praise the blueness of thy water,—
Less blue than Baltic waves or Aegean sea:
   But thou flowest ever beautifully thick,
   Leaving thy filthy slime to make Bath brick!
I've seen thee gentle as a child asleep,
I've seen thee rushing wild from either shore,
Bringing back health and freedom from the deep,—
Yet men have called thy swift return a *bore*!

E. H. Burrington

43   The Quantocks

these populous slopes
With all their groves and with their murmurous woods,
Giving a curious feeling to the mind
Of peopled solitude.

William Wordsworth

44   Seen from the Quantocks
(i)

(Coleridge, prevented by an accident from going with them, describes what his friends, among them Charles Lamb, will see during their evening walk on the Quantocks above Nether Stowey, in June 1797)

Well, they are gone, and here must I remain,
This lime-tree bower my prison! I have lost
Beauties and feelings, such as would have been
Most sweet to my remembrance even when age
Had dimmed mine eyes to blindness! They, meanwhile,
Friends, whom I never more may meet again,
On springy heath, along the hill-top edge,
Wander in gladness, and wind down, perchance,
To that still roaring dell, of which I told;
The roaring dell, o'erwooded, narrow, deep,
And only speckled by the mid-day sun;
Where its slim trunk the ash from rock to rock
Flings arching like a bridge;—that branchless ash,
Unsunned and damp, whose few poor yellow leaves
Ne'er tremble in the gale, yet tremble still,
Fanned by the water-fall! and there my friends
Behold the dark green file of long lank weeds,
That all at once (a most fantastic sight!)
Still nod and drip beneath the dripping edge
Of the blue clay-stone.

Now, my friends emerge
Beneath the wide wide Heaven—and view again
The many-steepled tract magnificent
Of hilly fields and meadows, and the sea,
With some fair bark, perhaps, whose sails light up
The slip of smooth clear blue betwixt two Isles
Of purple shadow! Yes! they wander on

In gladness all; but thou, methinks, most glad,
My gentle-hearted Charles! for thou hast pined
And hungered after Nature, many a year,
In the great City pent, winning thy way
With sad yet patient soul, through evil and pain
And strange calamity! Ah! slowly sink
Behind the western ridge, thou glorious Sun!
Shine in the slant beams of the sinking orb,
Ye purple heath-flowers! richlier burn, ye clouds!
Live in the yellow light, ye distant groves!
And kindle, thou blue Ocean! So my friend
Struck with deep joy may stand, as I have stood,
Silent with swimming sense; yea, gazing round
On the wide landscape, gaze till all doth seem
Less gross than bodily; and of such hues
As veil the Almighty Spirit, when yet he makes
Spirits perceive his presence.

(ii)
Looking down on Nether Stowey

But now the gentle dew-fall sends abroad
The fruit-like perfume of the golden furze:
The light has left the summit of the hill,
Though still a sunny gleam lies beautiful,
Aslant the ivied beacon. Now farewell,
Farewell, awhile, O soft and silent spot!
On the green sheep-track, up the heathy hill,
Homeward I wind my way; and lo! recalled
From bodings that have well-nigh wearied me,
I find myself upon the brow, and pause
Startled! And after lonely sojourning
In such a quiet and surrounded nook,
This burst of prospect, here the shadowy main,
Dim-tinted, there the mighty majesty
Of that huge amphitheatre of rich
And elmy fields, seems like society—
Conversing with the mind, and giving it
A livelier impulse and a dance of thought!
And now, beloved Stowey! I behold
Thy church-tower, and, methinks, the four huge elms
Clustering, which mark the mansion of my friend;

And close behind them, hidden from my view,
Is my own lowly cottage, where my babe
And my babe's mother dwell in peace! With light
And quickened footsteps thitherward I tend,
Remembering thee, O green and silent dell!
And grateful, that by nature's quietness
And solitary musings, all my heart
Is soften'd, and made worthy to indulge
Love, and the thoughts that yearn for human kind.

Nether Stowey, 20 April 1798   S. T. Coleridg

45   Bournemouth

Le long bois de sapins se tord jusqu'au rivage,
L'étroit bois de sapins, de lauriers et de pins,
Avec la ville autour déguisée en village:
Chalets éparpillés rouges dans le feuillage
Et les blanches villas des stations de bains.

Le bois sombre descend d'un plateau de bruyère,
Va, vient, creuse un vallon, puis monte vert et noir
Et redescend en fins bosquets où la lumière
Filtre et dore l'obscur sommeil du cimetière
Qui s'étage bercé d'un vague nonchaloir.

À gauche la tour lourde (elle attend une flèche)
Se dresse d'une église invisible d'ici;
L'estacade très loin; haute, la tour, et sèche:
C'est bien l'anglicanisme impérieux et rêche
À qui l'essor du cœur vers le ciel manque aussi.

Il fait un de ces temps ainsi que je les aime,
Ni brume ni soleil! le soleil deviné,
Pressenti, du brouillard mourant dansant à même
Le ciel très haut qui tourne et fuit, rose de crème;
L'atmosphère est de perle et la mer d'or fané.

De la tour protestante il part un chant de cloche,
Puis deux et trois et quatre, et puis huit à la fois,
Instinctive harmonie allant de proche en proche,
Enthousiasme, joie, appel, douleur, reproche,
Avec de l'or, du bronze et du feu dans la voix;

Bruit immense et bien doux que le long bois écoute!
La Musique n'est pas plus belle. Cela vient
Lentement sur la mer qui chante et frémit toute,
Comme sous une armée au pas sonne une route
Dans l'écho qu'un combat d'avant-garde retient.

La sonnerie est morte. Une rouge traînée
De grands sanglots palpite et s'éteint sur la mer,
L'éclair froid d'un couchant de la nouvelle année
Ensanglante là-bas la ville couronnée
De nuit tombante, et vibre à l'ouest encore clair.

Le soir se fonce. Il fait glacial. L'estacade
Frissonne et le ressac a gémi dans son bois
Chanteur, puis est tombé lourdement en cascade
Sur un rythme brutal comme l'ennui maussade
Qui martelait mes jours coupables d'autrefois:

Solitude du cœur dans le vide de l'âme,
Le combat de la mer et des vents de l'hiver,
L'Orgueil vaincu, navré, qui râle et qui déclame,
Et cette nuit où rampe un guet-apens infâme,
Catastrophe flairée, avant-goût de l'Enfer! . . .

Voici trois tintements comme trois coups de flûtes,
Trois encor! trois encor! l'*Angélus* oublié
Se souvient, le voici qui dit: Paix à ces luttes!
Le Verbe s'est fait chair pour relever tes chutes,
Une vierge a conçu, le monde est délié!

Ainsi Dieu parle par la voie de *sa* chapelle
Sise à mi-côte à droite et sur le bord du bois . . .
Ô Rome, ô Mère! Cri, geste qui nous rappelle
Sans cesse au bonheur seul et donne au cœur rebelle
Et triste le conseil pratique de la Croix.

—La nuit est de velours. L'estacade laissée
Tait par degrés son bruit sous l'eau qui refluait.
Une route assez droite, heureusement tracée,
Guide jusque chez moi ma retraite pressée
Dans ce noir absolu sous le long bois muet.

nvier 1877   Paul Verlaine

46   La Mer de Bournemouth

La mer est plus belle
Que les cathédrales,
Nourrice fidèle,
Berceuse de râles,
La mer sur qui prie
La Vierge Marie!

Elle a tous les dons
Terribles et doux.
J'entends ses pardons
Gronder ses courroux . . .
Cette immensité
N'a rien d'entêté.

Oh! si patiente,
Même quand méchante!
Un souffle ami hante
La vague, et nous chante:
«Vous sans espérance,
Mourez sans souffrance!»

Et puis sous les cieux
Qui s'y rient plus clairs,
Elle a des airs bleus,
Roses, gris et verts . . .
Plus belle que tous,
Meilleure que nous!

Paul Verlaine

47   Ad Henricum Wottonem*
(Bere Regis, Dorset)

Wotton, my little Bere dwells on a hill,
Under whose foot the silver trout doth swim,
The trout silver without and gold within,
Bibbing clear nectar, which doth aye distil
From Nulam's low head; there the birds are singing
And there the partial sun still gives occasion

* To Henry Wotton.

To the sweet dew's eternal generation:
There is green joy and pleasure ever springing.
   O iron age of men, O time of rue,
    Shame ye not that all things are gold but you.

Thomas Bastard

48   Domicilium
(his birthplace at Higher Bockhampton, Dorset)

It faces west, and round the back and sides
High beeches, bending, hang a veil of boughs,
And sweep against the roof. Wild honeysucks
Climb on the walls, and seem to sprout a wish
(If we may fancy wish of trees and plants)
To overtop the apple-trees hard by.

Red roses, lilacs, variegated box
Are there in plenty, and such hardy flowers
As flourish best untrained. Adjoining these
Are herbs and esculents; and farther still
A field; then cottages with trees, and last
The distant hills and sky.

Behind, the scene is wilder. Heath and furze
Are everything that seems to grow and thrive
Upon the uneven ground. A stunted thorn
Stands here and there, indeed; and from a pit
An oak uprises, springing from a seed
Dropped by some bird a hundred years ago.

               In days bygone—
Long gone—my father's mother, who is now
Blest with the blest, would take me out to walk.
At such a time I once inquired of her
How looked the spot when first she settled here.
The answer I remember. 'Fifty years
Have passed since then, my child, and change has marked
The face of all things. Yonder garden-plots
And orchards were uncultivated slopes
O'ergrown with bramble bushes, furze and thorn:
That road a narrow path shut in by ferns,
Which, almost trees, obscured the passer-by.
Our house stood quite alone, and those tall firs

And beeches were not planted. Snakes and efts
Swarmed in the summer days, and nightly bats
Would fly about our bedrooms. Heathcroppers
Lived on the hills, and were our only friends;
So wild it was when first we settled here.'

Thomas Hard

49   The Roman Road
(Dorset: Puddletown Heath)

The Roman Road runs straight and bare
As the pale parting-line in hair
Across the heath. And thoughtful men
Contrast its days of Now and Then,
And delve, and measure, and compare;

Visioning on the vacant air
Helmed legionaries, who proudly rear
The Eagle, as they pace again
                    The Roman Road.

But no tall brass-helmed legionnaire
Haunts it for me. Uprises there
A mother's form upon my ken,
Guiding my infant steps, as when
We walked that ancient thoroughfare,
                    The Roman Road.

Thomas Hard

50   Once at Swanage

The spray sprang up across the cusps of the moon,
        And all its light loomed green
        As a witch-flame's weirdsome sheen
At the minute of an incantation scene;
And it greened our gaze—that night at demilune.

Roaring high and roaring low was the sea
        Behind the headland shores:
        It symboled the slamming of doors,
Or a regiment hurrying over hollow floors. . . .
And there we two stood, hands clasped; I and she!

Thomas Hard

51   Overlooking the River Stour
(Dorset)

The swallows flew in the curves of an eight
        Above the river-gleam
        In the wet June's last beam:
Like little crossbows animate
The swallows flew in the curves of an eight
        Above the river-gleam.

Planing up shavings of crystal spray
        A moor-hen darted out
        From the bank thereabout,
And through the stream-shine ripped his way;
Planing up shavings of crystal spray
        A moor-hen darted out.

Closed were the kingcups; and the mead
        Dripped in monotonous green,
        Though the day's morning sheen
Had shown it golden and honeybee'd;
Closed were the kingcups; and the mead
        Dripped in monotonous green.

And never I turned my head, alack,
        While these things met my gaze
        Through the pane's drop-drenched glaze,
To see the more behind my back. . . .
O never I turned, but let, alack,
        These less things hold my gaze!

                                    Thomas Hardy

52   On Sturminster Footbridge
(Dorset)

Reticulations creep upon the slack stream's face
        When the wind skims irritably past,
The current clucks smartly into each hollow place
That years of flood have scrabbled in the pier's sodden base;
        The floating-lily leaves rot fast.

On a roof stand the swallows ranged in wistful waiting rows,
    Till they arrow off and drop like stones
Among the eyot-withies at whose foot the river flows:
And beneath the roof is she who in the dark world shows
    As a lattice-gleam when midnight moans.

                        Thomas Hardy

53   Wessex Heights

There are some heights in Wessex, shaped as if by a kindly hand
For thinking, dreaming, dying on, and at crises when I stand,
Say, on Ingpen Beacon eastward, or on Wylls-Neck westwardly,
I seem where I was before my birth, and after death may be.

In the lowlands I have no comrade, not even the lone man's
    friend—
Her who suffereth long and is kind; accepts what he is too weak
    to mend:
Down there they are dubious and askance; there nobody thinks
    as I,
But mind-chains do not clank where one's next neighbour is the
    sky.

In the towns I am tracked by phantoms having weird detective
    ways—
Shadows of beings who fellowed with myself of earlier days:
They hang about at places, and they say harsh heavy things—
Men with a wintry sneer, and women with tart disparagings.

Down there I seem to be false to myself, my simple self that
    was,
And is not now, and I see him watching, wondering what crass
    cause
Can have merged him into such a strange continuator as this,
Who yet has something in common with himself, my chrysalis.

I cannot go to the great grey Plain; there's a figure against the
    moon,
Nobody sees it but I, and it makes my breast beat out of tune;
I cannot go to the tall-spired town, being barred by the forms
    now passed
For everybody but me, in whose long vision they stand there
    fast.

here's a ghost at Yell'ham Bottom chiding loud at the fall of
    the night,
here's a ghost in Froom-side Vale, thin-lipped and vague, in a
    shroud of white,
here is one in the railway train whenever I do not want it near,
see its profile against the pane, saying what I would not hear.

s for one rare fair woman, I am now but a thought of hers,
nter her mind and another thought succeeds me that she
    prefers;
et my love for her in its fulness she herself even did not know;
ell, time cures hearts of tenderness, and now I can let her go.

I am found on Ingpen Beacon, or on Wylls-Neck to the west,
r else on homely Bulbarrow, or little Pilsdon Crest,
here men have never cared to haunt, nor women have walked
    with me,
nd ghosts then keep their distance; and I know some liberty.

96
                                         Thomas Hardy

54   To Dean-bourn, a Rude River in Devon, by which
                sometimes he lived

    Dean-bourn, farewell; I never look to see
    Dean, or thy warty incivility.
    Thy rocky bottom, that doth tear thy streams,
    And makes them frantic, ev'n to all extremes,
    To my content I never should behold,
    Were thy streams silver, or thy rocks all gold.
    Rocky thou art; and rocky we discover
    Thy men; and rocky are thy ways all over.
    O men, O manners; now, and ever known
    To be a rocky generation!
    A people currish, churlish as the seas,
    And rude (almost) as rudest savages—
    With whom I did, and may re-sojourn when
    Rocks turn to rivers, rivers turn to men.
                             Robert Herrick

55   A Devonshire Walk

As when some wayfaring man passing a wood,
Whose waving top hath long a sea-mark stood,
Goes jogging on, and in his mind nought hath,
But how the primrose finely strew the path,
Or sweetest violets lay down their heads
At some tree's root on mossy feather-beds,
Until his heel receives an adder's sting,
Whereat he starts, and back his head doth fling.

                              William Browne of Tavistoc

56   The Course of the Tavy
(Devonshire)

                    Right so this river storms:
But broken forth; as Tavy creeps upon
The western vales of fertile Albion,
Here dashes roughly on an aged rock,
That his intended passage doth up-lock;
There intricately 'mongst the woods doth wander,
Losing himself in many a wry meander:
Here amorously bent, clips some fair mead;
And then dispersed in rills, doth measures tread
Upon her bosom 'mongst her flow'ry ranks:
There in another place bears down the banks
Of some day-labouring wretch: here meets a rill,
And with their forces joined cuts out a mill
Into an island, then in jocund guise
Surveys his conquest, lauds his enterprise:
Here digs a cave at some high mountain's foot:
There undermines an oak, tears up his root:
Thence rushing to some country farm at hand,
Breaks o'er the yeoman's mounds, sweeps from his land
His harvest hope of wheat, of rye, or pease:
And makes that channel which was shepherd's lease:
Here, as our wicked age doth sacrilege,
Helps down an abbey, then a natural bridge
By creeping underground he frameth out,
As who should say he either went about
To right the wrong he did, or hid his face,
For having done a deed so vile and base:
So ran this river on.

                              William Browne of Tavisto

lease: pasturage, common

57   On Seeing a Fine Frigate at Anchor in a Bay off
              Mount Edgecumbe
              (Plymouth Sound)

Is she not beautiful? reposing there
    On her own shadow, with her white wings furl'd;
Moveless, as in the sleepy sunny air,
    Rests the meek swan in her own quiet world.

Is she not beautiful? her graceful bow
    Triumphant rising o'er the enamour'd tides
That, glittering in the noon-day sunbeam, now
    Just leap and die along her polished sides.

                                    N. T. Carrington

              58   Devonshire Scenes

    One morn I watch'd the rain subside;
        And then fared singly forth,
    Below the clouds, till eve to ride
        From Edgecumb to the North.
    Once, only once, I paused upon
        The sea-transcending height,
    And turn'd to gaze: far breakers shone,
        Slow gleams of silent light.
    Into my horse I struck the spur;
        Sad was the soul in me;
    Sore were my lids with tears for her
        Who slept beneath the sea.
    But soon I sooth'd my startled horse,
        And check'd that sudden grief,
    And look'd abroad on crag and gorse
        And Dartmoor's cloudy reef.
    Far forth the air was dark and clear,
        The crags acute and large,
    The clouds uneven, black, and near,
        And ragged at the marge.
    The spider, in his rainy mesh,
        Shook not, but, as I rode,
    The opposing air, sweet, sharp, and fresh,
        Against my hot lids flow'd.
    Peat-cutters pass'd me, carrying tools;
        Hawks glimmer'd on the wing;

The ground was glad with grassy pools,
   And brooklets galloping;
And sparrows chirp'd, with feathers spread,
   And dipp'd and drank their fill,
Where, down its sandy channel, fled
   The lessening road-side rill.

I cross'd the furze-grown table-land,
   And near'd the northern vales,
That lay perspicuously plann'd
   In lesser hills and dales.
Then rearward, in a slow review,
   Fell Dartmoor's jagged lines;
Around were dross-heaps, red and blue,
   Old shafts of gutted mines,
Impetuous currents copper-stain'd,
   Wheels stream-urged with a roar,
Sluice-guiding grooves, strong works that strain'd
   With freight of upheaved ore.
And then, the train, with shock on shock,
   Swift rush and birth-scream dire,
Grew from the bosom of the rock,
   And pass'd in noise and fire.
With brazen throb, with vital stroke,
   It went, far heard, far seen,
Setting a track of shining smoke
   Against the pastoral green.
Then, bright drops, lodged in budding trees,
   Were loos'd in sudden showers,
Touch'd by the novel western breeze,
   Friend of the backward flowers.
Then rose the Church at Tavistock,
   The rain still falling there;
But sunny Dartmoor seem'd to mock
   The gloom with cheerful glare.
About the West the gilt vane reel'd
   And pois'd; and, with sweet art,
The sudden, jangling changes peal'd,
   Until, around my heart,
Conceits of brighter times, of times
   The brighter for past storms,
Clung thick as bees, when brazen chimes
   Call down the hiveless swarms.

I rested at the Tiger Inn,
   There half-way on my ride,
And mused with joy of friends and kin
   Who did my coming bide.
The Vicar, in his sombre wear
   That shone about the knees,
Before me stood, his aspect fair
   With godly memories.
I heard again his kind 'Good-bye:
   Christ speed and keep thee still
From frantic passions, for they die
   And leave a frantic will.'
My fond, old Tutor, learn'd and meek!
   A soul, in strangest truth,
As wide as Asia and as weak;
   Not like his daughter Ruth.
A Girl of fullest heart she was;
   Her spirit's lovely flame
Nor dazzled nor surprised, because
   It always burn'd the same;
And in the maiden path she trod
   Fair was the wife foreshown,
A Mary in the house of God,
   A Martha in her own.
Charms for the sight she had; but these
   Were tranquil, grave, and chaste,
And all too beautiful to please
   A rash, untutor'd taste.

In love with home, I rose and eyed
   The rainy North; but there
The distant hill-top, in its pride,
   Adorn'd the brilliant air:
And, as I pass'd from Tavistock,
   The scatter'd dwellings white,
The Church, the golden weather-cock,
   Were whelm'd in happy light;
The children 'gan the sun to greet,
   With song and senseless shout;
The lambs to skip, their dams to bleat;
   In Tavy leapt the trout;
Across a fleeting eastern cloud,
   The splendid rainbow sprang,
And larks, invisible and loud,
   Within its zenith sang.

So lay the Earth that saw the skies
   Grow clear and bright above,
As the repentant spirit lies
   In God's forgiving love.
The lark forsook the waning day,
   And all loud songs did cease;
The Robin, from a wither'd spray,
   Sang like a soul at peace.
Far to the South, in sunset glow'd
   The peaks of Dartmoor ridge,
And Tamar, full and tranquil, flow'd
   Beneath the Gresson Bridge.
There, conscious of the numerous noise
   Of rain-awaken'd rills,

And gathering deep and sober joys
   From the heart-enlarging hills,
I sat, until the first white star
   Appear'd, with dewy rays,
And the fair moon began to bar
   With shadows all the ways.
O, well is thee, whate'er thou art,
   And happy shalt thou be,
If thou hast known, within thy heart,
   The peace that came to me.
O, well is thee, if aught shall win
   Thy spirit to confess,
God proffers all, 'twere grievous sin
   To live content in less!

Coventry Patmo

59   The Marble-Streeted Town
(Plymouth)

I reach the marble-streeted town,
   Whose 'Sound' outbreathes its air
     Of sharp sea-salts;
I see the movement up and down
   As when she was there.
Ships of all countries come and go,
   The bandsmen boom in the sun
     A throbbing waltz;
The schoolgirls laugh along the Hoe
   As when she was one.

I move away as the music rolls:
 The place seems not to mind
  That she—of old
The brightest of its native souls—
  Left it behind!
Over this green aforedays she
 On light treads went and came,
  Yea, times untold;
Yet none here knows her history—
  Has heard her name.

Thomas Hardy

60 Hardy's Plymouth

Revisiting your marble-paved sea-perfumed town
I find it, like the middle class family of that
Girl you married, much run down.

I know, bombs fell; but years ago.
Bombs smashed the Regency facades
Which led you uphill to the Hoe,

Whereon later no aching comfort could be found
In pacing the daisied ground, in a drizzle
Vapouring as usual from the Sound.

Now out of irregular rubbly open spaces
Dirty concrete rises and replaces your town's
Stuccoed dignities and maritime graces,

And only in a neglected dead-end lane
I've seen, striped black or rose, a slab or two
Of your old marble glittering in the rain.

The other slabs are uniformly matt and grey
As if your town were now re-paved with all
The more aching recollections of your stay.

Geoffrey Grigson

61   The River Lynher
(East Cornwall)

When sun the earth least shadow spares,
And highest stalls in heaven his seat,
Then Lynher's pebble bones he bares,
Who like a lamb, doth lowly bleat,
    And faintly sliding every rock,
    Plucks from his foamy fleece a lock:

Before, a river, now a rill,
Before, a fence, now scarce a bound:
Children him over-leap at will,
Small beasts his deepest bottom sound.
    The heavens with brass enarch his head,
    And earth of iron makes his bed.

But when the milder-mooded sky
His face in mourning weeds doth wrap,
For absence of his clearest eye,
And drops tears in his centre's lap,
    Lynher 'gins lion-like to roar,
    And scorns old banks should bound him
        more.

Then, second sea, he rolls, and bears
Rocks in his womb, ricks on his back.
Down-born bridges, up-torn weirs,
Witness and wail his force their wrack.
    Into men's houses fierce he breaks,
    And on each stop his rage he wreaks.

Shepherd adieus his swimming flock,
The hind his whelmed harvest hope,
The strongest rampire fears his shock,
Plains scarce can serve to give him scope,
    Nor hills a bar; whereso he stray'th
    Ensue loss, terror, ruin, death.

                                        Richard Care

62   Green Slates
(Penpethy Quarries, near Delabole)

It happened once, before the duller
  Loomings of life defined them,
I searched for slates of greenish colour
  A quarry where men mined them;

And saw, the while I peered around there,
  In the quarry standing
A form against the slate background there,
  Of fairness eye-commanding.

And now, though fifty years have flown me,
  With all their dreams and duties,
And strange-pipped dice my hand has thrown me,
  And dust are all her beauties,

Green slates—seen high on roofs, or lower
  In waggon, truck, or lorry—
Cry out: 'Our home was where you saw her
  Standing in the quarry!'

                                    Thomas Hardy

63   After a Journey
(North Cornwall, St Juliot)

Hereto I come to view a voiceless ghost;
  Whither, O whither will its whim now draw me?
Up the cliff, down, till I'm lonely, lost,
  And the unseen waters' ejaculations awe me.
Where you will next be there's no knowing,
  Facing round about me everywhere,
    With your nut-coloured hair,
And gray eyes, and rose-flush coming and going.

Yes: I have re-entered your olden haunts at last;
   Through the years, through the dead scenes I have tracked
      you;
What have you now found to say of our past—
   Scanned across the dark space wherein I have lacked you?
Summer gave us sweets, but autumn wrought division?
    Things were not lastly as firstly well
      With us twain, you tell?
But all's closed now, despite Time's derision.

I see what you are doing: you are leading me on
   To the spots we knew when we haunted here together,
The waterfall, above which the mist-bow shone
   At the then fair hour in the then fair weather,
And the cave just under, with a voice still so hollow
   That it seems to call out to me from forty years ago,
     When you were all aglow,
And not the thin ghost that I now frailly follow!

Ignorant of what there is flitting here to see,
   The waked birds preen and the seals flop lazily;
Soon you will have, Dear, to vanish from me,
   For the stars close their shutters and the dawn whitens hazily
Trust me, I mind not, though Life lours,
   The bringing me here; nay, bring me here again!
    I am just the same as when
Our days were a joy, and our paths through flowers.

                          Thomas Hardy

64   The Phantom Horsewoman
(North Cornwall, near Beeny Cliff)

I

Queer are the ways of a man I know:
      He comes and stands
      In a careworn craze,
      And looks at the sands
      And the seaward haze
      With moveless hands
      And face and gaze,
      Then turns to go ...
And what does he see when he gazes so?

II

They say he sees as an instant thing
    More clear than to-day,
    A sweet soft scene
    That was once in play
    By that briny green;
    Yes, notes alway
    Warm, real, and keen,
    What his back years bring—
A phantom of his own figuring.

III

Of this vision of his they might say more:
    Not only there
    Does he see this sight,
    But everywhere
    In his brain—day, night,
    As if on the air
    It were drawn rose-bright—
    Yea, far from that shore
Does he carry this vision of heretofore:

IV

A ghost girl-rider. And though, toil-tried,
    He withers daily,
    Time touches her not,
    But she still rides gaily
    In his rapt thought
    On that shagged and shaly
    Atlantic spot,
    And as when first eyed
Draws rein and sings to the swing of the tide.

                       Thomas Hardy

65   At Carbis Bay
     (Cornwall)

Out of the night of the sea,
Out of the turbulent night,
A sharp and hurrying wind
Scourges the waters white:
The terror by night.

Out of the doubtful dark,
Out of the night of the land,
What is it breathes and broods
Hoveringly at hand?
The menace of land.

Out of the night of heaven,
Out of the delicate sky,
Pale and serene the stars
In their silence reply:
The peace of the sky.

                                   Arthur Symons

66   Back Again for the Holidays
     (Trebetherick, North Cornwall)
                (i)

Oh what a host of questions in me rose:
Were spring tides here or neap? And who was down?
Had Mr. Rosevear built himself a house?
Was there another wreck upon Doom Bar?
The carriage lamps lit up the pennywort
And fennel in the hedges of the lane;
Huge slugs were crawling over slabs of slate;
Then, safe in bed, I watched the long-legg'd fly
With red transparent body tap the walls
And fizzle in the candle flame and drag
Its poisonous-looking abdomen away
To somewhere out of sight and out of mind,
While through the open window came the roar
Of full Atlantic rollers on the beach.
   Then before breakfast down toward the sea
I ran alone, monarch of miles of sand,
Its shining stretches satin-smooth and vein'd.
I felt beneath bare feet the lugworm casts
And walked where only gulls and oyster-catchers
Had stepped before me to the water's edge.
The morning tide flowed in to welcome me,
The fan-shaped scallop shells, the backs of crabs,
The bits of driftwood worn to reptile shapes,
The heaps of bladder-wrack the tide had left
(Which, lifted up, sent sandhoppers to leap

In hundreds round me) answered 'Welcome back!'
Along the links and under cold Bray Hill
Fresh water pattered from an iris marsh
And drowned the golf-balls on its stealthy way
Over the slates in which the elvers hid,
And spread across the beach. I used to stand,
A speculative water engineer—
Here I would plan a dam and there a sluice
And thus divert the stream, creating lakes,
A chain of locks descending to the sea.
Inland I saw, above the tamarisks,
From various villas morning breakfast smoke
Which warned me then of mine; so up the lane
I wandered home contented, full of plans,
Pulling a length of pink convolvulus
Whose blossoms, almost as I picked them, died.

(ii)

                              The afternoons
Brought coconut smell of gorse; at Mably's farm
Sweet scent of drying cowdung; then the moist
Exhaling of the earth in Shilla woods—
First earth encountered after days of sand.
Evening brought back the gummy smell of toys
And fishy stink of glue and Stickphast paste,
And sleep inside the laundriness of sheets.
    Eyes! See again the rock-face in the lane,
Years before tarmac and the motor-car.
Across the estuary Stepper Point
Stands, still unquarried, black against the sun;
On its Atlantic face the cliffs fall sheer.
Look down into the weed world of the lawn—
The devil's-coach-horse beetle hurries through,
Lifting its tail up as I bar the way
To further flowery jungles.
                              See once more
The Padstow ferry, worked by oar and sail,
Her outboard engine always going wrong,
Ascend the slippery quay's up-ended slate,
The sea-weed hanging from the harbour wall.
Hot was the pavement under, as I gazed
At lanterns, brass, rope and ships' compasses

In the marine-store window on the quay.
The shoe-shop in the square was cool and dark.
The Misses Quintrell, fancy stationers,
Had most to show me—dialect tales in verse
Published in Truro (Netherton and Worth)
And model lighthouses of serpentine.
Climb the steep hill to where that belt of elm
Circles the town and church tower, reached by lanes
Whose ferny ramparts shelter toadflax flowers
And periwinkles. See hydrangeas bloom
In warm back-gardens full of fuchsia bells.
To the returning ferry soon draws near
Our own low bank of sand-dunes; then the walk
Over a mile of quicksand evening-cold.

It all is there, excitement for the eyes,
Imagined ghosts on unfrequented roads
Gated and winding up through broom and gorse
Out of the parish, on to who knows where?
What pleasure, as the oil-lamp sparkled gold
On cut-glass tumblers and the flip of cards,
To feel protected from the night outside:
Safe Cornish holidays before the storm!

John Betjema

67   Tregardock
(North Cornwall)

A mist that from the moor arose
    In sea-fog wraps Port Isaac bay,
The moan of warning from Trevose
    Makes grimmer this October day.

Only the shore and cliffs are clear.
    Gigantic slithering shelves of slate
In waiting awfulness appear
    Like journalism full of hate.

On the steep path a bramble leaf
    Stands motionless and wet with dew,
The grass bends down, the bracken's brown,
    The grey-green gorse alone is new.

Cautious my sliding footsteps go
   To quarried rock and dripping cave;
The ocean, leaden-still below,
   Hardly has strength to lift a wave.

I watch it crisp into its height
   And flap exhausted on the beach,
The long surf menacing and white
   Hissing as far as it can reach.

The dunlin do not move, each bird
   Is stationary on the sand
As if a spirit in it heard
   The final end of sea and land.

And I on my volcano edge
   Exposed to ridicule and hate
Still do not dare to leap the ledge
   And smash to pieces on the slate.

                                   John Betjeman

                68   Tresco
            (in the Isles of Scilly)

A low-set island this September
   Holds me tight like a jail:
I am warded by roving water
   Under this equinoctial gale.

Uneasy draughts now raise,
   As the feet run in the wall,
The sad curtains of the heart,
   And slowly let them fall.

So in the rich Bolivian night
   A train clatters in the hills,
And its echo speaks to the sleepless
   All the language of his ills:

An infant whines in his cot,
   Still ignorant of the unseen,
A hand gropes for a latch-key,
   A body bubbles down through the green.

The lights are yellow in 'Lamorna',
   In 'Clovelly', and in 'The Nest',
A diabetic drives in a needle,
   And chatters on to his guest.

Or an owl whines in a pine tree,
   The lovers switch out the light,
The uninfluential planets shine,
   And wheel, and disappear with the night.

A councillor mutters his speech
   In a bilious, uneasy dream,
And out on the enormous aerodrome
   Waves, at intervals, a warning beam.

All, as so slowly rise
   Out on this island, and so slowly fall,
The gusty curtains of the heart,
   And the feet run in the wall.

                          Geoffrey Grigson

4 Oxford and the Midlands

69 A Love Sonnet
(an undergraduate outing: Oxford)

I loved a lass, a fair one,
   As fair as e'er was seen;
She was indeed a rare one,
   Another Sheba queen.
But, fool as then I was,
   I thought she loved me too,
But now, alas, she's left me,
   Falero, lero, loo.

Her hair like gold did glister,
   Each eye was like a star;
She did surpass her sister,
   Which passed all others far.
She would me 'honey' call,
   She'd, O! she'd kiss me too;
But now, alas, she's left me,
   Falero, lero, loo.

In summer time to Medley
   My love and I would go;
The boatmen there stood ready,
   My love and I to row.
For cream there would we call,
   For cakes, and for prunes too;
But now, alas, she's left me,
   Falero, lero, loo.

Many a merry meeting
    My love and I have had;
She was my only sweeting,
    She made my heart full glad,
The tears stood in her eyes,
    Like to the morning dew;
But now, alas, she's left me,
    Falero, lero, loo.

And as abroad we walked,
    As lovers' fashion is,
Oft as we sweetly talked
    The sun should steal a kiss,
The wind upon her lips
    Likewise most sweetly blew;
But now, alas, she's left me,
    Falero, lero, loo.

Her cheeks were like the cherry,
    Her skin as white as snow;
When she was blithe and merry,
    She angel-like did show.
Her waist exceeding small,
    The fives did fit her shoe;
But now, alas, she's left me,
    Falero, lero, loo.

In summer time or winter
    She had her heart's desire;
I still did scorn to stint her
    From sugar, sack, or fire;
The world went round about,
    No cares we ever knew;
But now, alas, she's left me,
    Falero, lero, loo.

As we walked home together
    At midnight through the town,
To keep away the weather
    O'er her I'd cast my gown.
No cold my love should feel,
    Whate'er the heavens could do;
But now, alas, she's left me,
    Falero, lero, loo.

Like doves we would be billing,
   And clip and kiss so fast,
Yet she would be unwilling
   That I should kiss the last;
They're Judas' kisses now,
   Since that they proved untrue.
For now, alas, she's left me,
   Falero, lero, loo.

To maidens' vows and swearing
   Henceforth no credit give,
You may give them the hearing
   But never them believe.
They are as false as fair,
   Unconstant, frail, untrue;
For mine, alas, has left me,
   Falero, lero, loo.

'Twas I that paid for all things,
   'Twas others drank the wine,
I cannot now recall things,
   Live but a fool to pine.
'Twas I that beat the bush,
   The bird to others flew,
For she, alas, hath left me,
   Falero, lero, loo.

If ever that Dame Nature,
   For this false lover's sake,
Another pleasing creature
   Like unto her would make,
Let her remember this,
   To make the other true,
For this, alas, hath left me,
   Falero, lero, loo.

No riches now can raise me,
   No want make me despair,
No misery amaze me,
   Nor yet for want I care;
I have lost a world itself,
   My earthly heaven, adieu,
Since she, alas, hath left me,
   Falero, lero, loo.

George Wither

70   Binsey Poplars
felled 1879
(Oxford)

My aspens dear, whose airy cages quelled,
Quelled or quenched in leaves the leaping sun,
All felled, felled, are all felled;
   Of a fresh and following folded rank
       Not spared, not one
       That dandled a sandalled
    Shadow that swam or sank
On meadow and river and wind-wandering weed-winding
   bank.

O if we but knew what we do
    When we delve or hew—
  Hack and rack the growing green!
    Since country is so tender
  To touch, her being só slender,
  That, like this sleek and seeing ball
  But a prick will make no eye at all,

Where we, even where we mean
    To mend her we end her,
  When we hew or delve:
After-comers cannot guess the beauty been.
  Ten or twelve, only ten or twelve
    Strokes of havoc únselve
    The sweet especial scene,
  Rural scene, a rural scene,
  Sweet especial rural scene.

                Gerard Manley Hopk

71   Philomela
(Oxford and Bagley Wood)

Procne, Philomela, and Itylus,
Your names are liquid, your improbable tale
Is recited in the classic numbers of the nightingale.
Ah, but our numbers are not felicitous,
It goes not liquidly for us.

Perched on a Roman ilex, and duly apostrophized,
The nightingale descanted unto Ovid;
She has even appeared to the Teutons, the swilled and
     gravid;
At Fontainebleau it may be the bird was gallicized;
Never was she baptized.

To England came Philomela with her pain,
Fleeing the hawk her husband; querulous ghost,
She wanders when he sits heavy on his roost,
Utters herself in the original again,
The untranslatable refrain.

Not to these shores she came! this other Thrace,
Environ barbarous to the royal Attic;
How could her delicate dirge run democratic,
Delivered in a cloudless boundless public place
To an inordinate race?

I pernoctated with the Oxford students once,
And in the quadrangles, in the cloisters, on the Cher,
Precociously knocked at antique doors ajar,
Fatuously touched the hems of the hierophants,
Sick of my dissonance.

I went out to Bagley Wood, I climbed the hill;
Even the moon had slanted off in a twinkling,
I heard the sepulchral owl and a few bells tinkling,
There was no more villainous day to unfulfil,
The diuturnity was still.

Out of the darkness where Philomela sat,
Her fairy numbers issued. What then ailed me?
My ears are called capacious but they failed me,
Her classics registered a little flat!
I rose, and venomously spat.

Philomela, Philomela, lover of song,
I am in despair if we may make us worthy,
A bantering breed sophistical and swarthy;
Unto more beautiful, persistently more young,
Thy fabulous provinces belong.

John Crowe Ransom

72 *from* The Scholar-Gipsy
(Oxford and Berkshire)

Go, for they call you, shepherd, from the hill;
　　Go, shepherd, and untie the wattled cotes!
　　　No longer leave thy wistful flock unfed,
　　Nor let thy bawling fellows rack their throats,
　　　Nor the cropped herbage shoot another head.
　　　　But when the fields are still,
And the tired men and dogs all gone to rest,
　　And only the white sheep are sometimes seen
　　Cross and recross the strips of moon-blanched green,
Come, shepherd, and again begin the quest!

Here, where the reaper was at work of late—
　　In this high field's dark corner, where he leaves
　　　His coat, his basket, and his earthen cruse,
　　And in the sun all morning binds the sheaves,
　　　Then here, at noon, comes back his stores to use—
　　　　Here will I sit and wait,
While to my ear from uplands far away
　　The bleating of the folded flocks is borne,
　　With distant cries of reapers in the corn—
All the live murmur of a summer's day.

Screened is this nook o'er the high, half-reaped field,
　　And here till sun-down, shepherd! will I be.
　　　Through the thick corn the scarlet poppies peep,
　　And round green roots and yellowing stalks I see
　　　Pale pink convolvulus in tendrils creep;
　　　　And air-swept lindens yield
Their scent, and rustle down their perfumed showers
　　Of bloom on the bent grass where I am laid,
　　And bower me from the August sun with shade;
And the eye travels down to Oxford's towers.

And near me on the grass lies Glanvil's book—
　　Come, let me read the oft-read tale again!
　　　The story of the Oxford scholar poor,
　　Of pregnant parts and quick inventive brain,

Who, tired of knocking at preferment's door,
  One summer-morn forsook
His friends, and went to learn the gipsy-lore,
  And roamed the world with that wild brotherhood,
  And came, as most men deemed, to little good,
But came to Oxford and his friends no more.

But once, years after, in the country-lanes,
  Two scholars, whom at college erst he knew,
  Met him, and of his way of life enquired;
Whereat he answered; that the gipsy-crew,
  His mates, had arts to rule as they desired
    The workings of men's brains,
And they can bind them to what thoughts they will.
  'And I,' he said, 'the secret of their art,
  When fully learned, will to the world impart;
But it needs heaven-sent moments for this skill.'

This said, he left them, and returned no more.—
  But rumours hung about the country-side,
  That the lost Scholar long was seen to stray,
Seen by rare glimpses, pensive and tongue-tied,
  In hat of antique shape, and cloak of grey,
    The same the gipsies wore.
Shepherds had met him on the Hurst in spring;
  At some lone alehouse in the Berkshire moors,
  On the warm ingle-bench, the smock-frocked boors
Had found him seated at their entering,

But, 'mid their drink and clatter, he would fly.
And I myself seem half to know thy looks,
  And put the shepherds, wanderer! on thy trace;
And boys who in lone wheatfields scare the rooks
  I ask if thou hast passed their quiet place;
    Or in my boat I lie
Moored to the cool bank in the summer-heats,
  'Mid wide grass meadows which the sunshine fills,
  And watch the warm, green-muffled Cumner hills,
And wonder if thou haunt'st their shy retreats.

For most, I know, thou lov'st retired ground!
   Thee at the ferry Oxford riders blithe,
      Returning home on summer-nights, have met
   Crossing the stripling Thames at Bab-lock-hithe,
      Trailing in the cool stream thy fingers wet,
         As the punt's rope chops round;
   And leaning backward in a pensive dream,
      And fostering in thy lap a heap of flowers
      Plucked in shy fields and distant Wychwood bowers,
   And thine eyes resting on the moonlit stream.

And then they land, and thou art seen no more!—
   Maidens, who from the distant hamlets come
      To dance around the Fyfield elm in May,
   Oft through the darkening fields have seen thee roam,
      Or cross a stile into the public way.
         Oft thou hast given them store
   Of flowers—the frail-leafed, white anemony,
      Dark bluebells drenched with dews of summer eves,
      And purple orchises with spotted leaves—
   But none hath words she can report of thee.

And, above Godstow Bridge, when hay-time's here
   In June, and many a scythe in sunshine flames,
      Men who through those wide fields of breezy grass
   Where black-winged swallows haunt the glittering Thames,
      To bathe in the abandoned lasher pass,
         Have often passed thee near
   Sitting upon the river bank o'ergrown;
      Marked thine outlandish garb, thy figure spare,
      Thy dark vague eyes, and soft abstracted air—
   But, when they came from bathing, thou wast gone!

At some lone homestead in the Cumner hills,
   Where at her open door the housewife darns,
      Thou hast been seen, or hanging on a gate
   To watch the threshers in the mossy barns.
      Children, who early range these slopes and late
         For cresses from the rills,
   Have known thee eying, all an April-day,
      The springing pastures and the feeding kine;
      And marked thee, when the stars come out and shine,
   Through the long dewy grass move slow away.

n autumn, on the skirts of Bagley Wood—
  Where most the gipsies by the turf-edged way
    Pitch their smoked tents, and every bush you see
  With scarlet patches tagged and shreds of grey,
    Above the forest-ground called Thessaly—
      The blackbird, picking food,
  Sees thee, nor stops his meal, nor fears at all;
    So often has he known thee past him stray,
    Rapt, twirling in thy hand a withered spray,
  And waiting for the spark from heaven to fall.

And once, in winter, on the causeway chill
  Where home through flooded fields foot-travellers go,
    Have I not passed thee on the wooden bridge,
  Wrapt in thy cloak and battling with the snow,
    Thy face toward Hinksey and its wintry ridge?
      And thou hast climbed the hill,
  And gained the white brow of the Cumner range;
    Turned once to watch, while thick the snowflakes fall,
    The line of festal light in Christ-Church hall—
  Then sought thy straw in some sequestered grange.

But what—I dream! Two hundred years are flown
  Since first thy story ran through Oxford halls,
    And the grave Glanvil did the tale inscribe
  That thou wert wandered from the studious walls
    To learn strange arts, and join a gipsy-tribe;
      And thou from earth art gone
  Long since, and in some quiet churchyard laid—
    Some country-nook, where o'er thy unknown grave
    Tall grasses and white flowering nettles wave,
  Under a dark, red-fruited yew-tree's shade.

—No, no, thou hast not felt the lapse of hours!
  For what wears out the life of mortal men?
    'Tis that from change to change their being rolls;
  'Tis that repeated shocks, again, again,
    Exhaust the energy of strongest souls
      And numb the elastic powers.
  Till having used our nerves with bliss and teen,
    And tired upon a thousand schemes our wit,
    To the just-pausing Genius we remit
  Our worn-out life, and are—what we have been.

                                    Matthew Arnold

73 *from* Thyrsis
(Oxford and Berkshire)

A Monody, to commemorate the author's friend, Arthur Hugh Clough, wh
died at Florence, 1861

How changed is here each spot man makes or fills!
In the two Hinkseys nothing keeps the same;
The village street its haunted mansion lacks,
And from the sign is gone Sibylla's name,
And from the roofs the twisted chimney-stacks—
Are ye too changed, ye hills?
See, 'tis no foot of unfamiliar men
To-night from Oxford up your pathway strays!
Here came I often, often, in old days—
Thyrsis and I; we still had Thyrsis then.

Runs it not here, the track by Childsworth Farm,
Past the high wood, to where the elm-tree crowns
The hill behind whose ridge the sunset flames?
The signal-elm, that looks on Ilsley Downs,
The Vale, the three lone weirs, the youthful
Thames?—
This winter-eve is warm,
Humid the air! leafless, yet soft as spring,
The tender purple spray on copse and briers!
And that sweet city with her dreaming spires,
She needs not June for beauty's heightening,

Lovely all times she lies, lovely to-night!—
Only, methinks, some loss of habit's power
Befalls me wandering through this upland dim.
Once passed I blindfold here, at any hour;
Now seldom come I, since I came with him.
That single elm-tree bright
Against the west—I miss it! is it gone?
We prized it dearly; while it stood, we said,
Our friend, the Gipsy-Scholar, was not dead;
While the tree lived, he in these fields lived on.

Too rare, too rare, grow now my visits here,
But once I knew each field, each flower, each stick;
And with the country-folk acquaintance made

By barn in threshing-time, by new-built rick.
　Here, too, our shepherd-pipes we first assayed.
　　Ah me! this many a year
My pipe is lost, my shepherd's holiday!
　Needs must I lose them, needs with heavy heart
　Into the world and wave of men depart;
But Thyrsis of his own will went away.

It irked him to be here, he could not rest.
　He loved each simple joy the country yields,
　　He loved his mates; but yet he could not keep,
For that a shadow loured on the fields,
　　Here with the shepherds and the silly sheep.
　　　Some life of men unblest
He knew, which made him droop, and filled his head.
　He went; his piping took a troubled sound
　Of storms that rage outside our happy ground;
He could not wait their passing, he is dead.

So, some tempestuous morn in early June,
　When the year's primal burst of bloom is o'er,
　　Before the roses and the longest day—
When garden-walks and all the grassy floor
　　With blossoms red and white of fallen May
　　　And chestnut-flowers are strewn—
So have I heard the cuckoo's parting cry,
　From the wet field, through the vext garden-trees,
　Come with the volleying rain and tossing breeze:
The bloom is gone, and with the bloom go I!

Too quick despairer, wherefore wilt thou go?
　Soon will the high Midsummer pomps come on,
　　Soon will the musk carnations break and swell,
Soon shall we have gold-dusted snapdragon,
　　Sweet-William with his homely cottage-smell,
　　　And stocks in fragrant blow;
Roses that down the alleys shine afar,
　And open, jasmine-muffled lattices,
　And groups under the dreaming garden-trees,
And the full moon, and the white evening-star.

He hearkens not! light comer, he is flown!
What matters it? next year he will return,
And we shall have him in the sweet spring-days,
With whitening hedges, and uncrumpling fern,
And blue-bells trembling by the forest-ways,
And scent of hay new-mown.
But Thyrsis never more we swains shall see;
See him come back, and cut a smoother reed,
And blow a strain the world at last shall heed—
For Time, not Corydon, hath conquered thee!

Alack, for Corydon no rival now!—
But when Sicilian shepherds lost a mate,
Some good survivor with his flute would go,
Piping a ditty sad for Bion's fate;
And cross the unpermitted ferry's flow,
And relax Pluto's brow,
And make leap up with joy the beauteous head
Of Proserpine, among whose crowned hair
Are flowers first opened on Sicilian air,
And flute his friend, like Orpheus, from the dead.

O easy access to the hearer's grace
When Dorian shepherds sang to Proserpine!
For she herself had trod Sicilian fields,
She knew the Dorian water's gush divine,
She knew each lily white which Enna yields,
Each rose with blushing face;
She loved the Dorian pipe, the Dorian strain.
But ah, of our poor Thames she never heard!
Her foot the Cumner cowslips never stirred;
And we should tease her with our plaint in vain!

Well! wind-dispersed and vain the words will be,
Yet, Thyrsis, let me give my grief its hour
In the old haunt, and find our tree-topped hill!
Who, if not I, for questing here hath power?
I know the wood which hides the daffodil,
I know the Fyfield tree,
I know what white, what purple fritillaries
The grassy harvest of the river-fields,
Above by Ensham, down by Sandford, yields,
And what sedged brooks are Thames's tributaries;

I know these slopes; who knows them if not I?—
  But many a dingle on the loved hill-side,
    With thorns once studded, old, white-blossomed
      trees,
    Where thick the cowslips grew, and far descried
      High towered the spikes of purple orchises,
        Hath since our day put by
  The coronals of that forgotten time;
    Down each green bank hath gone the ploughboy's
      team,
    And only in the hidden brookside gleam
  Primroses, orphans of the flowery prime.

Where is the girl, who by the boatman's door,
  Above the locks, above the boating throng,
    Unmoored our skiff when through the Wytham
      flats,
  Red loosestrife and blond meadow-sweet among
    And darting swallows and light water-gnats,
      We tracked the shy Thames shore?
  Where are the mowers, who, as the tiny swell
    Of our boat passing heaved the river-grass,
    Stood with suspended scythe to see us pass?—
They all are gone, and thou art gone as well!

                       Matthew Arnold

  74   Laleham: Matthew Arnold's Grave
        (Berkshire)

    Beside the broad, gray Thames one lies,
    With whom a spring of beauty dies:
    Among the willows, the pure wind
    Calls all his wistful song to mind;
    And, as the calm, strong river flows,
    With it his mightier music goes;
    But those winds cool, those waters lave,
    The country of his chosen grave.
    Go past the cottage flowers, and see,
    Where Arnold held it good to be!
    Half church, half cottage, comely stands
    An holy house, from Norman hands:
    By rustic Time well taught to wear
    Some lowly, meditative air:
    Long ages of a pastoral race

Have softened sternness into grace;
And many a touch of simpler use
From Norman strength hath set it loose.
Here, under old, red-fruited yews,
And summer suns, and autumn dews,
With his lost children at his side,
Sleeps Arnold: Still those waters glide,
Those winds blow softly down their breast:
But he, who loved them, is at rest.

Lionel John

75   To Oxford

(i)

New-dated from the terms that reappear,
More sweet-familiar grows my love to thee,
And still thou bind'st me to fresh fealty
With long-superfluous ties, for nothing here
Nor elsewhere can thy sweetness unendear.
This is my park, my pleasaunce; this to me
As public is my greater privacy,
All mine, yet common to my every peer.
Those charms accepted of my inmost thought,
The towers musical, quiet-walled grove,
The window-circles, these may all be sought
By other eyes, and other suitors move,
And all like me may boast, impeached not,
Their special-general title to thy love.

(ii)

Thus, I come underneath this chapel-side,
So that the mason's levels, courses, all
The vigorous horizontals, each way fall
In bows above my head, as falsified
By visual compulsion, till I hide
The steep-up roof at last behind the small
Eclipsing parapet; yet above the wall
The sumptuous ridge-crest leave to poise and ride.
None besides me this bye-ways beauty try.
Or if they try it, I am happier then:
The shapen flags and drillèd holes of sky,
Just seen, may be to many unknown men
The one peculiar of their pleasured eye,
And I have only set the same to pen.

Gerard Manley Hop

76   By Magdalen Bridge, Oxford

Beyond Mágdalen and by the Bridge, on a place called there
   the Plain,
  In Summer, in a burst of summertime
  Following falls and falls of rain,
When the air was sweet-and-sour of the flown fineflour of
Those goldnails and their gaylinks that hang along a lime

                        Gerard Manley Hopkins

77   Oxford Bells

  Like shuttles fleet the clouds, and after
  A drop of shade rolls over field and flock;
  The wind comes breaking here and there with laughter:
  The violet moves and copses rock.

   .   .   .   .

  When the wind drops you hear the skylarks sing;
  From Oxford comes the throng and hum of bells
  Breaking the.   .   .   . air of spring.

                        Gerard Manley Hopkins

78   Duns Scotus's Oxford

Towery city and branchy between towers;
Cuckoo-echoing, bell-swarmèd, lark-charmèd,
   rook-racked, river-rounded;
The dapple-eared lily below thee; that country and town
   did
Once encounter in, here coped and poisèd powers;

Thou hast a base and brickish skirt there, sours
That neighbour-nature thy grey beauty is grounded
Best in; graceless growth, thou hast confounded
Rural rural keeping—folk, flocks, and flowers.

Yet ah! this air I gather and I release
He lived on; these weeds and waters, these walls are what
He haunted who of all men most sways my spirits to
   peace;

Of realty the rarest-veinèd unraveller; a not
Rivalled insight, be rival Italy or Greece;
Who fired France for Mary without spot.

                        Gerard Manley Hopkins

79 Oxford

Over, the four long years! And now there rings
One voice of freedom and regret: *Farewell!*
Now old remembrance sorrows, and now sings:
But song from sorrow, now, I cannot tell.

City of weathered cloister and worn court;
Gray city of strong towers and clustering spires:
Where art's fresh loveliness would first resort;
Where lingering art kindled her latest fires.

Where on all hands, wondrous with ancient grace,
Grace touched with age, rise works of goodliest men:
Next Wykeham's art obtain their splendid place
The zeal of Inigo, the strength of Wren.

Where at each coign of every antique street,
A memory hath taken root in stone:
There, Raleigh shone; there, toil'd Franciscan feet;
There, Johnson flinch'd not, but endured alone.

There, Shelley dream'd his white Platonic dreams;
There, classic Landor throve on Roman thought;
There, Addison pursued his quiet themes;
There, smiled Erasmus, and there, Colet taught.

And there, O memory more sweet than all!
Lived he, whose eyes keep yet our passing light;
Whose crystal lips Athenian speech recall;
Who wears Rome's purple with least pride, most right.

That is the Oxford, strong to charm us yet:
Eternal in her beauty and her past.
What, though her soul be vexed? She can forget
Cares of an hour: only the great things last.

Only the gracious air, only the charm,
And ancient might of true humanities:
These, nor assault of man, nor time, can harm;
Not these, nor Oxford with her memories.

Together have we walked with willing feet
Gardens of plenteous trees, bowering soft lawn:
Hills whither Arnold wandered; and all sweet
June meadows, from the troubling world withdrawn:

Chapels of cedarn fragrance, and rich gloom
Poured from empurpled panes on either hand:
Cool pavements, carved with legends of the tomb;
Grave haunts, where we might dream, and understand.

Over, the four long years! And unknown powers
Call to us, going forth upon our way:
Ah! turn we, and look back upon the towers,
That rose above our lives, and cheered the day.

Proud and serene, against the sky, they gleam:
Proud and secure, upon the earth, they stand:
Our city hath the air of a pure dream,
And hers indeed is an Hesperian land.

Think of her so! the wonderful, the fair,
The immemorial, and the ever young:
The city, sweet with our forefathers' care;
The city, where the Muses all have sung.

Ill times may be; she hath no thought of time:
She reigns beside the waters yet in pride.
Rude voices cry: but in her ears the chime
Of full, sad bells brings back her old springtide.

Like to a queen in pride of place, she wears
The splendour of a crown in Radcliffe's dome.
Well fare she, well! As perfect beauty fares;
And those high places, that are beauty's home.

                                        Lionel Johnson

80   Autumn on the Upper Thames
            (Kelmscott)

Fair is the world, now autumn's wearing,
And the sluggard sun lies long abed;
Sweet are the days, now winter's nearing,
And all winds feign that the wind is dead.

Dumb is the hedge where the crabs hang yellow,
Bright as the blossoms of the spring;
Dumb is the close where the pears grow mellow,
And none but the dauntless redbreasts sing.

Fair was the spring, but amidst his greening
Grey were the days of the hidden sun;
Fair was the summer, but overweening,
So soon his o'er-sweet days were done.

Come then, love, for peace is upon us,
Far off is failing, and far is fear,
Here where the rest in the end hath won us,
In the garnering tide of the happy year.

Come from the grey old house by the water,
Where, far from the lips of the hungry sea,
Green groweth the grass o'er the field of the slaughter,
And all is a tale for thee and me.

William Morri

81   Elegy Written in a Country Churchyard
(Stoke Poges, Buckinghamshire)

The curfew tolls the knell of parting day,
The lowing herd wind slowly o'er the lea,
The ploughman homeward plods his weary way,
And leaves the world to darkness and to me.

Now fades the glimmering landscape on the sight,
And all the air a solemn stillness holds,
Save where the beetle wheels his droning flight,
And drowsy tinklings lull the distant folds;

Save that from yonder ivy-mantled tower
The moping owl does to the moon complain
Of such as, wandering near her secret bower,
Molest her ancient solitary reign.

Beneath those rugged elms, that yew-tree's shade,
Where heaves the turf in many a mouldering heap,
Each in his narrow cell for ever laid,
The rude forefathers of the hamlet sleep.

The breezy call of incense-breathing morn,
The swallow twittering from the straw-built shed,
The cock's shrill clarion or the echoing horn,
No more shall rouse them from their lowly bed.

For them no more the blazing hearth shall burn,
Or busy housewife ply her evening care:
No children run to lisp their sire's return,
Or climb his knees the envied kiss to share.

Oft did the harvest to their sickle yield,
Their furrow oft the stubborn glebe has broke;
How jocund did they drive their team afield!
How bowed the woods beneath their sturdy stroke!

Let not Ambition mock their useful toil,
Their homely joys and destiny obscure;
Nor Grandeur hear, with a disdainful smile,
The short and simple annals of the poor.

The boast of heraldry, the pomp of power,
And all that beauty, all that wealth e'er gave,
Awaits alike the inevitable hour.
The paths of glory lead but to the grave.

Nor you, ye Proud, impute to these the fault,
If Memory o'er their tomb no trophies raise,
Where through the long-drawn aisle and fretted vault
The pealing anthem swells the note of praise.

Can storied urn or animated bust
Back to its mansion call the fleeting breath?
Can Honour's voice provoke the silent dust,
Or Flattery soothe the dull cold ear of Death?

Perhaps in this neglected spot is laid
Some heart once pregnant with celestial fire;
Hands that the rod of empire might have swayed,
Or waked to ecstasy the living lyre.

But Knowledge to their eyes her ample page
Rich with the spoils of time did ne'er unroll;
Chill Penury repressed their noble rage,
And froze the genial current of the soul.

Full many a gem of purest ray serene
The dark unfathomed caves of ocean bear:
Full many a flower is born to blush unseen,
And waste its sweetness on the desert air.

Some village-Hampden that with dauntless breast
The little tyrant of his fields withstood;
Some mute inglorious Milton here may rest,
Some Cromwell guiltless of his country's blood.

The applause of listening senates to command,
The threats of pain and ruin to despise,
To scatter plenty o'er a smiling land,
And read their history in a nation's eyes,

Their lot forbade: nor circumscribed alone
Their growing virtues, but their crimes confined;
Forbade to wade through slaughter to a throne,
And shut the gates of mercy on mankind,

The struggling pangs of conscious truth to hide,
To quench the blushes of ingenuous shame,
Or heap the shrine of Luxury and Pride
With incense kindled at the Muse's flame.

Far from the madding crowd's ignoble strife
Their sober wishes never learned to stray;
Along the cool sequestered vale of life
They kept the noiseless tenor of their way.

Yet even these bones from insult to protect
Some frail memorial still erected nigh,
With uncouth rhymes and shapeless sculpture decked,
Implores the passing tribute of a sigh.

Their name, their years, spelt by the unlettered muse,
The place of fame and elegy supply:
And many a holy text around she strews,
That teach the rustic moralist to die.

For who to dumb Forgetfulness a prey,
This pleasing anxious being e'er resigned,
Left the warm precincts of the cheerful day,
Nor cast one longing lingering look behind?

On some fond breast the parting soul relies,
Some pious drops the closing eye requires;
Even from the tomb the voice of Nature cries,
Even in our ashes live their wonted fires.

For thee who, mindful of the unhonoured dead,
Dost in these lines their artless tale relate;
If chance, by lonely Contemplation led,
Some kindred spirit shall inquire thy fate,

Haply some hoary-headed swain may say,
'Oft have we seen him at the peep of dawn
Brushing with hasty steps the dews away
To meet the sun upon the upland lawn.

'There at the foot of yonder nodding beech
That wreathes its old fantastic roots so high,
His listless length at noontide would he stretch,
And pore upon the brook that babbles by.

'Hard by yon wood, now smiling as in scorn,
Muttering his wayward fancies he would rove,
Now drooping, woeful wan, like one forlorn,
Or crazed with care, or crossed in hopeless love.

'One morn I missed him on the customed hill,
Along the heath and near his favourite tree;
Another came; nor yet beside the rill,
Nor up the lawn, nor at the wood was he;

'The next with dirges due in sad array
Slow through the church-way path we saw him borne.
Approach and read (for thou canst read) the lay,
Graved on the stone beneath yon aged thorn.'

The Epitaph

Here rests his head upon the lap of earth
A youth to Fortune and to Fame unknown.
Fair Science frowned not on his humble birth,
And Melancholy marked him for her own.

Large was his bounty and his soul sincere,
Heaven did a recompense as largely send:
He gave to Misery all he had, a tear,
He gained from Heaven ('twas all he wished) a friend.

No farther seek his merits to disclose,
Or draw his frailties from their dread abode,
(There they alike in trembling hope repose)
The bosom of his Father and his God.

Thomas Gray

82   The Poplar-Field
(Olney, Buckinghamshire)

The poplars are fell'd, farewell to the shade
And the whispering sound of the cool colonnade,
The winds play no longer, and sing in the leaves,
Nor Ouse on his bosom their image receives.

Twelve years have elaps'd since I first took a view
Of my favourite field and the bank where they grew,
And now in the grass behold they are laid,
And the tree is my seat that once lent me a shade.

The blackbird has fled to another retreat
Where the hazels afford him a screen from the heat,
And the scene where his melody charm'd me before,
Resounds with his sweet-flowing ditty no more.

My fugitive years are all hasting away,
And I must ere long lie as lowly as they,
With a turf on my breast, and a stone at my head,
Ere another such grove shall arise in its stead.

'Tis a sight to engage me, if any thing can,
To muse on the perishing pleasures of man;
Though his life be a dream, his enjoyments, I see,
Have a being less durable even than he.

William Cowper

83   On Westwell Downs
(the Cotswolds)

When Westwell Downs I gan to tread,
Where cleanly winds the green did sweep,
Methought a landskip there was spread,
Here a bush and there a sheep:

The pleated wrinkles of the face
Of wave-swoll'n earth did lend such grace,
As shadowings in imag'ry
Which both deceive and please the eye.

The sheep sometimes did tread the maze
By often winding in and in,
And sometimes round about they trace
Which milkmaids call a fairy ring:
    Such semicircles have they run,
    Such lines across so trimly spun
    That shepherds learn whenere they please
    A new geometry with ease.

The slender food upon the down
Is always even, always bare,
Which neither spring nor winter's frown
Can aught improve or aught impair:
    Such is the barren eunuch's chin,
    Which thus doth evermore begin
    With tender down to be o'ercast
    Which never comes to hair at last.

Here and there two hilly crests
Amidst them hug a pleasant green,
And these are like two swelling breasts
That close a tender fall between.
    Here would I sleep, or read, or pray
    From early morn till flight of day:
    But hark! a sheep-bell calls me up
    Like Oxford college bells, to sup.

                        William Strode

84   The High Hills
(the Cotswolds)

The high hills have a bitterness
Now they are not known,
And memory is poor enough consolation
For the soul hopeless gone.
Up in the air there beech tangles widely in the wind—
That I can imagine.
But the speed, the swiftness, walking into clarity,
Like last year's briony, are gone.

                        Ivor Gurney

85 Possessions
(near Gloucester, on the Cotswold Scarp)

Sand has the ants, clay ferny weeds for play,
But what shall please the wind now the trees are away
War took on Witcombe steep?
It breathes there, and wonders at old night roarings;
October time all lights, and the new clearings
For memory are like to weep.
It was right for the beeches to stand over Witcombe reaches,
Until the wind roared and softened and died to sleep.

Ivor Gurney

86 Adlestrop
(the Cotswolds)

Yes. I remember Adlestrop—
The name, because one afternoon
Of heat the express-train drew up there
Unwontedly. It was late June.

The steam hissed. Someone cleared his throat
No one left and no one came
On the bare platform. What I saw
Was Adlestrop—only the name

And willows, willow-herb, and grass,
And meadowsweet, and haycocks dry,
No whit less still and lonely fair
Than the high cloudlets in the sky.

And for that minute a blackbird sang
Close by, and round him, mistier,
Farther and farther, all the birds
Of Oxfordshire and Gloucestershire.

Edward Thoma

87   Dawns I Have Seen
(over Cotswold)

erribly for mystery or glory my dawns have arisen
ver Cotswold in great light, or beginning of colour,
nd my body at them has trembled, for beauty enraptured
   shaken
My spirit for so long Beauty's friend, truest follower).
seemed the right of Severn to call from the East-heaving
f Cotswold, nobleness his own for his right of honour;
nd his birds have exulted as if newly let from prison.
o those claims have I read Shakespeare, and the grand wide
   reason
f Milton—the childlike wonder of Chaucer almost or grieving
t the beauty of dewy daisies in the May-time season,
awn overpowering me past my own power of making;
lorious as West Country dawns show, day's first most-sacred
   hour.
o music in me to fit that great life-in-flood awakening.

                                            Ivor Gurney

88   Song
(Severn meadows)

Only the wanderer
   Knows England's graces,
Or can anew see clear
   Familiar faces.

And who loves joy as he
   That dwells in shadows?
Do not forget me quite,
   O Severn meadows.

                                            Ivor Gurney

89   Elver Fishermen on the Severn:
Two Gloucester Fragments

(i)
Rainy Midnight

ong shines the line of wet lamps dark in gleaming,
he trees so still felt yet as strength not used,
bruary chills April, the cattle are housed,
nd night's grief from the highest things comes streaming.

The traffic is all gone, the elver-fishers gone
To string their lights 'long Severn like a wet Fair.
If it were fine the elvers would swim clear.
Clothes sodden, the out-of-work stay on.

(ii)
Elver Fishers

The white faces are lit below the high bank,
Deadwood on the brown ledge fishermen made,
The night around tempers to another shade.

Ivor Gurney

90   Bredon Hill
(Worcestershire)

In summertime on Bredon
    The bells they sound so clear;
Round both the shires they ring them
    In steeples far and near,
    A happy noise to hear.

Here of a Sunday morning
    My love and I would lie,
And see the coloured counties,
    And hear the larks so high
    About us in the sky.

The bells would ring to call her
    In valleys miles away:
'Come all to church, good people;
    Good people, come and pray.'
    But here my love would stay.

And I would turn and answer
    Among the springing thyme,
'Oh, peal upon our wedding,
    And we will hear the chime,
    And come to church in time.'

But when the snows at Christmas
  On Bredon top were strown,
My love rose up so early
  And stole out unbeknown
  And went to church alone.

They tolled the one bell only,
  Groom there was none to see,
The mourners followed after,
  And so to church went she,
  And would not wait for me.

The bells they sound on Bredon,
  And still the steeples hum.
'Come all to church, good people,'—
  Oh, noisy bells, be dumb;
  I hear you, I will come.

A. E. Housman

91   Larches
(Cotswold, Malvern, Bredon)

arches are most fitting to small red hills
hat rise like swollen ant-heaps likeably
nd modest before big things like near Malvern
r Cotswold's farther early Italian
lue arrangement, unassuming as the
owslips, celandines, buglewort and daisies
hat trinket out the green swerves like a child's game.
, never so careless or lavish as here.
thought, 'You beauty, I must rise soon one dawn time
nd ride to see the first beam strike on you
f gold or ruddy recognisance over
rickley level or Bredon sloping down smoother.
must play tunes like Burns, or sing like the King David,
 saying out of what the hill leaves unexprest,
he tale or song that lives in it, and is sole—
 round red thing, green upright things of flame'.
is May, and the conceited cuckoo toots and whoots his name.

Ivor Gurney

92   The Dwindling Forest of Arden
(Warwickshire)

Muse, first of Arden tell, whose footsteps yet are found
In her rough woodlands more than any other ground
That mighty Arden held even in her height of pride;
Her one hand touching Trent, the other, Severn's side.
The very sound of these the wood nymphs doth awake:
When thus of her own self the ancient forest spake:
'My many goodly sites when first I came to show,
Here opened I the way to mine own overthrow:
For when the world found out the fitness of my soil,
The gripple wretch began immediately to spoil
My tall and goodly woods, and did my grounds enclose:
By which, in little time, my bounds I came to lose.
When Britain first her fields with villages had filled,
Her people waxing still, and wanting where to build,
They oft dislodged the hart, and set their houses, where
He in the broom and brakes had long time made his lair.
Of all the forests here within this mighty isle,
If those old Britons then me sovereign did instile,
I needs must be the great'st, for greatness 'tis alone
That gives our kind the place: else were there many a one
For pleasantness of shade that far doth me excel.
But of our forests' kind the quality to tell,
We equally partake with woodland as with plain,
Alike with hill and dale; and every day maintain
The sundry kinds of beasts upon our copious wastes,
That men for profit breed, as well as those of chase.'
Here Arden of her self ceased any more to show;
And with her sylvan joys the Muse along doth go.

Michael Drayt

gripple: grasping, greedy

93   At Arley
(Worcestershire)

The Severn sweeping smooth and broad
A motion to the hillside gives
Till it too liquifies and lives,
For glancing from that rushing road
I see the solid hill
Flow backward for a moment and stand still.

Andrew You

94   I Remember, I Remember
(Coventry)

Coming up England by a different line
For once, early in the cold new year,
We stopped, and, watching men with number-plates
Sprint down the platform to familiar gates,
'Why, Coventry!' I exclaimed. 'I was born here.'

I leant far out, and squinnied for a sign
That this was still the town that had been 'mine'
So long, but found I wasn't even clear
Which side was which. From where those cycle-crates
Were standing, had we annually departed

For all those family hols? . . . A whistle went:
Things moved. I sat back, staring at my boots.
'Was that,' my friend smiled, 'where you "have your roots"?'
No, only where my childhood was unspent,
I wanted to retort, just where I started:

By now I've got the whole place clearly charted.
Our garden, first: where I did not invent
Blinding theologies of flowers and fruits,
And wasn't spoken to by an old hat.
And here we have that splendid family

I never ran to when I got depressed,
The boys all biceps and the girls all chest,
Their comic Ford, their farm where I could be
Really myself. I'll show you, come to that,
The bracken where I never trembling sat,

Determined to go through with it; where she
Lay back, and 'all became a burning mist'.
And, in those offices, my doggerel
Was not set up in blunt ten-point, nor read
By a distinguished cousin of the mayor,

Who didn't call and tell my father *There*
Before us, had we the gift to see ahead—
'You look as if you wished the place in Hell,'
My friend said, 'judging from your face.' 'Oh well,
I suppose it's not the place's fault,' I said.

'Nothing, like something, happens anywhere.'

Philip Larkin

95   Charnwood Forest
(Leicestershire)
(*The River Soar speaks of the Forest*)

   O Charnwood, be thou called the choicest of thy kind,
The like in any place, what flood hath happed to find?
No tract in all this isle, the proudest let her be,
Can show a sylvan nymph for beauty like to thee:
The satyrs and the fauns, by Dian set to keep,
Rough hills, and forest holts, were sadly seen to weep,
When thy high-palmed harts, the sport of bows and hounds,
By gripple borderers' hands, were banished thy grounds.
The dryads that were wont thy lawns to rove,
To trip from wood to wood, and scud from grove to grove,
On Sharpley that were seen, and Cademan's aged rocks,
Against the rising sun, to braid their silver locks,
And with the harmless elves, on heathy Bardon's height,
By Cynthia's colder beams to play them night by night,
Exiled their sweet abode, to poor bare commons fled,
They with the oaks that lived, now with the oaks are dead.
Who will describe to life a forest, let him take
Thy surface to himself, nor shall he need to make
Another form at all, where oft in thee is found
Fine sharp but easy hills, which reverently are crowned
With aged antique rocks, to which the goats and sheep
(To him that stands remote) do softly seem to creep,
To gnaw the little shrubs, on their steep sides that grow;
Upon whose other part, on some descending brow,
Huge stones are hanging out, as though they down would
        drop,
Where under-growing oaks on their old shoulders prop

high-palmed: high antlered   borderers: cottagers
gripple: greedy, grasping

e others' hoary heads, which still seem to decline,
d in a dimble near (even as a place divine,
r contemplation fit) an ivy-sealed bower,
   Nature had therein ordained some sylvan power.

Michael Drayton

le: hollow

96   Sir Gawayn Goes to Receive His Return
       Blow from the Green Knight
       (Ludchurch, Staffordshire)

Gawayn spurred on, and he picked out a path,
Thrust in by a slope alongside a shaw,
Then over a rough bank dropped to a dell.
It was wilderness there. No sign at all
Of shelter he saw, but leftward and right
Cliffs steep and tall, and knuckles
Of crags, below clouds which the jutting
Of rocks seemed to graze. Gawayn hoved,
And held his horse back. For a chapel
He looked, and none such was there: a tump
In a glade was all that he saw,
By a bank on the brim of a burn
In a furrow, which bubbled and boiled.
He urged Gryngolet forward, then neatly
Lit down, tied the horse by his reins
To the bough of a lime, and trod closer round,
In debate what to make of this holed,
Hollow hump, which was grassed here and there:
Some old cave could it be, some old cleft
In a crag? What it was rightly Gawayn could not
                    spell.
            'Christ,' the knight cried,
            'In this chapel of hell
            The devil at midnight
            His matins might tell.'

'Now indeed,' Gawayn said, 'it's desolate here.
Ill looks this bede-house, with herbage so grown,
And well it befits for his devil's devoirs

That wight geared in green. Now with my five
Wits I see it's the Fiend who has fixed
This tryst up to slaughter me here; by this
Chapel of doom checkmate may betide me,
At this cursedest kirk came I ever nigh to.'
With high helmet on head and lance in his hand
He roved to the roof of that ragged abode,
When he heard, from that hard height of rock past
The brook, a noise on a bank which came strangely and stron
Quat! it clattered as if the cliff cracked.
It seemed someone was grinding a scythe on a stone.
Wat! it seemed mill-water, whetting and whirring.
Wat! ruth to hear, that noise rushed and rang.
'God,' Gawayn said, 'it's for me that gear's now
Preparing—a knight's proper greeting, my welcome I
                know,
            God does what he will:
            It is no good crying *Woe*!
            Yet no noise can scare me
            Though my life I forego.'

Then the knight called out loudly 'Who is it
Bids me to tryst in this place?
Good Gawayn is here now, so let
Who will now reveal himself quickly,
And quick let him speed, now or never, his need.'
'Wait!' cried one on the height overhead.
'What I promised you once, you shall have soon.'
But fast he continued his grinding a bit;
Stops his whetting, lights down, makes a way
By a crag, comes out through a cleft,
And waves in his nook a fell weapon aloft,
A new Danish axe to give the blow back.
It curved to its haft, a blade of strong bite,
Filed with a filer, full four feet across
(No less long by its bright gleaming thong).
So that grim one, in green as at first,
Green of visage and legs and of beard and of locks
(Though graceful his walking around), sets
His steel to the ground, stalks therewith
To the water, and not wading the stream,
On his axe hops across, and fiercely comes on. . . .

                    Anon (translated from the Middle Engl

97   An Ode Written in the Peak

This while we are abroad,
  Shall we not touch our lyre?
Shall we not sing an ode?
  Shall that holy fire
In us that strongly glowed
  In this cold air expire?

Long since the summer laid
  Her lusty brav'ry down,
The autumn half is wayed
  And Boreas 'gins to frown,
Since now I did behold
  Great Brute's first builded town.

Though in the utmost Peak
  A while we do remain,
Amongst the mountains bleak
  Exposed to sleet and rain,
No sport our hours shall break
  To exercise our vein.

What though bright Phoebus' beams
  Refresh the southern ground
And though the princely Thames
  With beauteous nymphs abound,
And by old Camber's streams
  Be many wonders found,

Yet many rivers clear
  Here glide in silver swathes,
And what of all most dear,
  Buxton's delicious bathes,
Strong ale and noble cheer
  T'assuage breme winter's scathes.

Those grim and horrid caves,
  Whose looks affright the day,

at Brute's first builded town: London
ne: furious
hes: injuries

Wherein nice nature saves
    What she would not bewray,
Our better leisure craves,
    And doth invite our lay.

In places far or near,
    Or famous, or obscure,
Where wholesome is the air,
    Or where the most impure,
All times, and everywhere,
    The Muse is still in ure.

Michael Drayt⟨

ure: use, practice

98   The Trent

Near to the silver Trent
    Sirena dwelleth:
She to whom Nature lent
    All that excelleth:
By which the Muses late,
    And the neat Graces,
Have for their greater state
    Taken their places:
Twisting an anadem
    Wherewith to crown her,
As it belonged to them
    Most to renown her.

On thy bank,
    In a rank
    Let thy swans sing her,
And with their music
    Along let them bring her.

Tagus and Pactolus
    Are to thee debtor,
Nor for their gold to us
    Are they the better:
Henceforth of all the rest
    Be thou the river,

anadem: wreath of flowers

Which as the daintiest,
  Puts them down ever,
For as my precious one
  O'er thee doth travel,
She to pearl paragon
  Turneth thy gravel.

    On thy bank,
    In a rank,
      Let thy swans sing her,
And with their music
  Along let them bring her.

Our mournful Philomel,
  That rarest tuner,
Henceforth in Aperil
  Shall wake the sooner,
And to her shall complain
  From the thick cover,
Redoubling every strain
  Over and over:
For when my love too long
  Her chamber keepeth,
As though it suffered wrong,
  The morning weepeth.

    On thy bank,
    In a rank,
      Let thy swans sing her,
And with their musick
  Along let them bring her.

Oft have I seen the sun,
  To do her honour,
Fix himself at his noon
  To look upon her,
And hath gilt every grove,
  Every hill near her,
With his flames from above,
  Striving to cheer her,
And when she from his sight
  Hath herself turned,

He as it had been night,
  In clouds hath mourned.

    On thy bank,
    In a rank,
      Let thy swans sing her,
And with their music
  Along let them bring her.

The verdant meads are seen,
  When she doth view them,
In fresh and gallant green
  Straight to renew them,
And every little grass
  Broad itself spreadeth,
Proud that this bonny lass
  Upon it treadeth:
Nor flower is so sweet
  In this large cincture
But it upon her feet
  Leaveth some tincture.

    On thy bank,
    In a rank,
      Let thy swans sing her,
And with their music
  Along let them bring her.

    .   .   .   .

Fair Dove and Darwine clear
  Boast ye your beauties,
To Trent your mistress here
  Yet pay your duties.
My love was higher born
  Tow'rds the full fountains,
Yet doth she moorland scorn,
  And the Peak mountains;
Nor would she none should dream
  Where she abideth,
Humble as is the stream,
  Which by her slideth.

    On thy bank,
    In a rank,

Darwine: the Darwen

Let thy swans sing her,
And with their music
Along let them bring her.

Yet my poor rustic Muse,
Nothing can move her,
Nor the means I can use,
Though her true lover:
Many a long winter's night
Have I waked for her,
Yet this my piteous plight,
Nothing can stir her.
All thy sands, silver Trent,
Down to the Humber,
The sighs that I have spent
Never can number.

On thy bank,
In a rank,
Let thy swans sing her,
And with their music
Along let them bring her.

Michael Drayton

99   The Trent Again

What should I care at all from what my name I take,
That thirty doth impart, that thirty rivers make
My greatness what it is, or thirty abbeys great,
That on my fruitful banks times formerly did seat;
Or thirty kinds of fish that in my streams do live,
To me this name of Trent did from that number give.
What reck I: let great Thames, since by his fortune he
Is sovereign of us all that here in Britain be,
From Isis and old Tame his pedigree derive;
And for the second place proud Severn that doth thrive,
Fetch her descent from Wales, from that proud mountain sprung,
Plinillimon, whose praise is frequent them among,
Is of that princely maid whose name she boasts to bear,
Bright Sabrin, which she holds as her undoubted heir.
Let these imperious floods draw down their long descent
From these so famous stocks, and only say of Trent

That moorlands' barren earth me first to light did bring,
Which though she be but brown, my clear complexioned spring
Gained with the nymphs such grace that when I first did rise
The Naiads on my brim danced wanton hydegies,
And on her spacious breast with heaths that doth abound
Encircled my fair fount with many a lusty round:
And of the British floods though but the third I be,
Yet Thames and Severn both in this come short of me,
For that I am the meare of England, that divides
The north part from the south, on my so either sides,
That reckoning how these tracts in compass be extent,
Men bound them on the north, or on the south of Trent.
Their banks are barren sands, if but compared with mine,
Through my perspicuous breast the pearly pebbles shine.
I throw my crystal arms along the flow'ry valleys,
Which lying sleek, and smooth, as any garden alleys,
Do give me leave to play, whilst they do court my stream,
And crown my winding banks with many an anademe.

Michael Drayto

hydegies: hay-de-Guys, formal dances   anademe: wreath of flowers
meare: boundary

100   The Retirement
(Dovedale, Derbyshire)

I

Farewell, thou busy world, and may
        We never meet again:
Here can I eat, and sleep, and pray,
And do more good in one short day,
Than he who his whole age out wears
Upon the most conspicuous theatres,
Where nought but vice and vanity do reign.

II

Good God! how sweet are all things here!
How beautiful the fields appear!
How cleanly do we feed and lie!
Lord! what good hours do we keep!
        How quietly we sleep!
What peace, what unanimity!
How innocent from the lewd fashion
Is all our bus'ness, all our conversation!

III

Oh how happy here's our leisure!
Oh how innocent our pleasure!
Oh ye valleys, oh ye mountains!
Oh ye groves and crystal fountains,
     How I love at liberty,
By turns to come and visit ye!

IV

    O Solitude, the soul's best friend,
That man acquainted with himself dost make,
And all his Maker's wonders to intend;
With thee I here converse at will,
And would be glad to do so still;
For it is thou alone, that keep'st the soul awake.

V

How calm and quiet a delight
    It is, alone
To read, and meditate, and write,
By none offended, nor offending none;
To walk, ride, sit, or sleep at one's own ease,
And pleasing a man's self, none other to displease!

VI

Oh my beloved nymph! fair Dove,
Princess of rivers, how I love
    Upon thy flow'ry banks to lie,
    And view thy silver stream,
When gilded by a summer's beam!
And in it, all thy wanton fry
    Playing at liberty,
And with my angle upon them
    The all of treachery
I ever learn'd to practise and to try!

VII

Such streams Rome's yellow Tiber cannot show,
Th' Iberian Tagus, nor Ligurian Po;
    The Meuse, the Danube, and the Rhine,
Are puddle-water all compar'd with thine;
And Loire's pure streams yet too polluted are
    With thine much purer to compare:

The rapid Garonne, and the winding Seine
  Are both too mean,
   Beloved Dove, with thee
   To vie priority;
Nay, Tame and Isis, when conjoin'd, submit,
And lay their trophies at thy silver feet.

                    VIII

Oh my beloved rocks! that rise
To awe the earth, and brave the skies,
From some aspiring mountain's crown
            How dearly do I love,
            Giddy with pleasure, to look down,
And from the vales to view the noble heights above

                    IX

Oh my beloved caves! from dog-star heats,
And hotter persecution safe retreats,
What safety, privacy, what true delight,
            In the artificial night,
            Your gloomy entrails make,
            Have I taken, do I take!
  How oft, when grief has made me fly
  To hide me from society,
  Even of my dearest friends, have I
            In your recesses' friendly shade
            All my sorrows open laid,
And my most secret woes entrusted to your privac

                    X

      Lord! would men let me alone,
      What an over-happy one
      Should I think my self to be,
      Might I in this desert place,
   Which most men by their voice disgrace,
      Live but undisturb'd and free!
      Here in this despis'd recess
            Would I maugre winter's cold,
      And the summer's worst excess,
Try to live out to sixty full years old,
            And all the while
            Without an envious eye
On any thriving under Fortune's smile,
Contented live, and then contented die.
                              Charles Cott

5 London

101 To the City of London

London, thou art of townes A *per se*.
  Soveraign of cities, semeliest in sight,
Of high renoun, riches, and royaltie;
  Of lordis, barons, and many goodly knyght;
  Of most delectable lusty ladies bright;
Of famous prelatis in habitis clericall;
  Of merchauntis full of substaunce and myght:
London, thou art the flour of Cities all.

Gladdith anon, thou lusty Troy Novaunt,
  Citie that some tyme cleped was New Troy,
In all the erth, imperiall as thou stant,
  Pryncesse of townes, of pleasure, and of joy,
  A richer restith under no Christen roy;
For manly power, with craftis naturall,
  Fourmeth none fairer sith the flode of Noy:
London, thou art the flour of Cities all.

Gemme of all joy, jasper of jocunditie,
  Most myghty carbuncle of vertue and valour;
Strong Troy in vigour and in strenuytie;
  Of royall cities rose and geraflour;
  Empresse of townes, exalt in honour;
In beawtie beryng the crone imperiall;
  Swete paradise precelling in pleasure;
London, thow art the floure of Cities all.

Above all ryvers thy Ryver hath renowne,
  Whose beryall stremys, pleasaunt and preclare,
Under thy lusty wallys renneth down,
  Where many a swanne doth swymme with wyngis fare;
  Where many a barge doth saile, and row with are,
Where many a ship doth rest with toppe-royall.
  O! towne of townes, patrone and not-compare:
London, thou art the floure of Cities all.

Upon thy lusty Brigge of pylers white
  Been merchauntis full royall to behold;
Upon thy stretis goth many a semely knyght
  In velvet gownes and cheynes of fyne gold.
  By Julyus Cesar thy Tour founded of old
May be the hous of Mars victoryall,
  Whos artillary with tonge may not be told;
London, thou art the flour of Cities all.

Strong be thy wallis that about the standis;
  Wise be the people that within the dwellis;
Fresh is thy ryver with his lusty strandis;
  Blith be thy chirches, wele sownyng be thy bellis;
  Riche be thy merchauntis in substaunce that excellis;
Fair be thy wives, right lovesom, white and small;
  Clere be thy virgyns, lusty under kellis:
London, thow art the flour of Cities all.

Thy famous Maire, by pryncely governaunce,
  With swerd of justice the rulith prudently.
No Lord of Parys, Venyce, or Floraunce
  In dignytie or honoure goeth to hym nye.
  He is exampler, loode-ster, and guye;
Principall patrone and roose orygynalle,
  Above all Maires as maister moost worthy:
London, thou art the flour of Cities all.

William Dunb

beryall: beryl   guye: guide
are: oar   roose: rose
kellis: coifs

102   London Lickpenny

In London there I was bent,
I saw myself, where truth should be atteint,
Fast to Westminster ward I went
To a man of law, to make my complaint;
I said, 'For Mary's sake, that holy saint,
Have pity on the poor that would proceed;
I would give silver, but my purse is faint:
For lack of money I may not speed.'

As I thrust throughout the throng
Among them all, my hood was gone;
Nathless I let not long
To King's Bench till I come.
Before a judge I kneeled anon,
I prayed him for God's sake he would take heed;
Full ruefully to him I gan make my moan:
'For lack of money I may not speed.'

Beneath him sat clerks, a great rout;
Fast they were written by one assent;
There stood up one, and cried round about,
'Richard, Robert, and one of Kent!'
I wist not well what he meant,
He cried so thich there indeed;
There were strong thieves shamed and shent,
But they that lacked money might mo speed.

Unto the Common Place I yowed thoo,
Where sat one with a silken hood;
I did him reverence as me ought to do,
I told him my case as well as I could,
And said all my goods by nowrd and soude;
I am defrauded with great falshed:
He would not give me a momme of his mouth;
For lack of money I may not speed.

ent: punished   nowrd, soude: north, south
owed thoo: went then   momme: mumble

Then I went me unto the Rollis,
Before the clerks of the Chancerie,
There were many *qui tollis*
But I heard no man speak of me;
Before them I kneeled upon my knee,
Showed them my evidence and they began to read;
They said truwe things might there never be—
But for lack of money I may not speed.

In Westminster Hall I found one
Went in a long gown of ray;
I crouched, I kneeled before them anon,
For Mary's love, of help I gan them pray.
As he had been wroth, he voided away
Backward, his hand he gan me bid:
'I wot not what thou meanest,' gan he say,
'Lay down silver, or here thou may not speed.'

In all Westminster Hall I could find never a one
That for me would do, though I should die:
Without the doors were Flemings great wone,
Upon me fast they gan to cry,
And said 'Master, what will ye copen or buy,
Fine felt hats, spectacles for to read
Of this gay gear?'—a great cause why
For lack of money I might not speed.

Then to Westminster gate I went,
When the sun was at high prime:
Cooks to me they took good intent,
Called me near for to dine,
And proffered me good bread, ale and wine;
A fair cloth they began to spread,
Ribs of beef both fat and fine;
But for want of money I might not speed.

---

many *qui tollis*: many takers up of causes (from the Litany, *Agnus Dei, qui tollis peccat*
mundi, Lamb of God, who takest away the sins of the world)
ray: striped cloth
great wone: very many   read of: inspect, estimate
copen: buy   high prime: nine in the morning

Into London I gan me hie,
Of all the land it beareth the prize;
'Hot peascods!' one gan cry,
'Strawberry ripe!', and 'Cherry in the rice!'
One bad me come near and buy some spice,
Pepper and saffron they gan me bede,
Clove, grains, and flower of rice;
For lack of money I might not speed.

Then into Cheap I gan me drawn,
Where I saw stand much people;
One bad me come near, and buy fine cloth of lawn,
Paris thread, cotton and umple;
I said thereupon I could no skill,
I am not wont thereto indeed;
One bad me buy a hure, my head to hele:
For lack of money I might not speed.

Then went I forth by London Stone,
Throughout all Canywike Street;
Drapers to me they called anon,
Great cheap of cloth they gan me hete;
Then come there one and cried 'Hot sheep's feet!'
'Rushes fair and green!' another gan to grete,
Both melwell and mackerel I gan meet,
But for lack of money I might not speed.

Then I hied me into Eastcheap;
One cried 'Ribs of beef, and many a pie!'
Pewter pots they clattered on a heap;
There was harp, pipe, and sawtry;
'Yea, by cock, nay, by cock' some began to cry;
Some sang of Jenken and Julian, to get themselves
    meed;
Full fain I would had of that minstrelsy,
But for lack of money I could not speed.

e rice: on the branch
: offer
s: a favourite medieval spice, Grains of Paradise, from Africa
le: fine linen   Canywike Street: Cannon Street
ld no skill: I had no knowledge   cheap: bargain
: cap   hete: offer
 cover   melwell: cod

Into Cornhill anon I yode,
Where is much stolen gear among;
I saw where hung mine own hood
That I had lost in Westminster among the throng!
Then I beheld it with looks full long;
I kenned it as well as I did my Creed:
To buy mine own hood again methought it wrong,
But for lack of money I might not speed.

Then came the taverner, and took me by the sleeve,
And said 'Sir, a pint of wine would you assay?'
'Sir,' quod I, 'it may not grieve,
For a penny may do no more than it may.'
I drank a pint, and therefor gan pay;
Sore a-hungered away I yede.
Farewell, London, Lickpenny, for once and aye!
For lack of money I may not speed.

Then I hied me to Billingsgate,
And cried 'Wag, wag, go hence!'
I prayed a bargeman for God's sake,
That they would spare me mine expense.
He said 'Rise up, man, and get thee hence!
What, weenist thou I will do on thee my alms deed?
Here scapeth no man beneath two pence!'
For lack of money I might not speed.

Then I conveyed me into Kent,
For of the law would I meddle no more;
Because no man to me would take intent,
I dight me to the plough, even as I did before.
Jesus save London, that in Bethlehem was bore!
And every true man of law God grant him his
　　　soul's meed,
And they that be other, God their state restore,
For he that lacketh money, with them he shall not
　　　speed.

15th century　　　　　　　　　　　　　　　　　　　　　　A

yode: went
Wag, wag, go hence: ? the customary cry for ferry or ferryman
meed: reward

103   Prothalamion

Calm was the day, and through the trembling air
Sweet breathing Zephyrus did softly play,
A gentle spirit, that lightly did delay
Hot Titan's beams, which then did glister fair;
When I whose sullen care,
Through discontent of my long fruitless stay
In prince's court, and expectation vain
Of idle hopes, which still do fly away
Like empty shadows, did afflict my brain,
Walked forth to ease my pain
Along the shore of silver streaming Thames,
Whose rutty bank, the which his river hems,
Was painted all with variable flowers,
And all the meads adorned with dainty gems,
Fit to deck maidens' bowers,
And crown their paramours,
Against the bridal day, which is not long:
    Sweet Thames, run softly, till I end my song.

There, in a meadow, by the river's side,
A flock of nymphs I chanced to espy,
All lovely daughters of the flood thereby,
With goodly greenish locks all loose untied,
As each had been a bride;
And each one had a little wicker basket,
Made of fine twigs entrailed curiously,
In which they gathered flowers to fill their flasket,
And with fine fingers cropped full featously
The tender stalks on high.
Of every sort, which in that meadow grew,
They gathered some; the violet pallid blue,
The little daisy, that at evening closes,
The virgin lily, and the primrose true,
With store of vermeil roses,
To deck their bridegrooms' posies,
Against the bridal day, which was not long:
    Sweet Thames, run softly, till I end my song.

With that, I saw two swans of goodly hue
Come softly swimming down along the Lee;
Two fairer birds I yet did never see.
The snow, which doth the top of Pindus strew,
Did never whiter shew,
Nor Jove himself, when he a swan would be
For love of Leda, whiter did appear:
Yet Leda was they say as white as he,
Yet not so white as these, nor nothing near.
So purely white they were,
That even the gentle stream, the which them bare,
Seemed foul to them, and bade his billows spare
To wet their silken feathers, lest they might
Soil their fair plumes with water not so fair,
And mar their beauties bright,
That shone as heaven's light,
Against their bridal day, which was not long:
    Sweet Thames, run softly, till I end my song.

Eftsoons the nymphs, which now had flowers their f
Ran all in haste, to see that silver brood,
As they came floating on the crystal flood.
Whom when they saw, they stood amazed still,
Their wondering eyes to fill.
Them seemed they never saw a sight so fair,
Of fowls so lovely, that they sure did deem
Them heavenly born, or to be that same pair
Which through the sky draw Venus' silver team;
For sure they did not seem
To be begot of any earthly seed,
But rather angels or of angels' breed:
Yet were they bred of Somers-heat they say,
In sweetest season, when each flower and weed
The earth did fresh array,
So fresh they seemed as day,
Even as their bridal day, which was not long:
    Sweet Thames, run softly, till I end my song.

Somers-heat: summer's heat, Somerset

Then forth they all out of their baskets drew
Great store of flowers, the honour of the field,
That to the sense did fragrant odours yield,
All which upon those goodly birds they threw,
And all the waves did strew,
That like old Peneus' waters they did seem,
When down along by pleasant Tempe's shore,
Scattered with flowers, through Thessaly they stream,
That they appear through lilies' plenteous store,
Like a bride's chamber floor.
Two of those nymphs, meanwhile, two garlands
    bound,
Of freshest flowers which in that mead they found,
The which presenting all in trim array,
Their snowy foreheads therewithal they crowned,
Whilst one did sing this lay,
Prepared against that day,
Against their bridal day, which was not long:
    Sweet Thames, run softly, till I end my song.

'Ye gentle birds, the world's fair ornament,
And heaven's glory, whom this happy hour
Doth lead unto your lovers' blissful bower,
Joy may you have and gentle heart's content
Of your love's couplement:
And let fair Venus, that is queen of love,
With her heart-quelling son upon you smile,
Whose smile, they say, hath virtue to remove
All love's dislike, and friendship's faulty guile
For ever to assoil.
Let endless peace your steadfast hearts accord,
And blessed plenty wait upon your board,
And let your bed with pleasures chaste abound,
That fruitful issue may to you afford,
Which may your foes confound,
And make your joys redound,
Upon your bridal day, which is not long:
    Sweet Thames, run softly, till I end my song.'

So ended she; and all the rest around
To her redoubled that her undersong,
Which said, their bridal day should not be long.
And gentle echo from the neighbour ground
Their accents did resound.
So forth those joyous birds did pass along,
Adown the Lee, that to them murmured low,
As he would speak, but that he lacked a tongue,
Yet did by signs his glad affection show,
Making his stream run slow.
And all the fowl which in his flood did dwell
'Gan flock about these twain, that did excel
The rest so far as Cynthia doth shend
The lesser stars. So they, enraged well,
Did on those two attend,
And their best service lend,
Against their wedding day, which was not long:
    Sweet Thames, run softly, till I end my song.

At length they all to merry London came,
To merry London, my most kindly nurse,
That to me gave this life's first native source;
Though from another place I take my name,
An house of ancient fame.
There when they came, whereas those bricky towers,
The which on Thames' broad aged back do ride,
Where now the studious lawyers have their bowers
There whilom wont the Templar Knights to bide,
Till they decayed through pride:
Next whereunto there stands a stately place,
Where oft I gained gifts and goodly grace
Of that great lord, which therein wont to dwell,
Whose want too well now feels my friendless case.
But ah! here fits not well
Old woes but joys to tell
Against the bridal day, which is not long:
    Sweet Thames, run softly, till I end my song.

shend: shame

Yet therein now doth lodge a noble peer,
Great England's glory and the world's wide wonder,
Whose dreadful name late through all Spain did
    thunder,
And Hercules' two pillars standing near
Did make to quake and fear.
Fair branch of honour, flower of chivalry,
That fillest England with thy triumph's fame,
Joy have thou of thy noble victory,
And endless happiness of thine own name
That promiseth the same:
That through thy prowess and victorious arms,
Thy country may be freed from foreign harms;
And great Elisa's glorious name may ring
Through all the world, filled with thy wide alarms,
Which some brave Muse may sing
To ages following,
Upon the bridal day, which is not long:
  Sweet Thames, run softly, till I end my song.

From those high towers this noble lord issuing,
Like radiant Hesper when his golden hair
In th' Ocean billows he hath bathed fair,
Descended to the river's open viewing,
With a great train ensuing.
Above the rest were goodly to be seen
Two gentle knights of lovely face and feature
Beseeming well the bower of any queen,
With gifts of wit and ornaments of nature,
Fit for so goodly stature;
That like the twins of Jove they seemed in sight,
Which deck the baldric of the heavens bright.
They two forth pacing to the river's side,
Received those two fair birds, their love's delight,
Which at th'appointed tide
Each one did make his bride,
Against their bridal day, which is not long:
  Sweet Thames, run softly, till I end my song.

Edmund Spenser

104   Twicknam Garden

Blasted with sighs, and surrounded with tears,
  Hither I come to seek the spring,
  And at mine eyes, and at mine ears,
Receive such balms, as else cure everything;
  But O, self traitor, I do bring
The spider love, which transubstantiates all,
  And can convert manna to gall,
And that this place may thoroughly be thought
  True paradise, I have the serpent brought.

'Twere wholesomer for me, that winter did
  Benight the glory of this place,
  And that a grave frost did forbid
These trees to laugh, and mock me to my face;
  But that I may not this disgrace
Endure, nor yet leave loving, Love, let me
  Some senseless piece of this place be;
Make me a mandrake, so I may groan here,
  Or a stone fountain weeping out my year.

Hither with crystal vials, lovers come,
  And take my tears, which are love's wine,
And try your mistress' tears at home,
For all are false, that taste not just like mine;
  Alas, hearts do not in eyes shine,
Nor can you more judge woman's thoughts by
    tears,
  Than by her shadow, what she wears.
O perverse sex, where none is true but she,
  Who's therefore true, because her truth kills me

                    John Donn

105   His Tears to Thamasis

I send, I send here my supremest kiss
To thee, my silver-footed Thamasis.
No more shall I reiterate thy Strand,
Whereon so many stately structures stand;
Nor in the summer's sweeter evenings go
To bathe in thee (as thousand others do).

No more shall I along thy crystal glide,
In barge (with boughs and rushes beautified)
With soft-smooth virgins (for our chaste disport)
To Richmond, Kingston, and to Hampton Court.
Never again shall I with finny oar
Put from, or draw unto thy faithful shore;
And landing here, or safely landing there,
Make way to my beloved Westminster;
Or to the golden Cheapside, where the earth
Of Julia Herrick gave to me my birth.
May all clean nymphs and curious water dames,
With swanlike state, float up and down thy streams,
No drought upon thy wanton waters fall
To make them lean, and languishing at all.
No ruffling winds come hither to disease
Thy pure, and silver-wristed Naiades.
Keep up your state, ye streams; and as ye spring,
Never make sick your banks by surfeiting.
Grow young with tides, and though I see ye never,
Receive this vow, *So fare ye well for ever.*

Robert Herrick

106   His Return to London

From the dull confines of the drooping West,
To see the day spring from the pregnant East,
Ravished in spirit, I come, nay more, I fly
To thee, blest place of my nativity!
Thus, thus with hallowed foot I touch the
    ground,
With thousand blessings by thy fortune crowned.
O fruitful Genius! that bestowest here
An everlasting plenty, year by year.
O Place! O People! Manners! framed to please
All nations, customs, kindreds, languages!
I am a freeborn Roman; suffer then
That I amongst you live a citizen.
London my home is: though by hard fate sent
Into a long and irksome banishment;
Yet since called back; henceforward let me be,
O native country, repossessed by thee!

For rather than I'll to the West return
I'll beg of thee first here to have mine urn.
Weak I am grown, and must in short time fall;
Give thou my sacred relics burial.

Robert Herrick

107   Of London Bridge, and the Stupendous Sight, and Structure Thereof

When Neptune from his billows London spied,
  Brought proudly thither by a high spring-tide,
  As through a floating wood he steer'd along,
  And dancing castles cluster'd in a throng;
  When he beheld a mighty bridge give law
  Unto his surges, and their fury awe,
  When such a shelf of cataracts did roar,
  As if the Thames with Nile had chang'd her shore,
  When he such massy walls, such tow'rs did eye,
  Such posts, such irons upon his back to lie,
  When such vast arches he observ'd, that might
  Nineteen Rialtos make for depth and height,
  When the Cerulean God these things survey'd,
  He shook his trident, and astonish'd said,
  Let the whole Earth now all her wonders count.
  This Bridge of Wonders is the paramount.

James Howell

108   London in 1646

Should we go now a-wand'ring, we should meet
With catchpoles, whores, and carts in ev'ry street:
Now when each narrow lane, each nook and cave,
Signposts, and shop doors, pimp for ev'ry knave,
When riotous sinful plush, and tell-tale spurs
Walk Fleet Street, and the Strand, when the soft stirs
Of bawdy, ruffled silks turn night to day;
And the loud whip, and coach scolds all the way;
When lusts of all sorts, and each itchy blood
From the Tower Wharf to Cymbeline, and Lud,
Hunts for a mate, and the tired footman reels
'Twixt chairmen, torches, and the hackney wheels.

Henry Vaughan

109   Solitude and Reason, in the Village

Thou the faint beams of reason's scattered light,
    Dost like a burning-glass unite,
    Dost multiply the feeble heat,
And fortify the strength, till thou dost bright
    And noble fires beget.

Whilst this hard truth I teach, methinks I see
    This monster, London, laugh at me,
    I should at thee too, foolish City,
If it were fit to laugh at misery,
    But thy estate I pity.

Let but thy wicked men from out thee go,
    And all the fools that crowd thee so,
    Even thou who dost thy millions boast,
A village less than Islington will grow,
    A solitude almost.

Abraham Cowley

110   About in London
(i)
Before it Rains

The seasons operate on ev'ry breast;
'Tis hence that fawns are brisk, and ladies dressed.
When on his box the nodding coachman snores,
And dreams of fancied fares; when tavern doors
The chairmen idly crowd; then ne'er refuse
To trust thy busy steps in thinner shoes.

  But when the swinging signs your ears offend
With creaky noise, then rainy floods impend;
Soon shall the kennels swell with rapid streams;
And rush in muddy torrents to the Thames.
The bookseller, whose shop's an open square,
Foresees the tempest, and with early care
Of learning strips the rails; the rowing crew
To tempt a fare, clothe all their tilts in blue:

nels: open runnels in the street   tilts: awnings

On hosiers' poles depending stockings tied
Flag with the slackened gale from side to side;
Church monuments foretell the changing air;
Then Niobe dissolves into a tear,
And sweats with secret grief: you'll hear the sounds
Of whistling winds, ere kennels break their bounds;
Ungrateful odours common shores diffuse,
And dropping vaults distil unwholesome dews
Before tiles rattle with the smoking show'r,
And spouts on heedless men their torrents pour.

(ii)
London at Night

When night first bids the twinkling stars appear,
Or with her cloudy veil enwraps the air,
Then swarms the busy street; with caution tread
Where the shop-windows falling threat thy head;
Now lab'rers home return, and join their strength
To bear the tott'ring plank, or ladder's length;
Still fix thy eyes intent upon the throng,
And as the passes open, wind along.

Where the fair columns of St Clement stand,
Whose straitened bounds encroach upon the Strand;
Where the low penthouse bows the walker's head,
And the rough pavement wounds the yielding tread;
Where not a post protects the narrow space,
And strung in twines, combs dangle in thy face;
Summon at once thy courage, rouse thy care,
Stand firm, look back, be resolute, beware.
Forth issuing from steep lanes, the collier's steeds
Drag the black load; another cart succeeds,
Team follows team, crowds heaped on crowds appear,
And wait impatient till the road grow clear.
Now all the pavement sounds with trampling feet,
And the mixed hurry barricades the street.
Entangled here, the waggon's lengthened team
Cracks the tough harness; here a pond'rous beam
Lies overturned athwart; for slaughter fed
Here lowing bullocks raise their horned head.

common shores: sewers

Now oaths grow loud, with coaches coaches jar,
And the smart blow provokes the sturdy war;
From the high box they whirl the thong around,
And with the twining lash their shins resound:
Their rage ferments, more dangerous wounds they try,
And the blood gushes down their painful eye,
And now on foot the frowning warriors light,
And with their pond'rous fists renew the fight;
Blow answers blow, their cheeks are smeared with
 blood,
Till down they fall, and grappling roll in mud.
So when two boars, in wild Ytene* bred,
Or on Westphalia's fatt'ning chestnuts fed,
Gnash their sharp tusks, and roused with equal fire,
Dispute the reign of some luxurious mire;
In the black flood they wallow o'er and o'er,
Till their armed jaws distil with foam and gore.

   Where the mob gathers, swiftly shoot along,
Nor idly mingle with the noisy throng.
Lured by the silver hilt, amid the swarm,
The subtil artist will thy side disarm.
Nor is thy flaxen wig with safety worn;
High on the shoulder in a basket born
Lurks the fly boy; whose hand to rapine bred,
Plucks off the curling honours of thy head.

                                        John Gay

w Forest in Hampshire, anciently so called.

111   Hampton Court

Close by those meads, for ever crowned with flowers,
Where Thames with pride surveys his rising towers,
There stands a structure of majestic frame,
Which from the neighb'ring Hampton takes its name.
Here Britain's statesmen oft the fall foredoom
Of foreign tyrants and of nymphs at home;
Here thou, great Anna! whom three realms obey,
Dost sometimes counsel take—and sometimes tea.
Hither the heroes and the nymphs resort,
To taste awhile the pleasures of a court;

In various talk the instructive hours they passed,
Who gave the ball, or paid the visit last;
One speaks the glory of the British Queen,
And one describes a charming Indian screen;
A third interprets motions, looks, and eyes;
At every word a reputation dies.
Snuff, or the fan, supply each pause of chat,
With singing, laughing, ogling, and all that.
Meanwhile, declining from the noon of day,
The sun obliquely shoots his burning ray;
The hungry judges soon the sentence sign,
And wretches hang that jury-men may dine;
The merchant from the Exchange returns in peace,
And the long labours of the toilet cease.

                                        Alexander Pope

112   London Suburbs

Suburban villas, highway-side retreats,
That dread th'encroachment of our growing streets,
Tight boxes, neatly sash'd, and in a blaze
With all a July sun's collected rays,
Delight the citizen, who, gasping there,
Breathes clouds of dust, and calls it country air.
Oh sweet retirement, who would balk the thought,
That could afford retirement, or could not?
'Tis such an easy walk, so smooth and straight,
The second milestone fronts the garden gate;
A step if fair, and, if a shower approach,
You find safe shelter in the next stage-coach.
There, prison'd in a parlour snug and small,
Like bottled wasps upon a southern wall,
The man of bus'ness and his friends compress'd,
Forget their labours, and yet find no rest;
But still 'tis rural—trees are to be seen
From ev'ry window, and the fields are green;
Ducks paddle in the pond before the door,
And what could a remoter scene show more?

                                        William Cowper

113 London

I wander thro' each charter'd street,
Near where the charter'd Thames does flow,
And mark in every face I meet
Marks of weakness, marks of woe.

In every cry of every Man,
In every Infant's cry of fear,
In every voice, in every ban,
The mind-forg'd manacles I hear.

How the Chimney-sweeper's cry
Every black'ning Church appalls;
And the hapless Soldier's sigh
Runs in blood down Palace walls.

But most thro' midnight streets I hear
How the youthful Harlot's curse
Blasts the new born Infant's tear,
And blights with plagues the Marriage hearse.

William Blake

114 The Young Wordsworth's London

Oh wond'rous power of words, how sweet they are
According to the meaning which they bring!
Vauxhall and Ranelagh, I then had heard
Of your green groves, and wilderness of lamps,
Your gorgeous Ladies, fairy cataracts,
And pageant fireworks; nor must we forget
Those other wonders different in kind,
Though scarcely less illustrious in degree,
The River proudly bridged, the giddy top
And Whispering Gallery of St. Paul's, the Tombs
Of Westminster, the Giants of Guildhall,
Bedlam, and the two maniacs at its Gates,
Streets without end, and Churches numberless,
Statues, with flowery gardens in vast Squares,
The Monument, and Armoury of the Tower.

These fond imaginations of themselves
Had long before given way in season due,
Leaving a throng of others in their stead;
And now I looked upon the real scene,
Familiarly perus'd it day by day
With keen and lively pleasure even there
Where disappointment was the strongest, pleas'd
Through courteous self-submission, as a tax
Paid to the object by prescriptive right,
A thing that ought to be. Shall I give way,
Copying the impression of the memory,
Though things unnumber'd idly do half seem
The work of fancy, shall I, as the mood
Inclines me, here describe, for pastime's sake
Some portion of that motley imagery,
A vivid pleasure of my Youth, and now
Among the lonely places that I love
A frequent day-dream for my riper mind?
—And first the look and aspect of the place
The broad high-way appearance, as it strikes
On Strangers of all ages, the quick dance
Of colours, lights and forms, the Babel din
The endless stream of men, and moving things,
From hour to hour the illimitable walk
Still among streets with clouds and sky above,
The wealth, the bustle and the eagerness,
The glittering Chariots with their pamper'd Steeds,
Stalls, Barrows, Porters; midway in the Street
The Scavenger, who begs with hat in hand,
The labouring Hackney Coaches, the rash speed
Of Coaches travelling far, whirl'd on with horn
Loud blowing, and the sturdy Drayman's Team,
Ascending from some Alley of the Thames
And striking right across the crowded Strand
Till the fore Horse veer round with punctual skill:
Here there and everywhere a weary throng
The Comers and the Goers face to face,
Face after face; the string of dazzling Wares,
Shop after shop, with Symbols, blazon'd Names,
And all the Tradesman's honours overhead;
Here, fronts of houses, like a title-page
With letters huge inscribed from top to toe;
Station'd above the door, like guardian Saints,

There, allegoric shapes, female or male;
Or physiognomies of real men,
Land-Warriors, Kings, or Admirals of the Sea,
Boyle, Shakspear, Newton, or the attractive head
Of some Scotch doctor, famous in his day.

    Meanwhile the roar continues, till at length,
Escaped as from an enemy, we turn
Abruptly into some sequester'd nook
Still as a shelter'd place when winds blow loud:
At leisure thence, through tracts of thin resort,
And sights and sounds that come at intervals,
We take our way: a raree-show is here
With children gather'd round, another Street
Presents a company of dancing Dogs,
Or Dromedary, with an antic pair
Of Monkies on his back, a minstrel Band
Of Savoyards, or, single and alone,
An English Ballad-singer. Private Courts,
Gloomy as Coffins, and unsightly Lanes
Thrill'd by some female Vender's scream, belike
The very shrillest of all London Cries,
May then entangle us awhile,
Conducted through those labyrinths unawares
To privileg'd Regions and inviolate,
Where from their airy lodges studious Lawyers
Look out on waters, walks, and gardens green.

    Thence back into the throng, until we reach,
Following the tide that slackens by degrees,
Some half-frequented scene where wider Streets
Bring straggling breezes of suburban air;
Here files of ballads dangle from dead walls,
Advertisements of giant-size, from high
Press forward in all colours on the sight;
These, bold in conscious merit; lower down
That, fronted with a most imposing word,
Is, peradventure, one in masquerade.
As on the broadening Causeway we advance,
Behold a Face turn'd up toward us, strong
In lineaments, and red with over-toil;
'Tis one perhaps, already met elsewhere,
A travelling Cripple, by the trunk cut short,

And stumping with his arms: in Sailor's garb
Another lies at length beside a range
Of written characters, with chalk inscrib'd
Upon the smooth flat stones: the Nurse is here,
The Bachelor that loves to sun himself,
The military Idler, and the Dame,
That field-ward takes her walk in decency.

  Now homeward through the thickening hubbub,
     where
See, among less distinguishable shapes,
The Italian, with his frame of Images
Upon his head; with Basket at his waist
The Jew; the stately and slow-moving Turk
With freight of slippers piled beneath his arm.
Briefly, we find, if tired of random sights
And haply to that search our thoughts should turn,
Among the crowd, conspicuous less or more,
As we proceed, all specimens of Man
Through all the colours which the sun bestows,
And every character of form and face,
The Swede, the Russian; from the genial South,
The Frenchman and the Spaniard; from remote
America, the Hunter-Indian; Moors,
Malays, Lascars, the Tartar and Chinese,
And Negro Ladies in white muslin gowns.

William Wordswo

115   Composed upon Westminster Bridge, Sept. 3, 1802

Earth has not anything to show more fair:
Dull would he be of soul who could pass by
A sight so touching in its majesty:
This City now doth, like a garment, wear
The beauty of the morning; silent, bare,
Ships, towers, domes, theatres, and temples lie
Open unto the fields, and to the sky;
All bright and glittering in the smokeless air.
Never did sun more beautifully steep
In his first splendour, valley, rock, or hill;
Ne'er saw I, never felt, a calm so deep!
The river glideth at his own sweet will:
Dear God! the very houses seem asleep;
And all that mighty heart is lying still!

William Wordsw

116   London, from Hampstead Heath

Our haughty life is crowned with darkness,
Like London with its own black wreath,
On which with thee, O Crabbe! forth-looking,
I gazed from Hampstead's breezy heath.

William Wordsworth

117   Lines Written in Kensington Gardens

In this lone, open glade I lie,
Screened by deep boughs on either hand;
And at its end, to stay the eye,
Those black-crowned, red-boled pine-trees stand!

Birds here make song, each bird has his,
Across the girdling city's hum.
How green under the boughs it is!
How thick the tremulous sheep-cries come!

Sometimes a child will cross the glade
To take his nurse his broken toy;
Sometimes a thrush flit overhead
Deep in her unknown day's employ.

Here at my feet what wonders pass,
What endless, active life is here!
What blowing daisies, fragrant grass!
An air-stirred forest, fresh and clear.

Scarce fresher is the mountain-sod
Where the tired angler lies, stretched out,
And, eased of basket and of rod,
Counts his day's spoil, the spotted trout.

In the huge world, which roars hard by,
Be others happy if they can!
But in my helpless cradle I
Was breathed on by the rural Pan.

I, on men's impious uproar hurled,
Think often, as I hear them rave,
That peace has left the upper world
And now keeps only in the grave.

Yet here is peace for ever new!
When I who watch them am away,
Still all things in this glade go through
The changes of their quiet day.

Then to their happy rest they pass!
The flowers upclose, the birds are fed,
The night comes down upon the grass,
The child sleeps warmly in his bed.

Calm soul of all things! make it mine
To feel, amid the city's jar,
That there abides a peace of thine,
Man did not make, and cannot mar.

Matthew Arno

118   London Snow

When men were all asleep the snow came flying,
In large white flakes falling on the city brown,
Stealthily and perpetually settling and loosely lying,
    Hushing the latest traffic of the drowsy town;
Deadening, muffling, stifling its murmurs failing;
Lazily and incessantly floating down and down:
    Silently sifting and veiling road, roof and railing;
Hiding difference, making unevenness even,
Into angles and crevices softly drifting and sailing.
    All night it fell, and when full inches seven
It lay in the depth of its uncompacted lightness,
The clouds blew off from a high and frosty heaven;
    And all woke earlier for the unaccustomed brightness
Of the winter dawning, the strange unheavenly glare:
The eye marvelled—marvelled at the dazzling whiteness;
    The ear hearkened to the stillness of the solemn air;
No sound of wheel rumbling nor of foot falling,
And the busy morning cries came thin and spare.
    Then boys I heard, as they went to school, calling,
They gathered up the crystal manna to freeze
Their tongues with tasting, their hands with snowballing;
    Or rioted in a drift, plunging up to the knees;
Or peering up from under the white-mossed wonder,
'O look at the trees!' they cried, 'O look at the trees!'
    With lessened load a few carts creak and blunder,

ollowing along the white deserted way,
A country company long dispersed asunder:
When now already the sun, in pale display
standing by Paul's high dome, spread forth below
His sparkling beams, and awoke the stir of the day.
For now doors open, and war is waged with the snow;
And trains of sombre men, past tale of number,
Tread long brown paths, as toward their toil they go:
But even for them awhile no cares encumber
Their minds diverted; the daily word is unspoken,
The daily thoughts of labour and sorrow slumber
At the sight of the beauty that greets them, for the charm they
      have broken.

Robert Bridges

119 À Germain Nouveau

Ce fut à Londres, ville où l'Anglaise domine,
Que nous nous sommes vus pour la première fois,
Et, dans King's Cross mêlant ferrailles, pas et voix,
Reconnus dès l'abord sur notre bonne mine.

Puis, la soif nous creusant à fond comme une mine,
De nous précipiter, dès libres des convois,
Vers des bars attractifs comme les vieilles fois,
Où de longues misses plus blanches que l'hermine

Font couler l'ale et le bitter dans l'étain clair
Et le cristal chanteur et léger comme l'air,
—Et de boire sans soif à l'amitié future!

Notre toast a tenu sa promesse. Voici
Que vieillis quelque peu depuis cette aventure,
Nous n'avons ni le cœur ni le coude transi.

Paul Verlaine

120 Londres
    . . . *un grave Anglais correct, bien mis, beau linge.*
                          (VICTOR HUGO)

Un dimanche d'été, quand le soleil s'en mêle,
Londres forme un régal offert aux délicats:
Les arbres forts et ronds sur la verdure frêle,
Vert tendre, ont l'air bien loin des brumes et des gaz,

Tant ils semblent plantés en terre paysanne.
Un soleil clair, léger dans le ciel fin, bleuté
À peine. On est comme en un bain où se pavane
Le parfum d'une lente infusion de thé.

Dix heures et demie, heure des longs services
Divins. Les cloches par milliers chantent dans l'air
Sonore et volatil sur d'étranges caprices,
Les psaumes de David s'ébrouent en brouillard clair.

Argentines comme on n'en entend pas en France,
Pays de sonnerie intense, bronze amer,
Font un concert très doux de joie et d'espérance,
Trop doux peut-être, il faut la crainte de l'Enfer.

L'après-midi, cloches encor. Des files d'hommes,
De femmes et d'enfants bien mis glissent plutôt
Qu'ils ne marchent, muets, on dirait économes
De leur voix réservée aux amen de tantôt.

Tout ce monde est plaisant dans sa raide attitude
Gardant, bien qu'erroné, le geste de la foi
Et son protestantisme à la fois veule et rude
Met quelqu'un tout de même au-dessus de la loi.

Espoir du vrai chrétien, riche vivier de Pierre,
Poisson prêt au pêcheur qui peut compter dessus,
Saint-Esprit, Dieu puissant, versez-leur la lumière
Pour qu'ils apprennent à comprendre enfin Jésus.

Six heures. Les buveurs regagnent leur buvette,
La famille son home et la rue est à Dieu:
Et dans le ciel sali quelque étoile seulette
Pronostique la pluie aux gueux sans feu ni lieu.

1876?   Paul Verlai

121

L'immensité de l'humanité,
Le Temps passé, vivace et bon père,
Une entreprise à jamais prospère:
Quelle puissante et calme cité!

Il semble ici qu'on vit dans l'histoire.
Tout est plus fort que l'homme d'un jour.
De lourds rideaux d'atmosphère noire
Font richement la nuit alentour.

Ô civilisés que civilise
L'Ordre obéi, le Respect sacré!
Ô, dans ce champ si bien préparé,
Cette moisson de la seule Église!

                                        Paul Verlaine

122   A Ballad of London

Ah, London! London! our delight,
Great flower that opens but at night,
Great City of the Midnight Sun,
Whose day begins when day is done.

Lamp after lamp against the sky
Opens a sudden beaming eye,
Leaping alight on either hand,
The iron lilies of the Strand.

Like dragonflies, the hansoms hover,
With jewelled eyes, to catch the lover;
The streets are full of lights and loves,
Soft gowns, and flutter of soiled doves.

The human moths about the light
Dash and cling close in dazed delight,
And burn and laugh, the world and wife,
For this is London, this is life!

Upon thy petals butterflies,
But at thy root, some say, there lies
A world of weeping trodden things,
Poor worms that have not eyes or wings.

From out corruption of their woe
Springs this bright flower that charms us so,
Men die and rot deep out of sight
To keep this jungle-flower bright.

Paris and London, World-Flowers twain
Wherewith the World-Tree blooms again,
Since Time hath gathered Babylon,
And withered Rome still withers on.

Sidon and Tyre were such as ye,
How bright they shone upon the Tree!
But Time hath gathered, both are gone,
And no man sails to Babylon.

Ah, London! London! our delight,
For thee, too, the eternal night,
And Circe Paris hath no charm
To stay Time's unrelenting arm.

Time and his moths shall eat up all.
Your chiming towers proud and tall
He shall most utterly abase,
And set a desert in their place.

Richard le Gallienne

123   There

«Angels»! seul coin luisant dans ce Londres du soir,
Où flambe un peu de gaz et jase quelque foule,
C'est drôle que, semblable à tel très dur espoir,
Ton souvenir m'obsède et puissamment enroule
Autour de mon esprit un regret rouge et noir:

Devantures, chansons, omnibus et les danses
Dans le demi-brouillard où flue un goût de rhum,
Décence, toutefois, le souci des cadences,
Et même dans l'ivresse un certain décorum,
Jusqu'à l'heure où la brume et la nuit se font denses.

«Angels»! jours déjà loin, soleils morts, flots taris;
Mes vieux péchés longtemps ont rôdé par tes voies,
Tout soudain rougissant, misère! et tout surpris
De se plaire vraiment à tes honnêtes joies,
Eux, pour tout le contraire arrivés de Paris!

'Angels': i.e. the district around The Angel, Islington

Souvent l'incompressible Enfance ainsi se joue,
Fût-ce dans ce rapport infinitésimal,
Du monstre intérieur qui nous crispe la joue
Au froid ricanement de la haine et du mal,
Ou gonfle notre lèvre amère en lourde moue.

L'Enfance baptismale émerge du pécheur,
Inattendue, alerte, et nargue ce farouche
D'un sourire non sans franchise ou sans fraîcheur,
Qui vient, quoi qu'il en ait, se poser sur sa bouche
À lui, par un prodige exquisement vengeur.

C'est la Grâce qui passe aimable et nous fait signe.
Ô la simplicité primitive, elle encor!
Cher recommencement bien humble! Fuite insigne
De l'heure vers l'azur mûrisseur de fruits d'or!
«Angels»! ô nom *revu*, calme et frais comme un cygne!

Paul Verlaine

124   Symphony in Yellow

An omnibus across the bridge
   Crawls like a yellow butterfly,
   And, here and there, a passer-by
Shows like a little restless midge.

Big barges full of yellow hay
   Are moored against the shadowy wharf,
   And, like a yellow silken scarf,
The thick fog hangs along the quay.

The yellow leaves begin to fade
   And flutter from the Temple elms,
   And at my feet the pale green Thames
Lies like a rod of rippled jade.

Oscar Wilde

125   Sonnet Boiteux

Ah! vraiment c'est triste, ah! vraiment ça finit trop mal.
Il n'est pas permis d'être à ce point infortuné.
Ah! vraiment c'est trop la mort du naïf animal
Qui voit tout son sang couler sous son regard fané.

Londres fume et crie. Ô quelle ville de la Bible!
Le gaz flambe et nage et les enseignes sont vermeilles.
Et les maisons dans leur ratatinement terrible
Épouvantent comme un sénat de petites vieilles.

Tout l'affreux passé saute, piaule, miaule et glapit
Dans le brouillard rose et jaune et sale des Sohos
Avec des *indeeds* et des *all rights* et des *haôs*.

Non vraiment c'est trop un martyre sans espérance,
Non vraiment cela finit trop mal, vraiment c'est triste
Ô le feu du ciel sur cette ville de la Bible!

Paul Verlaine

126   London Town

Let others chaunt a country praise,
Fair river walks and meadow ways;
Dearer to me my sounding days
          In *London Town*:
To me the tumult of the street
Is no less music, than the sweet
Surge of the wind among the wheat,
          By dale or down.

Three names mine heart with rapture hails,
With homage: *Ireland, Cornwall, Wales*:
Lands of lone moor, and mountain gales,
          And stormy coast:
Yet *London's* voice upon the air
Pleads at mine heart, and enters there;
Sometimes I wellnigh love and care
          For *London* most.

Listen upon the ancient hills:
All silence! save the lark, who trills
Through sunlight, save the rippling rills:
     There peace may be.
But listen to great *London!* loud,
As thunder from the purple cloud,
Comes the deep thunder of the crowd,
     And heartens me.

O gray, O gloomy skies! What then?
Here is a marvellous world of men;
More wonderful than *Rome* was, when
     The world was *Rome!*
See the great stream of life flow by!
Here thronging myriads laugh and sigh,
Here rise and fall, here live and die:
     In this vast home.

In long array they march toward death,
Armies, with proud or piteous breath:
Forward! the spirit in them saith,
     Spirit of life:
Here the triumphant trumpets blow;
Here mourning music sorrows low;
Victors and vanquished, still they go
     Forward in strife.

Who will not heed so great a sight?
Greater than marshalled stars of night,
That move to music and with light:
     For these are men!
These move to music of the soul;
Passions, that madden or control:
These hunger for a distant goal,
     Seen now and then.

Is mine too tragical a strain,
Chaunting a burden full of pain,
And labour, that seems all in vain?
     I sing but truth.
Still, many a merry pleasure yet,
To many a merry measure set,
Is ours, who need not to forget
     Summer and youth.

Do *London* birds forget to sing?
Do *London* trees refuse the spring?
Is *London* May no pleasant thing?
    Let country fields,
To milking maid and shepherd boy,
Give flowers, and song, and bright employ:
Her children also can enjoy,
    What *London* yields.

Gleaming with sunlight, each soft lawn
Lies fragrant beneath dew of dawn;
The spires and towers rise, far withdrawn,
    Through golden mist:
At sunset, linger beside *Thames:*
See now, what radiant lights and flames!
That ruby burns: that purple shames
    The amethyst.

Winter was long, and dark, and cold:
Chill rains! grim fogs, black fold on fold,
Round street, and square, and river rolled!
    Ah, let it be:
Winter is gone! Soon comes July,
With wafts from hayfields by-and-by:
While in the dingiest courts you spy
    Flowers fair to see.

Take heart of grace: and let each hour
Break gently into bloom and flower:
Winter and sorrow have no power
    To blight all bloom.
One day, perchance, the sun will see
London's entire felicity:
And all her loyal children be
    Clear of all gloom.

A dream? Dreams often dreamed come true:
Our world would seem a world made new
To those, beneath the churchyard yew
    Laid long ago!
When we beneath like shadows bide,
Fair *London,* throned upon *Thames'* side,
May be our children's children's pride:
    And we shall know.

Lionel Johnson

127   Vœux du Poète

Lorsque je serai mort depuis plusieurs années,
Et que dans le brouillard les cabs se heurteront,
Comme aujourd'hui (les choses n'étant pas changées)
Puissé-je être une main fraîche sur quelque front!
Sur le front de quelqu'un qui chantonne en voiture
Au long de Brompton Road, Marylebone ou Holborn,
Et regarde en songeant à la littérature
Les hauts monuments noirs dans l'air épais et jaune.
Oui, puissé-je être la pensée obscure et douce
Qu'on porte avec secret dans le bruit des cités,
Le repos d'un instant dans le vent qui nous pousse,
Enfants perdus parmi la foire aux vanités;
Et qu'on mette à mes débuts dans l'éternité,
L'ornement simple, à la Toussaint, d'un peu de
    mousse.

Valery Larbaud

128   Londres

Après avoir aimé des yeux dans Burlington Arcade,
Je redescends Piccadilly à pied, doucement.
O bouffées de printemps mêlées à des odeurs d'urine,
Entre les grilles du Green Park et la station des cabs,
Combien vous êtes émouvantes!

Puis, je suis Rotten Row, vers Kensington, plus calme,
Moins en poésie, moins sous le charme
De ces couleurs, de ces odeurs et de ce grondement de
    Londres.
(O Johnson, je comprends ton cœur, savant Docteur,
Ce cœur tout résonnant des bruits de la grand'ville:
L'horizon de Fleet Street suffisait à tes yeux.)

O jardins verts et bleus, brouillards blancs, voiles
    mauves!
Barrant l'eau de platine morne du Bassin,
Qui dort sous l'impalpable gaze d'une riche brume,
Le long sillage d'un oiseau d'eau couleur de rouille...

Il y a la Tamise, que Madame d'Aulnoy
Trouvait «un des plus beaux cours d'eau du monde».
Ses personnages historiques y naviguaient, l'été,
Au soir tombant, froissant le reflet blanc
Des premières étoiles;
Et les barges, tendues de soie, chargées de princes
Et de dames couchés sur les carreaux brodés,
Et Buckingham et les menines de la Reine,
S'avançaient doucement, comme un rêve, sur l'eau,
Ou comme notre cœur se bercerait longtemps
Aux beaux rythmes des vers royaux d'Albert Samain.
La rue luisante où tout se mire;
Le bus multicolore, le cab noir, la girl en rose
Et même un peu de soleil couchant, on dirait. . .
Les toits lavés, le square bleuâtre et tout fumant. . .
Les nuages de cuivre sali qui s'élèvent lentement. . .
Accalmie et tiédeur humide, et odeur de miel du tabac;
La dorure de ce livre
Devient plus claire à chaque instant: un essai de soleil
     sans doute.
(Trop tard, la nuit le prendra fatalement.)
Et voici qu'éclate l'orgue de Barbarie après l'averse.

                              Valery Larbau

129   Regent's Park Terrace

The noises round my house. On cobbles bounding
Victorian-fashioned drays laden with railway goods;
their hollow sound like stones in rolling barrels:
the stony hoofing of dray horses.

Further, the trains themselves; among them the violent,
screaming like frightened animals, clashing metal;
different the pompous, the heavy breathers, the aldermen
or those again which speed with the declining
sadness of crying along the distant routes
knitting together weathers and dialects.

Between these noises the little teeth
of a London silence.

Finally the lions grumbling over the park,
angry in the night hours,
cavernous as though their throats were openings up from
     the earth:
hooves, luggage, engines, tumbrils, lions,
hollow noises, noises of travel, hourly these unpick
the bricks of a London terrace, make the ear
their road, and have their audience in whatever
hearing the heart or the deep of the belly owns.

                                        Bernard Spencer

            130   The Rainbow
                  (Essex)

                         See on one hand
He drops his bright roots in the water'd sward,
And rosing part, on part dispenses green;
But with his other foot three miles beyond
He rises from the flocks of villages
That bead the plain; did ever Havering church-tower
Breathe in such ether? or the Quickly elms
⎰ With such a violet slight their distanced green?
⎱ Slight with such violet their bright-mask'd green?

Mask'd with such violet disallow their green?
                              Gerard Manley Hopkins

            131   In Epping Forest

How beautiful this hill of fern swells on!
So beautiful the chapel peeps between
The hornbeams—with its simple bell. Alone
I wander here, hid in a palace green.
Mary is absent—but the forest queen,
Nature, is with me. Morning, noon and gloaming,
I write my poems in these paths unseen;
And when among these brakes and beeches roaming,
I sigh for truth, and home, and love and woman.

I sigh for one and two—and still I sigh,
For many are the whispers I have heard
From beauty's lips. Love's soul in many an eye
Hath pierced my heart with such intense regard,
I looked for joy and pain was the reward.
I think of them I love, each girl and boy,
Babes of two mothers,—on this velvet sward,
And Nature thinks—in her so sweet employ,
While dews fall on each blossom, weeping joy.

Here is the chapel yard enclosed with pales,
And oak trees nearly top its little bell.
Here is the little bridge with guiding rail
That leads me on to many a pleasant dell.
The fern owl chitters like a startled knell
To nature—yet 'tis sweet at evening still.
A pleasant road curves round the gentle swell,
Where Nature seems to have her own sweet will,
Planting her beech and thorn about the sweet fern
　　hill

                                        John Clare

132　London versus Epping Forest

The brakes, like young stag's horns, come up in
　　Spring,
And hide the rabbit holes and fox's den;
They crowd about the forest everywhere;
The ling and holly-bush, and woods of beach,
With room enough to walk and search for flowers;
Then look away and see the Kentish heights.
Nature is lofty in her better mood,
She leaves the world and greatness all behind;
Thus London, like a shrub among the hills,
Lies hid and lower than the bushes here.
I could not bear to see the tearing plough
Root up and steal the Forest from the poor,
But leave to Freedom all she loves, untamed,
The Forest walk enjoyed and loved by all!

                                        John Clare

133   The Green Roads
(Essex: Hainault Forest)

The green roads that end in the forest
Are strewn with white goose feathers this June,

Like marks left behind by some one gone to the
    forest
To show his track. But he has never come back.

Down each green road a cottage looks at the forest.
Round one the nettle towers; two are bathed in
    flowers.

An old man along the green road to the forest
Strays from one, from another a child alone.

In the thicket bordering the forest,
All day long a thrush twiddles his song.

It is old, but the trees are young in the forest,
All but one like a castle keep, in the middle deep.

That oak saw the ages pass in the forest:
They were a host, but their memories are lost,

For the tree is dead: all things forget the forest
Excepting perhaps me, when now I see

The old man, the child, the goose feathers at the
    edge of the forest,
And hear all day long the thrush repeat his song.

                                    Edward Thomas

6   Cambridge and the Eastern Counties

134   Cambridge and the Cam

By yellow Chame, where all the Muses reign,
And with their tow'rs his reedy head embrave.

Phineas Fletch

135   Residence at Cambridge
(i)

It was a dreary morning when the Chaise
Roll'd over the flat Plains of Huntingdon
And, through the open windows, first I saw
The long-back'd Chapel of King's College rear
His pinnacles above the dusky groves.

Soon afterwards, we espied upon the road,
A student cloth'd in Gown and tassell'd Cap;
He pass'd; nor was I master of my eyes
Till he was left a hundred yards behind.
The Place, as we approach'd, seem'd more and mo
To have an eddy's force, and suck'd us in
More eagerly at every step we took.
Onward we drove beneath the Castle, down
By Magdalene Bridge we went and cross'd the Cai
And at the *Hoop* we landed, famous Inn.

My spirit was up, my thoughts were full of hop
Some Friends I had, acquaintances who there
Seem'd Friends, poor simple Schoolboys, now hun
   round
With honour and importance; in a world
Of welcome faces up and down I rov'd;

Questions, directions, counsel and advice
Flow'd in upon me from all sides, fresh day
Of pride and pleasure! to myself I seem'd
A man of business and expense, and went
From shop to shop about my own affairs,
To Tutors or to Tailors, as befel,
From street to street with loose and careless heart.

I was the Dreamer, they the Dream; I roam'd
Delighted, through the motley spectacle;
Gowns grave or gaudy, Doctors, Students, Streets,
Lamps, Gateways, Flocks of Churches, Courts and
      Towers:
Strange transformation for a mountain Youth,
A northern Villager. As if by word
Of magic or some Fairy's power, at once
Behold me rich in monies, and attir'd
In splendid clothes, with hose of silk, and hair
Glittering like rimy trees when frost is keen.
My lordly Dressing-gown I pass it by,
With other signs of manhood which supplied
The lack of beard.—The weeks went roundly on,
With invitations, suppers, wine, and fruit,
Smooth housekeeping within, and all without
Liberal and suiting Gentleman's array!

The Evangelist St. John my Patron was,
Three gloomy Courts are his; and in the first
Was my abiding-place, a nook obscure!
Right underneath, the College kitchens made
A humming sound, less tuneable than bees,
But hardly less industrious; with shrill notes
Of sharp command and scolding intermix'd.
Near me was Trinity's loquacious Clock,
Who never let the Quarters, night or day,
Slip by him unproclaim'd, and told the hours
Twice over with a male and female voice.
Her pealing organ was my neighbour too;
And, from my Bedroom, I in moonlight nights
Could see, right opposite, a few yards off,
The Antechapel, where the Statue stood
Of Newton, with his Prism and silent Face.

(ii)

Caverns there were within my mind, which sun
Could never penetrate, yet did there not
Want store of leafy arbours where the light
Might enter in at will. Companionships,
Friendships, acquaintances, were welcome all;
We saunter'd, play'd, we rioted, we talk'd
Unprofitable talk at morning hours,
Drifted about along the streets and walks,
Read lazily in lazy books, went forth
To gallop through the country in blind zeal
Of senseless horsemanship, or on the breast
Of Cam sail'd boisterously; and let the stars
Come out, perhaps without one quiet thought.

   Such was the tenor of the opening act
In this new life. Imagination slept,
And yet not utterly. I could not print
Ground where the grass had yielded to the steps
Of generations of illustrious Men,
Unmov'd; I could not always lightly pass
Through the same Gateways; sleep where they had
     slept,
Wake where they wak'd, range that enclosure old
That garden of great intellects undisturb'd.
Place also by the side of this dark sense
Of nobler feeling, that those spiritual Men,
Even the great Newton's own etherial Self,
Seem'd humbled in these precincts; thence to be
The more belov'd; invested here with tasks
Of life's plain business, as a daily garb;
Dictators at the plough, a change that left
All genuine admiration unimpair'd.

   Beside the pleasant Mills of Trompington
I laugh'd with Chaucer; in the hawthorn shade
Heard him (while birds were warbling) tell his tale
Of amorous passion. And that gentle Bard,
Chosen by the Muses for their Page of State,
Sweet Spenser, moving through his clouded heaven
With the moon's beauty and the moon's soft pace
I call'd him Brother, Englishman, and Friend.

Yea, our blind Poet, who, in his later day,
Stood almost single, uttering odious truth,
Darkness before, and danger's voice behind;
Soul awful! if the earth has ever lodg'd
An awful Soul, I seem'd to see him here
Familiarly, and in his Scholar's dress
Bounding before me, yet a stripling Youth,
A Boy, no better, with his rosy cheeks
Angelical, keen eye, courageous look,
And conscious step of purity and pride.

                                    William Wordsworth

136   He Revisits Cambridge

I past beside the reverend walls
   In which of old I wore the gown;
   I roved at random through the town,
And saw the tumult of the halls;

And heard once more in college fanes
   The storm their high-built organs make,
   And thunder-music, rolling, shake
The prophet blazoned on the panes;

And caught once more the distant shout,
   The measured pulse of racing oars
   Among the willows; paced the shores
And many a bridge, and all about

The same gray flats again, and felt
   The same, but not the same; and last
   Up that long walk of limes I past
To see the rooms in which he dwelt.

Another name was on the door:
   I lingered; all within was noise
   Of songs, and clapping hands, and boys
That crashed the glass and beat the floor;

Where once we held debate, a band
   Of youthful friends, on mind and art,
   And labour, and the changing mart,
And all the framework of the land;

When one would aim an arrow fair,
  But send it slackly from the string;
  And one would pierce an outer ring,
And one an inner, here and there;

And last the master-bowman, he,
  Would cleave the mark. A willing ear
  We lent him. Who, but hung to hear
The rapt oration flowing free

From point to point, with power and grace
  And music in the bounds of law,
  To those conclusions when we saw
The God within him light his face,

And seem to lift the form, and glow
  In azure orbits heavenly-wise;
  And over those ethereal eyes
The bar of Michael Angelo.

Alfred Tennyson

137   The Old Vicarage, Grantchester
(Café des Westens, Berlin, May 1912)

  Just now the lilac is in bloom,
  All before my little room;
  And in my flower-beds, I think,
  Smile the carnation and the pink;
  And down the borders, well I know,
  The poppy and the pansy blow ...
  Oh! there the chestnuts, summer through,
  Beside the river make for you
  A tunnel of green gloom, and sleep
  Deeply above; and green and deep
  The stream mysterious glides beneath,
  Green as a dream and deep as death.
  —Oh, damn! I know it! and I know
  How the May fields all golden show,
  And when the day is young and sweet,
  Gild gloriously the bare feet
  That run to bathe ...
                    Du lieber Gott!

Here am I, sweating, sick, and hot,
And there the shadowed waters fresh
Lean up to embrace the naked flesh.
Temperamentvoll German Jews
Drink beer around;—and *there* the dews
Are soft beneath a morn of gold.
Here tulips bloom as they are told;
Unkempt about those hedges blows
An English unofficial rose;
And there the unregulated sun
Slopes down to rest when day is done,
And wages a vague unpunctual star,
A slippered Hesper; and there are
Meads towards Haslingfield and Coton
Where *das Betreten*'s not *verboten*.

εἴθε γενοίμην ... would I were
In Grantchester, in Grantchester!—
Some, it may be, can get in touch
With Nature there, or Earth, or such.
And clever modern men have seen
A Faun a-peeping through the green,
And felt the Classics were not dead,
To glimpse a Naiad's reedy head,
Or hear the Goat-foot piping low: ...
But these are things I do not know.
I only know that you may lie
Day-long and watch the Cambridge sky,
And, flower-lulled in sleepy grass,
Hear the cool lapse of hours pass,
Until the centuries blend and blur
In Grantchester, in Grantchester....
Still in the dawnlit waters cool
His ghostly Lordship swims his pool,
And tries the strokes, essays the tricks,
Long learnt on Hellespont, or Styx.
Dan Chaucer hears his river still
Chatter beneath a phantom mill.
Tennyson notes, with studious eye,
How Cambridge waters hurry by ...
And in that garden, black and white,
Creep whispers through the grass all night;

And spectral dance, before the dawn,
A hundred Vicars down the lawn;
Curates, long dust, will come and go
On lissom, clerical, printless toe;
And oft between the boughs is seen
The sly shade of a Rural Dean ...
Till, at a shiver in the skies,
Vanishing with Satanic cries,
The prim ecclesiastic rout
Leaves but a startled sleeper-out,
Grey heavens, the first bird's drowsy calls,
The falling house that never falls.

God! I will pack, and take a train,
And get me to England once again!
For England's the one land, I know,
Where men with Splendid Hearts may go;
And Cambridgeshire, of all England,
The shire for Men who Understand;
And of *that* district I prefer
The lovely hamlet Grantchester.
For Cambridge people rarely smile,
Being urban, squat, and packed with guile;
And Royston men in the far South
Are black and fierce and strange of mouth;
At Over they fling oaths at one,
And worse than oaths at Trumpington,
And Ditton girls are mean and dirty,
And there's none in Harston under thirty,
And folks in Shelford and those parts
Have twisted lips and twisted hearts,
And Barton men make Cockney rhymes,
And Coton's full of nameless crimes,
And things are done you'd not believe
At Madingley, on Christmas Eve.
Strong men have run for miles and miles,
When one from Cherry Hinton smiles;
Strong men have blanched, and shot their wive
Rather than send them to St Ives;
Strong men have cried like babes, bydam,
To hear what happened at Babraham.
But Grantchester! ah, Grantchester!
There's peace and holy quiet there,

Great clouds along pacific skies,
And men and women with straight eyes,
Lithe children lovelier than a dream,
A bosky wood, a slumbrous stream,
And little kindly winds that creep
Round twilight corners, half asleep.
In Grantchester their skins are white;
They bathe by day, they bathe by night;
The women there do all they ought;
The men observe the Rules of Thought.
They love the Good; they worship Truth;
They laugh uproariously in youth;
(And when they get to feeling old,
They up and shoot themselves, I'm told) . . .

Ah God! to see the branches stir
Across the moon at Grantchester!
To smell the thrilling-sweet and rotten
Unforgettable, unforgotten
River-smell, and hear the breeze
Sobbing in the little trees.
Say, do the elm-clumps greatly stand
Still guardians of that holy land?
The chestnuts shade, in reverend dream,
The yet unacademic stream?
Is dawn a secret shy and cold
Anadyomene, silver-gold?
And sunset still a golden sea
From Haslingfield to Madingley?
And after, ere the night is born,
Do hares come out about the corn?
Oh, is the water sweet and cool,
Gentle and brown, above the pool?
And laughs the immortal river still
Under the mill, under the mill?
Say, is there Beauty yet to find?
And Certainty? and Quiet kind?
Deep meadows yet, for to forget
The lies, and truths, and pain? . . . oh! yet
Stands the Church clock at ten to three?
And is there honey still for tea?

                              Rupert Brooke

138   Sunrise in Summer
(over the Northamptonshire Fens)

The summer's morning sun creeps up the blue
O'er the flat meadows' most remotest view:
A bit at first peeps from the splendid ball,
Then more, and more, until we see it all.
And then so ruddy and so cool it lies,
The gazer views it with unwatering eyes,
And cattle opposite its kindly shine
Seem something feeding in a land divine:
Ruddy at first, yet ere a minute's told
Its burning red keeps glowing into gold,
And o'er the fenny level richly flows,
Till seeded dock in shade a giant grows;
Then blazing bright with undefinèd day
He turns the morning's earnest gaze away.

John Cla

139   Northamptonshire Fens

The lake that held a mirror to the sun
Now curves with wrinkles in the stillest place.
The autumn wind sounds hollow as a gun,
And water stands in every swampy place.
Yet in these fens peace, harmony, and grace,
The attributes of nature, are allied.
The barge with naked mast, in sheltered place
Beside the brig, close to the bank is tied,
While small waves plash by its bulky side.

John Cla

140   Bedford Level
(Cambridgeshire)

Yet much may be performed, to check the force
Of nature's rigour: the high heath, by trees
Warm-sheltered, may despise the rage of storms:
Moors, bogs, and weeping fens, may learn to smile,
And leave in dykes their soon-forgotten tears.
Labour and art will ev'ry aim achieve
Of noble bosoms. Bedford Level, erst
A dreary pathless waste, the coughing flock

Was wont with hairy fleeces to deform;
And, smiling with her lure of summer flow'rs,
The heavy ox, vain-struggling, to ingulph;
Till one, of that high-honoured patriot name,
RUSSELL, arose, who drained the rushy fen,
Confined the waves, bid groves and gardens bloom,
And through his new creation led the Ouze,
And gentle Camus, silver-winding streams:
Godlike beneficence; from chaos drear
To raise the garden and the shady grove.

John Dyer

141   A Lament for the Priory of Walsingham
          (Norfolk)

In the wracks of Walsingham
  Whom should I chuse,
But the Queen of Walsingham,
  To be guide to my muse.

Then, thou Prince of Walsingham,
  Graunt me to frame
Bitter plaints to rue thy wrong,
  Bitter woe for thy name.

Bitter was it oh to see
  The seely sheep
Murdered by the ravening wolves
  While the shepherds did sleep.

Bitter was it oh to view
  The sacred vine,
Whiles the gardeners played all close,
  Rooted up by the swine.

Bitter, bitter oh to behold
  The grass to grow,
Where the walls of Walsingham
  So stately did show.

Such were the works of Walsingham
  Whiles she did stand,
Such are the wracks as now do show
  Of that holy land.

Level, level with the ground
  The towers do lie,
Which with their golden glittering tops
  Pierced once to the sky.

Where were gates no gates are now,
  The ways unknowen
Where the press of peers did pass
  While her fame far was blowen.

Owls do scrike where the sweetest hymns
  Lately were song,
Toads and serpents hold their dens
  Where the palmers did throng.

Weep, weep, O Walsingham,
  Whose days are nights,
Blessing turned to blasphemies,
  Holy deeds to despites.

Sin is where our Lady sat,
  Heaven turned is to hell,
Sathan sits where our Lord did sway,
  Walsingham, Oh farewell!

Ano

peers: companions

142   In Suffolk

How stately stand yon pines upon the hill;
How soft the murmurs of that living rill;
And o'er the park's tall paling, scarcely higher,
Peeps the low Church and shows the modest spire.
Unnumber'd violets on those banks appear,
And all the first-born beauties of the year;
The grey-green blossoms of the willows bring
The large wild bees upon the labouring wing.
Then comes the Summer with augmented pride,
Whose pure small streams along the valleys glide;
Her richer Flora their brief charms display,
And, as the fruit advances, fall away.

Then shall th' autumnal yellow clothe the leaf,
What time the reaper binds the burden'd sheaf;
Then silent groves denote the dying year,
The morning frost, and noon-tide gossamer;
And all be silent in the scene around—
All, save the distant sea's uncertain sound,
Or here and there the gun, whose loud report
Proclaims to man that Death is but his sport.
And then the wintry winds begin to blow;
Then fall the flaky stars of gathering snow;
When on the thorn the ripening sloe, yet blue,
Takes the bright varnish of the morning dew;
The aged moss grows brittle on the pale;
The dry boughs splinter in the windy gale;
And every changing season of the year
Stamps on the scene its English character.

George Crabbe

143   East Anglian Fen

Far to the left he saw the huts of men,
Half hid in mist, that hung upon the fen;
Before him swallows, gathering for the sea,
Took their short flights, and twitter'd on the lea;
And near the bean-sheaf stood, the harvest done,
And slowly blacken'd in the sickly sun;
All these were sad in nature, or they took
Sadness from him, the likeness of his look,
And of his mind—he ponder'd for a while,
Then met his Fanny with a borrow'd smile.

George Crabbe

144   Peter Grimes at Aldeburgh

Alas! for Peter not a helping hand,
So was he hated, could he now command;
Alone he row'd his boat; alone he cast
His nets beside, or made his anchor fast;
To hold a rope or hear a curse was none—
He toil'd and rail'd; he groan'd and swore alone.
Thus by himself compell'd to live each day,
To wait for certain hours the tide's delay;

At the same times the same dull views to see,
The bounding marsh-bank and the blighted tree;
The water only when the tides were high;
When low, the mud half-cover'd and half-dry;
The sun-burnt tar that blisters on the planks,
And bank-side stakes in their uneven ranks;
Heaps of entangled weeds that slowly float,
As the tide rolls by the impeded boat.
    When tides were neap, and, in the sultry day,
Through the tall bounding mud-banks made their
        way,
Which on each side rose swelling, and below
The dark warm flood ran silently and slow:
There anchoring, Peter chose from man to hide,
There hang his head, and view the lazy tide
In its hot slimy channel slowly glide;
Where the small eels that left the deeper way
For the warm shore, within the shallows play;
Where gaping muscles, left upon the mud,
Slope their slow passage to the fallen flood:—
Here dull and hopeless he'd lie down and trace
How sidelong crabs had scrawl'd their crooked
        race;
Or sadly listen to the tuneless cry
Of fishing gull or clanging golden-eye;
What time the sea-birds to the marsh would come
And the loud bittern, from the bull-rush home,
Gave from the salt-ditch side the bellowing boom
He nursed the feelings these dull scenes produce,
And loved to stop beside the opening sluice;
Where the small stream, confined in narrow boun
Ran with a dull, unvaried, sadd'ning sound;
Where all presented to the eye or ear
Oppress'd the soul with misery, grief, and fear.

                                    George Crab

145   The Suffolk Shore

They feel the calm delight, and thus proceed
Through the green lane—then linger in the mead—
Stray o'er the heath in all its purple bloom—
And pluck the blossom where the wild bees hum;

Then through the broomy bound with ease they pass,
And press the sandy sheep-walk's slender grass,
Where dwarfish flowers among the gorse are spread,
And the lamb browses by the linnet's bed;
Then 'cross the bounding brook they make their way
O'er its rough bridge—and there behold the bay!—
The ocean smiling to the fervid sun—
The waves that faintly fall and slowly run—
The ships at distance and the boats at hand;
And now they walk upon the sea-side sand,
Counting the number and what kind they be,
Ships softly sinking in the sleepy sea;
Now arm in arm, now parted, they behold
The glitt'ring waters on the shingles roll'd;
The timid girls, half dreading their design,
Dip the small foot in the retarded brine,
And search for crimson weeds, which spreading flow,
Or lie like pictures on the sand below;
With all those bright red pebbles that the sun
Through the small waves so softly shines upon;
And those live lucid jellies which the eye
Delights to trace as they swim glitt'ring by:
Pearl-shells and rubied star-fish they admire,
And will arrange above the parlour-fire.

George Crabbe

146   Evening by the Sea
           (Suffolk)

It was between the night and day,
    The trees looked weary—one by one
Against the west they seemed to sway,
    And yet were steady. The sad sun
In a sick doubt of colour lay
    Across the water's belt of dun.

On the weak wind scarce flakes of foam
    There floated, hardly borne at all
From the rent edge of water—some
    Between slack gusts the wind let fall,
The white brine could not overcome
    That pale grass on the southern wall.

That evening one could always hear
    The sharp hiss of the shingle, rent
As each wave settled heavier,
    The same rough way. This noise was blent
With many sounds that hurt the air
    As the salt sea-wind came and went.

The wind wailed once and was not. Then
    The white sea touching its salt edge
Dropped in a slow low sigh: again
    The ripples deepened to the ledge,
Across the beach from marsh and fen
    Came a faint smell of rotten sedge.

Like a hurt thing that will not die
    The sea lay moaning; waifs of weed
Strove thro' the water painfully
    Or lay flat, like drenched hair indeed,
Rolled over with the pebbles, nigh
    Low places where the rock-fish feed.

                              A. C. Swinburn

147   Where Dunwich Used To Be
         (Suffolk)

Death, and change, and darkness everlasting,
    Deaf, that hears not what the daystar saith,
Blind, past all remembrance and forecasting,
    Dead, past memory that it once drew breath;
These, above the washing tides and wasting,
    Reign, and rule this land of utter death.

Change of change, darkness of darkness, hidden,
    Very death of very death, begun
When none knows,—the knowledge is forbidden—
    Self-begotten, self-proceeding, one,
Born, not made—abhorred, unchained, unchidden,
    Night stands here defiant of the sun.

Change of change, and death of death begotten,
  Darkness born of darkness, one and three,
Ghostly godhead of a world forgotten,
  Crowned with heaven, enthroned on land and sea,
Here, where earth with dead men's bones is rotten,
  God of Time, thy likeness worships thee.

Lo, thy likeness of thy desolation,
  Shape and figure of thy might, O Lord,
Formless form, incarnate miscreation,
  Served of all things living and abhorred;
Earth herself is here thine incarnation,
  Time, of all things born on earth adored.

All that worship thee are fearful of thee;
  No man may not worship thee for fear:
Prayers nor curses prove not nor disprove thee,
  Move nor change thee with our change of cheer:
All at last, though all abhorred thee, love thee,
  God, the sceptre of whose throne is here.

Here thy throne and sceptre of thy station,
  Here the palace paven for thy feet;
Here thy sign from nation unto nation
  Passed as watchword for thy guards to greet,
Guards that go before thine exaltation,
  Ages, clothed with bitter years and sweet.

Here, where sharp the sea-bird shrills his ditty,
  Flickering flame-wise through the clear live calm,
Rose triumphal, crowning all a city,
  Roofs exalted once with prayer and psalm,
Built of holy hands for holy pity,
  Frank and fruitful as a sheltering palm.

Church and hospice wrought in faultless fashion,
  Hall and chancel bounteous and sublime,
Wide and sweet and glorious as compassion,
  Filled and thrilled with force of choral chime,
Filled with spirit of prayer and thrilled with passion,
  Hailed a God more merciful than Time.

Ah, less mighty, less than Time prevailing,
   Shrunk, expelled, made nothing at his nod,
Less than clouds across the sea-line sailing,
   Lies he, stricken by his master's rod.
'Where is man?' the cloister murmurs wailing;
   Back the mute shrine thunders—'Where is God?'

Here is all the end of all his glory—
   Dust, and grass, and barren silent stones.
Dead, like him, one hollow tower and hoary
   Naked in the sea-wind stands and moans,
Filled and thrilled with its perpetual story:
   Here, where earth is dense with dead men's bones.

Low and loud and long, a voice for ever,
   Sounds the wind's clear story like a song.
Tomb from tomb the waves devouring sever,
   Dust from dust as years relapse along;
Graves where men made sure to rest, and never
   Lie dismantled by the seasons' wrong.

Now displaced, devoured and desecrated,
   Now by Time's hands darkly disinterred,
These poor dead that sleeping here awaited
   Long the archangel's re-creating word,
Closed about with roofs and walls high-gated
   Till the blast of judgment should be heard,

Naked, shamed, cast out of consecration,
   Corpse and coffin, yea the very graves,
Scoffed at, scattered, shaken from their station,
   Spurned and scourged of wind and sea like slaves,
Desolate beyond man's desolation,
   Shrink and sink into the waste of waves.

Tombs, with bare white piteous bones protruded,
   Shroudless, down the loose collapsing banks,
Crumble, from their constant place detruded,
   That the sea devours and gives not thanks.
Graves where hope and prayer and sorrow brooded
   Gape and slide and perish, ranks on ranks.

Rows on rows and line by line they crumble,
  They that thought for all time through to be.
Scarce a stone whereon a child might stumble
  Breaks the grim field paced alone of me.
Earth, and man, and all their gods wax humble
  Here, where Time brings pasture to the sea.

                                    A. C. Swinburne

148   Suffolk: by the North Sea

Miles, and miles, and miles of desolation!
  Leagues on leagues on leagues without a change!
Sign or token of some eldest nation
  Here would make the strange land not so strange.
Time-forgotten, yea since time's creation,
  Seem these borders where the sea-birds range.

Slowly, gladly, full of peace and wonder
  Grows his heart who journeys here alone.
Earth and all its thoughts of earth sink under
  Deep as deep in water sinks a stone.
Hardly knows it if the rollers thunder,
  Hardly whence the lonely wind is blown.

Tall the plumage of the rush-flower tosses,
  Sharp and soft in many a curve and line
Gleam and glow the sea-coloured marsh-mosses
  Salt and splendid from the circling brine.
Streak on streak of glimmering seashine crosses
  All the land sea-saturate as with wine.

Far, and far between, in divers orders,
  Clear grey steeples cleave the low grey sky;
Fast and firm as time-unshaken warders,
  Hearts made sure by faith, by hope made high.
These alone in all the wild sea-borders
  Fear no blast of days and nights that die.

All the land is like as one man's face is,
  Pale and troubled still with change of cares.
Doubt and death pervade her clouded spaces:
  Strength and length of life and peace are theirs;
Theirs alone amid these weary places,
  Seeing not how the wild world frets and fares.

Firm and fast where all is cloud that changes
    Cloud-clogged sunlight, cloud by sunlight thinned
Stern and sweet, above the sand-hill ranges
    Watch the towers and tombs of men that sinned
Once, now calm as earth whose only change is
    Wind, and light, and wind, and cloud, and wind.

                                        A. C. Swinburne

149   Horsey Gap
(Norfolk)

When the sea comes in at Horsey Gap
    Without any previous warning,
A swan shall build its rushy nest
    On the roof of the Swan at Horning.

And a bald headed crow, contented and merry,
Shall feast on the corpses that float by the ferry.

                                        Anon

150   Lincolnshire: from the Wolds to the Fens

ALKEN: Know ye the witch's dell?
SCATHLOCK: No more than I do know the walks of Hell
ALKEN: Within a gloomy dimble she doth dwell
            Down in a pit, o'ergrown with brakes and briars
            Close by the ruins of a shaken abbey
            Torn, with an earthquake, down unto the ground
            'Mongst graves, and grotts, near an old charnel
                house,
            Where you shall find her sitting in her form,
            As fearful, and melancholic, as that
            She is about; with caterpillar's kells,
            And knotty cobwebs, rounded in with spells;
            Thence she steals forth to relief, in the fogs,
            And rotten mists, upon the fens, and bogs,
            Down to the drowned lands of Lincolnshire;
            To make ewes cast their lambs.

                                        Ben Jonson

kells: cocoons
relief: seek food

151   The Fen-men of Lincolnshire's Holland

(...lland speaks)

> The toiling fisher here is tewing of his net:
> The fowler is employed his limed twigs to set.
> One underneath his horse, to get a shoot doth stalk;
> Another over dykes upon his stilts doth walk:
> There others with their spades the peats are squaring
>   out,
> And others from their carrs are busily about,
> To draw out sedge and reed, for thatch and stover fit,
> That whosoever would a landskip rightly hit,
> Beholding but my fens shall with more shapes be
>   stored
> Than Germany, or France, or Thuscan can afford.
>
>   Michael Drayton

...ing: dragging
...ver: winter feed for animals

152   Lincolnshire's Holland Speaks of Her Waterfowl

Here in my vaster pools, as white as snow or milk,
(In water black as Styx) swims the wild Swan, the Ilke,
Of Hollanders so termed, no niggard of his breath,
(As poets say of swans, which only sing in death)
But oft as other birds is heard his tunes to rote,
Which like a trumpet comes from his long arched throat,
And tow'rds this wat'ry kind, about the flashes' brim,
Some cloven-footed are, by nature not to swim.
There stalks the stately Crane, as though he marched in
      war,
By him that hath the Hern, which (by the fishy carr)
Can fetch with their long necks, out of the rush and reed,
Snigs, fry, and yellow frogs, whereon they often feed:
And under them again (that water never take,
But by some ditch's side, or little shallow lake
Lie dabbling night and day) the palate-pleasing Snite,
The Bidcock, and like them the Redshanks, that delight

...s: small eels   bidcock: water-rail
...: snipe

Together still to be, in some small reedy bed,
In which these little fowls in summer's time were bred.
The buzzing Bitter sits, which through his hollow bill
A sudden bellowing sends, which many times doth fill
The neighbouring marsh with noise, as though a bull did
    roar.
But scarcely have I yet recited half my store:
And with my wondrous flocks of Wild Geese come I ther
Which look as though alone they peopled all the fen,
Which here in winter time, when all is overflowed,
And want of solid sward enforceth them abroad,
Th' abundance then is seen that my full fens do yield,
That almost through the isle do pester every field.

Michael Drayto

bitter: bittern

153   The High Tide on the Coast of Lincolnshire (1571)

The old mayor climbed the belfry tower,
    The ringers ran by two, by three;
'Pull, if ye never pulled before;
    Good ringers, pull your best,' quoth he.
'Play uppe, play uppe, O Boston bells!
Ply all your changes, all your swells,
      Play uppe "The Brides of Enderby".'

Men say it was a stolen tyde—
    The Lord that sent it, He knows all;
But in myne ears doth still abide
    The message that the bells let fall:
And there was nought of strange, beside
The flights of mews and peewits pied
    By millions crouched on the old sea wall.

I sat and spun within the doore,
    My thread brake off, I raised myne eyes;
The level sun, like ruddy ore,
    Lay sinking in the barren skies;
And dark against day's golden death
She moved where Lindis wandereth,
My sonne's faire wife, Elizabeth.

'Cusha! Cusha! Cusha!' calling,
Ere the early dews were falling,
Farre away I heard her song.
'Cusha! Cusha!' all along;
Where the reedy Lindis floweth,
    Floweth, floweth,
From the meads where melick groweth
Faintly came her milking song—

'Cusha! Cusha! Cusha!' calling,
'For the dews will soone be falling;
Leave your meadow grasses mellow,
    Mellow, mellow;
Quit your cowslips, cowslips yellow;
Come uppe Whitefoot, come uppe Lightfoot;
Quit the stalks of parsley hollow,
    Hollow, hollow;
Come uppe Jetty, rise and follow,
From the clovers lift your head;
Come uppe Whitefoot, come uppe Lightfoot,
Come uppe Jetty, rise and follow,
Jetty, to the milking shed.'

If it be long, ay, long ago,
    When I beginne to think howe long,
Againe I hear the Lindis flow,
    Swift as an arrowe, sharpe and strong;
And all the aire, it seemeth mee,
Bin full of floating bells (sayth shee),
That ring the tune of Enderby.

Alle fresh the level pasture lay,
    And not a shadowe mote be seene,
Save where full fyve good miles away
    The steeple towered from out the greene,
And lo! the great bell farre and wide
Was heard in all the country side
That Saturday at eventide.

The swanherds where their sedges are
  Moved on in sunset's golden breath,
The shepherde lads I heard afarre,
  And my sonne's wife, Elizabeth;
Till floating o'er the grassy sea
Came downe that kyndly message free,
The 'Brides of Mavis Enderby'.

Then some looked uppe into the sky,
  And all along where Lindis flows
To where the goodly vessels lie,
  And where the lordly steeple shows.
They sayde, 'And why should this thing be?
What danger lowers by land or sea?
They ring the tune of Enderby!

'For evil news from Mablethorpe,
  Of pyrate galleys warping down;
For shippes ashore beyond the scorpe,
  They have not spared to wake the towne:
But while the west bin red to see,
And storms be none, and pyrates flee,
Why ring "The Brides of Enderby"?'

I looked without, and lo! my sonne
  Came riding downe with might and main:
He raised a shout as he drew on,
  Till all the welkin rang again,
'Elizabeth! Elizabeth!'
(A sweeter woman ne'er drew breath
Than my sonne's wife, Elizabeth.)

'The olde sea wall (he cried) is downe,
  The rising tide comes on apace,
And boats adrift in yonder towne
  Go sailing uppe the market-place.'
He shook as one that looks on death:
'God save you, mother!' straight he saith;
'Where is my wife, Elizabeth?'

'Good sonne, where Lindis winds away,
  With her two bairns I marked her long;
And ere yon bells beganne to play
  Afar I heard her milking song.'
He looked across the grassy lea,
To right, to left, 'Ho Enderby!'
They rang 'The Brides of Enderby'!

With that he cried and beat his breast;
  For, lo! along the river's bed
A mighty eygre reared his crest,
  And uppe the Lindis raging sped.
It swept with thunderous noises loud;
Shaped like a curling snow-white cloud,
Or like a demon in a shroud.

And rearing Lindis backward pressed
  Shook all her trembling bankes amaine;
Then madly at the eygre's breast
  Flung uppe her weltering walls again.
Then bankes came downe with ruin and rout—
Then beaten foam flew round about—
Then all the mighty floods were out.

So farre, so fast the eygre drave,
  The heart had hardly time to beat,
Before a shallow seething wave
  Sobbed in the grasses at oure feet:
The feet had hardly time to flee
Before it brake against the knee,
And all the world was in the sea.

Upon the roofe we sate that night,
  The noise of bells went sweeping by:
I marked the lofty beacon light
  Stream from the church tower, red and high—
A lurid mark and dread to see;
And awsome bells they were to mee,
That in the dark rang 'Enderby'.

They rang the sailor lads to guide
    From roofe to roofe who fearless rowed;
And I—my sonne was at my side,
    And yet the ruddy beacon glowed;
And yet he moaned beneath his breath,
'O come in life, or come in death!
O lost! my love, Elizabeth.'

And didst thou visit him no more?
    Thou didst, thou didst, my daughter deare;
The waters laid thee at his doore,
    Ere yet the early dawn was clear.
Thy pretty bairns in fast embrace,
The lifted sun shone on thy face,
Downe drifted to thy dwelling-place.

That flow strewed wrecks about the grass,
    That ebbe swept out the flocks to sea;
A fatal ebbe and flow, alas!
    To manye more than myne and mee:
But each will mourn his own (she saith);
And sweeter woman ne'er drew breath
Than my sonne's wife, Elizabeth.

    I shall never hear her more
    By the reedy Lindis shore,
    'Cusha! Cusha! Cusha!' calling,
    Ere the early dews be falling;
    I shall never hear her song,
    'Cusha! Cusha!' all along
    Where the sunny Lindis floweth,
        Goeth, floweth;
    From the meads where melick groweth,
    When the water winding down,
    Onward floweth to the town.

    I shall never see her more
    Where the reeds and rushes quiver,
        Shiver, quiver;
    Stand beside the sobbing river,
    Sobbing, throbbing, in its falling
    To the sandy lonesome shore;
    I shall never hear her calling,

'Leave your meadow grasses mellow,
    Mellow, mellow;
Quit your cowslips, cowslips yellow;
Come uppe Whitefoot, come uppe Lightfoot;
Quit your pipes of parsley hollow,
    Hollow, hollow;
Come uppe Lightfoot, rise and follow;
    Lightfoot, Whitefoot,
From your clovers lift the head;
Come uppe Jetty, follow, follow,
Jetty to the milking shed.'

Jean Ingelow

154   Paysage en Lincolnshire

L'échelonnement des haies
Moutonne à l'infini, mer
Claire dans le brouillard clair
Qui sent bon les jeunes baies.

Des arbres et des moulins
Sont légers sur le vert tendre
Où vient s'ébattre et s'étendre
L'agilité des poulains.

Dans ce vague d'un Dimanche
Voici se jouer aussi
De grandes brebis aussi
Douces que leur laine blanche.

Tout à l'heure déferlait
L'onde, roulée en volutes,
De cloches comme des flûtes
Dans le ciel comme du lait.

Paul Verlaine

155   Boston, Lincolnshire

Oh, Boston, Boston, thou hast nought to boast on
But a grand sluice and a high steeple
And a coast as souls are lost on.

Anon

156   Lincolnshire Shores (at Mablethorpe)

(i)
Lines

Here often, when a child, I lay reclined,
  I took delight in this locality.
Here stood the infant Ilion of the mind,
  And here the Grecian ships did seem to be.
And here again I come, and only find
  The drain-cut levels of the marshy lea,—
Gray sandbanks, and pale sunsets,—dreary wind,
  Dim shores, dense rains, and heavy-clouded sea!

(ii)

A still salt pool, locked in with bars of sand,
  Left on the shore; that hears all night
The plunging seas draw backward from the land
  Their moon-led waters white.

(iii)

As the crest of some slow-arching wave,
Heard in dead night along that table-shore,
Drops flat, and after the great waters break
Whitening for half a league, and thin themselves,
Far over sands marbled with moon and cloud,
From less and less to nothing.

Alfred Tennyson

157   Somersby, Lincolnshire: after Leaving the Rectory

Unwatched, the garden bough shall sway,
  The tender blossom flutter down,
  Unloved, that beech will gather brown,
This maple burn itself away;

Unloved, the sun-flower, shining fair,
  Ray round with flames her disk of seed,
  And many a rose-carnation feed
With summer spice the humming air;

Unloved, by many a sandy bar,
    The brook shall babble down the plain,
    At noon or when the lesser wain
Is twisting round the polar star;

Uncared for, gird the windy grove,
    And flood the haunts of hern and crake;
    Or into silver arrows break
The sailing moon in creek and cove;

Till from the garden and the wild
    A fresh association blow,
    And year by year the landscape grow
Familiar to the stranger's child;

As year by year the labourer tills
    His wonted glebe, or lops the glades;
    And year by year our memory fades
From all the circle of the hills.

                                    Alfred Tennyson

158   Lincolnshire Wolds and Lincolnshire Sea

Calm is the morn without a sound,
    Calm as to suit a calmer grief,
    And only thro' the faded leaf
The chestnut pattering to the ground;

Calm and deep peace on this high wold,
    And on these dews that drench the furze,
    And all the silvery gossamers
That twinkle into green and gold;

Calm and still light on yon great plain
    That sweeps with all its autumn bowers,
    And crowded farms and lessening towers,
To mingle with the bounding main;

Calm and deep peace in this wide air,
    These leaves that redden to the fall,
    And in my heart, if calm at all,
If any calm, a calm despair;

Calm on the seas, and silver sleep,
  And waves that sway themselves in rest,
  And dead calm in the noble breast
Which heaves but with the heaving deep.

Alfred Tennyso

7   Wales and the Marches

159   The Snowdon Sunrise

In one of these excursions, travelling then
Through Wales on foot, and with a youthful Friend,
I left Bethhelert's huts at couching-time,
And westward took my way to see the sun
Rise from the top of Snowdon. Having reach'd
The Cottage at the Mountain's foot, we there
Rouz'd up the Shepherd, who by ancient right
Of office is the Stranger's usual guide;
And after short refreshment sallied forth.

  It was a Summer's night, a close warm night,
Wan, dull and glaring, with a dripping mist
Low-hung and thick that cover'd all the sky,
Half threatening storm and rain; but on we went
Uncheck'd, being full of heart and having faith
In our tried Pilot. Little could we see
Hemm'd round on every side with fog and damp,
And, after ordinary travellers' chat
With our Conductor, silently we sank
Each into commerce with his private thoughts:
Thus did we breast the ascent, and by myself
Was nothing either seen or heard the while
Which took me from my musings, save that once
The Shepherd's Cur did to his own great joy
Unearth a hedgehog in the mountain crags
Round which he made a barking turbulent.
This small adventure, for even such it seemed
In that wild place and at the dead of night,
Being over and forgotten, on we wound
In silence as before. With forehead bent
Earthward, as if in opposition set

Against an enemy, I panted up
With eager pace, and no less eager thoughts.
Thus might we wear perhaps an hour away,
Ascending at loose distance each from each,
And I, as chanced, the foremost of the Band;
When at my feet the ground appear'd to brighten,
And with a step or two seem'd brighter still;
Nor had I time to ask the cause of this,
For instantly a Light upon the turf
Fell like a flash: I looked about, and lo!
The Moon stood naked in the Heavens, at height
Immense above my head, and on the shore
I found myself of a huge sea of mist,
Which, meek and silent, rested at my feet:
A hundred hills their dusky backs upheaved
All over this still Ocean, and beyond,
Far, far beyond, the vapours shot themselves,
In headlands, tongues, and promontory shapes,
Into the Sea, the real Sea, that seem'd
To dwindle, and give up its majesty,
Usurp'd upon as far as sight could reach.
Meanwhile, the Moon look'd down upon this shew
In single glory, and we stood, the mist
Touching our very feet; and from the shore
At distance not the third part of a mile
Was a blue chasm; a fracture in the vapour,
A deep and gloomy breathing-place through which
Mounted the roar of waters, torrents, streams
Innumerable, roaring with one voice.
The universal spectacle throughout
Was shaped for admiration and delight,
Grand in itself alone, but in that breach
Through which the homeless voice of waters rose,
That dark deep thoroughfare had Nature lodg'd
The Soul, the Imagination of the whole.

                                    William Wordsworth

160   The Primrose, being at Montgomery Castle,
         upon the hill, on which it is situate

              Upon this primrose hill,
                Where, if heaven would distil
         A shower of rain, each several drop might go
         To his own primrose, and grow manna so;
         And where their form, and their infinity
                Make a terrestrial galaxy,
                As the small stars do in the sky:
         I walk to find a true love; and I see
         That 'tis not a mere woman, that is she,
         But must, or more, or less than woman be.

              Yet know I not, which flower
                I wish; a six, or four;
         For should my true love less than woman be,
         She were scarce anything; and then, should she
         Be more than woman, she would get above
                All thought of sex, and think to move
                My heart to study her, not to love;
         Both these were monsters; since there must reside
         Falsehood in woman, I could more abide,
         She were by art, than nature falsified.

              Live primrose then, and thrive
                With thy true number, five;
         And women, whom this flower doth represent,
         With this mysterious number be content;
         Ten is the farthest number; if half ten
                Belong unto each woman, then
                Each woman may take half us men;
         Or if this will not serve their turn, since all
         Numbers are odd, or even, and they fall
         First into this, five, women may take us all.

                                                    John Donne

161 Upon the Priory Grove, His Usual Retirement
(Brecon)

Hail sacred shades! cool, leavy house!
Chaste treasurer of all my vows,
And wealth! on whose soft bosom laid
My love's fair steps I first betrayed:
  Henceforth no melancholy flight,
No sad wing, or hoarse bird of night,
Disturb this air, no fatal throat
Of raven, or owl, awake the note
Of our laid echo, no voice dwell
Within these leaves, but Philomel.
The poisonous ivy here no more
His false twists on the oak shall score,
Only the woodbine here may twine,
As th' emblem of her love, and mine;
The amorous Sun shall here convey
His best beams, in thy shades to play;
The active air, the gentlest show'rs,
Shall from his wings rain on thy flow'rs;
And the Moon from her dewy locks
Shall deck thee with her brightest drops:
Whatever can a fancy move,
Or feed the eye, be on this grove;
  And when at last the winds, and tears
Of Heaven, with the consuming years,
Shall these green curls bring to decay,
And clothe thee in an aged gray:
(If ought a lover can foresee,
Or if we poets, prophets be)
From hence transplanted, thou shalt stand
A fresh grove in th' Elysian land;
Where (most blest pair!) as here on earth
Thou first didst eye our growth, and birth;
So there again, thou 'lt see us move
In our first innocence, and love:
And in thy shades, as now, so then.
We'll kiss, and smile, and walk agen.

Henry Vaughan

laid: sleeping (laid asleep)

162   The Shower
(at Llangorse Lake, Breconshire)

'Twas so, I saw thy birth: that drowsy lake
From her faint bosom breathed thee, the disease
Of her sick waters, and infectious ease.
                But, now at even
                Too gross for heaven,
Thou fall'st in tears, and weep'st for thy mistake.

Ah! it is so with me; oft have I pressed
Heaven with a lazy breath, but fruitless this
Pierced not; Love only can with quick access
                Unlock the way,
                When all else stray
The smoke, and exhalations of the breast.

Yet, if as thou dost melt, and with thy train
Of drops make soft the earth, my eyes could weep
O'er my hard heart, that's bound up, and asleep,
                Perhaps at last
                (Some such showers past,)
My God would give a sun-shine after rain.

                                    Henry Vaughan

163   The Storm
(Breconshire)

    I see the Usk, and know my blood
            Is not a sea,
    But a shallow, bounded flood
            Though red as he;
    Yet have I flows, as strong as his,
            And boiling streams that rave
    With the same curling force, and hiss,
            As doth the mountained wave.

But when his waters billow thus,
     Dark storms, and wind
Incite them to that fierce discuss,
     Else not inclined,
Thus the enlarged, enraged air
     Uncalms these to a flood,
But still the weather that's most fair
     Breeds tempests in my blood;

Lord, then round me with weeping clouds,
     And let my mind
In quick blasts sigh beneath those shrouds
     A spirit-wind,
So shall that storm purge this *recluse*
     Which sinful ease made foul,
And *wind*, and *water* to thy use
     Both *wash*, and *wing* my soul.

                                        Henry Vaugh

164   To the River Isca
            (the Usk)

When Daphne's lover here first wore the bays,
Eurotas' secret streams heard all his lays.
And holy Orpheus, Nature's busy child
By headlong Hebrus his deep hymns compiled.
Soft Petrarch (thawed by Laura's flames) did weep
On Tiber's banks, when she (proud fair!) could sleep
Mosella boasts Ausonius, and the Thames
Doth murmur SIDNEY'S Stella to her streams,
While Severn swoln with joy and sorrow, wears
Castara's smiles mixed with fair Sabrin's tears.
Thus poets (like the nymphs, their pleasing themes)
Haunted the bubbling springs and gliding streams,
And happy banks! whence such fair flowers have
     sprung,
But happier those where they have sate and sung!
Poets (like Angels) where they once appear
Hallow the place, and each succeeding year
Adds reverence to't, such as at length doth give
This aged faith, that there their genii live.
Hence the ancients say, that, from this sickly air
They pass to regions more refined and fair,

To meadows strowed with lilies and the rose,
And shades whose youthful green no old age knows,
Where all in white they walk, discourse, and sing
Like bees' soft murmurs, or a chiding spring.
    But Isca, whensoe'r those shades I see,
And thy loved arbours must no more know me,
When I am laid to rest hard by thy streams,
And my sun sets, where first it sprang in beams,
I'll leave behind me such a large, kind light,
As shall redeem thee from oblivious night,
And in these vows which (living yet) I pay
Shed such a previous and enduring ray,
As shall from age to age thy fair name lead
'Till rivers leave to run, and men to read.
First, may all bards born after me
(When I am ashes) sing of thee!
May thy green banks and streams (or none)
Be both their Hill and Helicon;
May vocal groves grow there, and all
The shades in them prophetical,
Where (laid) men shall more fair truths see
Than fictions were of Thessaly.
May thy gentle swains (like flowers)
Sweetly spend their youthful hours,
And thy beauteous nymphs (like doves)
Be kind and faithful to their loves;
Garlands, and Songs, and Roundelays,
Mild, dewy nights, and sun-shine days,
The turtle's voice, joy without fear,
Dwell on thy bosom all the year!
May the evet and the toad
Within thy banks have no abode,
Nor the wily, winding snake
Her voyage through thy waters make.
In all thy journey to the main
No nitrous clay, nor brimstone-vein
Mix with thy streams, but may they pass
Fresh as the air, and clear as glass,
And where the wandering crystal treads
Roses shall kiss, and couple heads.
The factor-wind from far shall bring
The odours of the scattered spring,
And loaden with the rich arrear,

Spend it in spicy whispers there.
No sullen heats, nor flames that are
Offensive, and canicular,
Shine on thy sands, nor pry to see
Thy scaly, shading family,
But noons as mild as Hesper's rays,
Or the first blushes of fair days.
What gifts more Heaven or Earth can add
With all those blessings be thou clad!
    Honour, Beauty,
    Faith and Duty,
    Delight and Truth,
    With Love, and Youth
Crown all about thee! And what ever Fate
Impose elsewhere, whether the graver state,
Or some toy else, may those loud, anxious cares
For dead and dying things (the common wares
And shows of time) ne'er break thy peace, nor make
Thy reposed arms to a new war awake!
    But freedom, safety, joy and bliss
    United in one loving kiss
    Surround thee quite, and style thy borders
The land redeemed from all disorders!

                      Henry Vaugha

165   'So Have I Spent on the Banks of
       Ysca Many a Serious Hour'
       (Breconshire)

'Tis day, my crystal Usk: now the sad night
Resigns her place as tenant to the light.
See the amazed mists begin to fly
And the victorious sun hath got the sky.
How shall I recompense thy streams, that keep
Me and my soul awaked when others sleep?
I watch my stars, I move on with the skies
And weary all the planets with mine eyes.
Shall I seek thy forgotten birth and see
What days are spent since thy nativity?
Didst serve with ancient Kishon? Canst thou tell
So many years as holy Hiddekel?

Thou art not paid in this: I'll levy more
Such harmless contributions from thy store
And dress my soul by thee as thou dost pass,
As I would do my body by my glass.
What a clear, running crystal here I find:
Sure I will strive to gain as clear a mind,
And have my spirits—freed from dross—made light,
That no base puddle may allay their flight.
How I admire thy humble banks: nought's here
But the same simple vesture all the year.
I'll learn simplicity of thee and when
I walk the streets I will not storm at men,
Nor look as if I had a mind to cry:
It is my valiant cloth of gold and I.
Let me not live, but I'm amazed to see
What a clear type thou art of piety.
Why should thy floods enrich those shores, that sin
Against thy liberty and keep thee in?
Thy waters nurse that rude land which enslaves
And captivates thy free and spacious waves.
Most blessed tutors, I will learn of those
To shew my charity unto my foes,
And strive to do some good unto the poor,
As thy streams do unto the barren shore.
    All this from thee, my Ysca? Yes, and more;
I am for many virtues on thy score.
Trust me thy waters yet: why—wilt not so?
Let me but drink again and I will go.
I see thy course anticipates my plea:
I'll haste to God, as thou dost to the sea;
And when my eyes in waters drown their beams,
The pious imitations of thy streams,
May every holy, happy, hearty tear
Help me to run to Heaven, as thou dost there.

                                        Thomas Vaughan

166   The Waterfall
(Breconshire)

With what deep murmurs through time's silent stealth
Doth thy transparent, cool and watery wealth
      Here flowing fall,
      And chide, and call,
As if his liquid, loose retinue stayed
Ling'ring, and were of this steep place afraid,
      The common pass
      Where, clear as glass,
      All must descend
      Not to an end:
But quickened by this deep and rocky grave,
Rise to a longer course more bright and brave.
Dear stream! dear bank, where often I
Have sat, and pleased my pensive eye,
Why, since each drop of thy quick store
Runs thither, whence it flowed before,
Should poor souls fear a shade or night,
Who came (sure) from a sea of light?
Or since those drops are all sent back
So sure to thee, that none doth lack,
Why should frail flesh doubt any more
That what God takes, he'll not restore?
O useful element and clear!
My sacred wash and cleanser here,
My first consigner unto those
Fountains of life, where the Lamb goes?
What sublime truths, and wholesome themes,
Lodge in thy mystical, deep streams!
Such as dull man can never find
Unless that Spirit lead his mind,
Which first upon thy face did move,
And hatched all with his quickening love.
As this loud brook's incessant fall
In streaming rings restagnates all,
Which reach by course the bank, and then
Are no more seen, just so pass men.
O my invisible estate,
My glorious liberty, still late!
Thou art the channel my soul seeks,
Not this with cataracts and creeks.

                         Henry Vaughan

167   The Brecon Beacons and the
          Black Mountains

Fair, shining mountains of my pilgrimage,
    And flow'ry vales, whose flow'rs were stars:
The days and nights of my first happy age;
    An age without distaste and wars:
When I by thoughts ascend your sunny heads,
    And mind those sacred midnight lights,
By which I walked, when curtained rooms and beds
    Confined, or sealed up others' sights:
            O then how bright
            And quick a light
    Doth brush my heart and scatter night;
            Chasing that shade
            Which my sins made,
    While I so spring, as if I could not fade!

                                        Henry Vaughan

        168   Grongar Hill
        (Carmarthenshire)

    Silent nymph, with curious eye!
    Who, the purple evening, lie
    On the mountain's lonely van,
    Beyond the noise of busy man,
    Painting fair the form of things,
    While the yellow linnet sings;
    Or the tuneful nightingale
    Charms the forest with her tale;
    Come with all thy various hues,
    Come, and aid thy sister Muse;
    Now while Phœbus riding high
    Gives lustre to the land and sky!
    Grongar Hill invites my song,
    Draw the landscape bright and strong;
    Grongar, in whose mossy cells
    Sweetly-musing Quiet dwells;
    Grongar, in whose silent shade,
    For the modest Muses made,
    So oft I have, the even still,
    At the fountain of a rill,
    Sate upon a flowery bed,
    With my hand beneath my head;

And strayed my eyes o'er Towy's flood,
Over mead and over wood,
From house to house, from hill to hill,
'Till Contemplation had her fill.

   About his chequered sides I wind,
And leave his brooks and meads behind,
And groves, and grottos where I lay,
And vistas shooting beams of day:
Wider and wider spreads the vale,
As circles on a smooth canal:
The mountains round, unhappy fate!
Sooner or later, of all height,
Withdraw their summits from the skies,
And lessen as the others rise:
Still the prospect wider spreads,
Adds a thousand woods and meads,
Still it widens, widens still,
And sinks the newly-risen hill.

   Now I gain the mountain's brow,
What a landscape lies below!
No clouds, no vapours intervene,
But the gay, the open scene
Does the face of Nature show,
In all the hues of heaven's bow!
And, swelling to embrace the light,
Spreads around beneath the sight.

   Old castles on the cliffs arise,
Proudly towering in the skies!
Rushing from the woods, the spires
Seem from hence ascending fires!
Half his beams Apollo sheds
On the yellow mountain-heads!
Gilds the fleeces of the flocks:
And glitters on the broken rocks!

   Below me trees unnumbered rise,
Beautiful in various dyes:
The gloomy pine, the poplar blue,
The yellow beech, the sable yew,
The slender fir that taper grows,
The sturdy oak with broad-spread boughs.
And beyond the purple grove,
Haunt of Phillis, queen of love!

Gaudy as the opening dawn,
Lies a long and level lawn,
On which a dark hill, steep and high,
Holds and charms the wandering eye!
Deep are his feet in Towy's flood,
His sides are cloth'd with waving wood,
And ancient towers crown his brow,
That cast an awful look below;
Whose ragged walls the ivy creeps,
And with her arms from falling keeps;
So both a safety from the wind
On mutual dependence find.
　　'Tis now the raven's bleak abode;
'Tis now the apartment of the toad;
And there the fox securely feeds;
And there the poisonous adder breeds,
Concealed in ruins, moss and weeds,
While, ever and anon, there falls
Huge heaps of hoary mouldered walls.
Yet Time has seen, that lifts the low,
And level lays the lofty brow,
Has seen this broken pile complete,
Big with the vanity of state;
But transient is the smile of fate!
A little rule, a little sway,
A sunbeam in a winter's day,
Is all the proud and mighty have
Between the cradle and the grave.
　　And see the rivers how they run,
Through woods and meads; in shade and sun,
Sometimes swift, sometimes slow,
Wave succeeding wave, they go
A various journey to the deep,
Like human life to endless sleep!
Thus is Nature's vesture wrought,
To instruct our wandering thought;
Thus she dresses green and gay,
To disperse our cares away.
　　Ever charming, ever new,
When will the landscape tire the view!
The fountain's fall, the river's flow,
The woody valleys, warm and low;

The windy summit, wild and high,
Roughly rushing on the sky!
The pleasant seat, the ruined tower,
The naked rock, the shady bower;
The town and village, dome and farm,
Each give each a double charm,
As pearls upon an Æthiop's arm.

See on the mountain's southern side,
Where the prospect opens wide,
Where the evening gilds the tide;
How close and small the hedges lie!
What streaks of meadows cross the eye!
A step methinks may pass the stream,
So little distant dangers seem;
So we mistake the future's face,
Eyed through hope's deluding glass;
As yon summits soft and fair,
Clad in colours of the air,
Which to those who journey near,
Barren, brown, and rough appear;
Still we tread the same coarse way,
The present's still a cloudy day.

O may I with myself agree,
And never covet what I see:
Content me with an humble shade,
My passions tamed, my wishes laid;
For while our wishes wildly roll,
We banish quiet from the soul:
'Tis thus the busy beat the air;
And misers gather wealth and care.

Now, even now, my joys run high,
As on the mountain-turf I lie;
While the wanton Zephyr sings,
And in the vale perfumes his wings;
While the waters murmur deep;
While the shepherd charms his sheep;
While the birds unbounded fly,
And with music fill the sky,
Now, even now, my joys run high.

Be full, ye courts, be great who will;
Search for peace with all your skill:
Open wide the lofty door,
Seek her on the marble floor,

In vain you search, she is not there;
In vain ye search the domes of Care!
Grass and flowers Quiet treads,
On the meads, and mountain-heads,
Along with Pleasure, close allied,
Ever by each other's side:
And often, by the murmuring rill,
Hears the thrush, while all is still,
Within the groves of Grongar Hill.

John Dyer

169 Pont-y-Wern
(Denbighshire)

When soft September brings again
  To yonder gorse its golden glow,
And Snowdon sends its autumn rain
  To bid thy current livelier flow;
Amid that ashen foliage light
When scarlet beads are glistering bright,
While alder boughs unchanged are seen
In summer livery of green;
When clouds before the cooler breeze
Are flying, white and large; with these
Returning, so may I return,
And find thee changeless, Pont-y-wern.

Arthur Hugh Clough

170 Cader Idris at Sunset

Last autumn, as we sat, ere fall of night,
Over against old Cader's rugged face,
We mark'd the sunset from its secret place
Salute him with a fair and sudden light.
Flame-hued he rose, and vast, without a speck
Of life upon his flush'd and lonely side;
A double rainbow o'er him bent, to deck
What was so bright before, thrice glorified!
How oft, when pacing o'er those inland plains,
I see that rosy rock of Northern Wales
Come up before me! then its lustre wanes,
And all the frith and intermediate vales
Are darken'd, while our little group remains
Half-glad, half-tearful, as the vision pales!

Charles Tennyson Turner

171   The Artist on Penmaenmawr

That first September day was blue and warm,
Flushing the shaly flanks of Penmaenmawr;
While youths and maidens, in the lucid calm
Exulting, bathed or bask'd from hour to hour;
What colour-passion did the artist feel!
While evermore the jarring trains went by,
Now, as for evermore, in fancy's eye,
Smutch'd with the cruel fires of Abergele;
Then fell the dark o'er the great crags and downs,
And all the night-struck mountain seem'd to say,
'Farewell! these happy skies, this peerless day!
And these fair seas—and fairer still than they,
The white-arm'd girls in dark blue bathing-gowns,
Among the snowy gulls and summer spray.'

Charles Tennyson Turner

172   At a Welsh Waterfall

It was a hard thing to undo this knot.
The rainbow shines, but only in the thought
Of him that looks. Yet not in that alone,
For who makes rainbows by invention?
And many standing round a waterfall
See one bow each, yet not the same to all,
But each a hand's breadth further than the next.
The sun on falling waters writes the text
Which yet is in the eye or in the thought.
It was a hard thing to undo this knot.

Gerard Manley Hopkins

Maentwrog

173   Moonrise
(Denbighshire)

I awoke in the Midsummer not-to-call night, ' in the white
    and the walk of the morning:
The moon, dwindled and thinned to the fringe ' of a fingernail
    held to the candle,
Or paring of paradisaïcal fruit, ' lovely in waning but
    lustreless,
Stepped from the stool, drew back from the barrow, ' of dark
    Maenefa the mountain;

A cusp still clasped him, a fluke yet fanged him, ' entangled
    him, not quit utterly.
This was the prized, the desirable sight, ' unsought, presented
    so easily,
Parted me leaf and leaf, divided me, ' eyelid and eyelid of
    slumber.

Gerard Manley Hopkins

174   Hurrahing in Harvest
(Denbighshire)

Summer ends now; now, barbarous in beauty, the stooks
    rise
Around; up above, what wind-walks! what lovely behaviour
Of silk-sack clouds! has wilder, wilful-wavier
Meal-drift moulded ever and melted across skies?

I walk, I lift up, I lift up heart, eyes,
Down all that glory in the heavens to glean our Saviour;
And, éyes, heárt, what looks, what lips yet gave you a
Rapturous love's greeting of realer, of rounder replies?

And the azurous hung hills are his world-wielding shoulder
Majestic—as a stallion stalwart, very-violet-sweet!—
These things, these things were here and but the beholder
Wanting; which two when they once meet,
The heart rears wings bold and bolder
And hurls for him, O half hurls earth for him off under his
    feet.

Gerard Manley Hopkins

175   Days that Have Been
(South Wales)

Can I forget the sweet days that have been,
    When poetry first began to warm my blood;
When from the hills of Gwent I saw the earth
    Burned into two by Severn's silver flood:

When I would go alone at night to see
    The moonlight, like a big white butterfly,
Dreaming on that old castle near Caerleon,
    While at its side the Usk went softly by:

When I would stare at lovely clouds in Heaven,
　　Or watch them when reported by deep streams;
When feeling pressed like thunder, but would not
　　Break into that grand music of my dreams?

Can I forget the sweet days that have been,
　　The villages so green I have been in;
Llantarnam, Magor, Malpas, and Llanwern,
　　Liswery, old Caerleon, and Alteryn?

Can I forget the banks of Malpas Brook,
　　Or Ebbw's voice in such a wild delight,
As on he dashed with pebbles in his throat,
　　Gurgling towards the sea with all his might?

Ah, when I see a leafy village now,
　　I sigh and ask it for Llantarnam's green;
I ask each river where is Ebbw's voice—
　　In memory of the sweet days that have been.

　　　　　　　　　　　　　　　　　W. H. Dav

176　Lines Composed a Few Miles above Tintern Abbey, o
revisiting the banks of the Wye during a tour, 13th July 1798

Five years have past; five summers, with the length
Of five long winters! and again I hear
These waters, rolling from their mountain-springs
With a soft inland murmur.—Once again
Do I behold these steep and lofty cliffs,
That on a wild secluded scene impress
Thoughts of more deep seclusion; and connect
The landscape with the quiet of the sky.
The day is come when I again repose
Here, under this dark sycamore, and view
These plots of cottage-ground, these orchard-tufts,
Which at this season, with their unripe fruits,
Are clad in one green hue, and lose themselves
'Mid groves and copses. Once again I see
These hedge-rows, hardly hedge-rows, little lines
Of sportive wood run wild: these pastoral farms,
Green to the very door; and wreaths of smoke
Sent up, in silence, from among the trees!

With some uncertain notice, as might seem
Of vagrant dwellers in the houseless woods,
Or of some Hermit's cave, where by his fire
The Hermit sits alone.
                                        These beauteous forms
Through a long absence, have not been to me
As is a landscape to a blind man's eye:
But oft, in lonely rooms, and 'mid the din
Of towns and cities, I have owed to them
In hours of weariness, sensations sweet,
Felt in the blood, and felt along the heart;
And passing even into my purer mind,
With tranquil restoration:—feelings too
Of unremembered pleasure: such, perhaps,
As have no slight or trivial influence
On that best portion of a good man's life,
His little, nameless, unremembered, acts
Of kindness and of love. Nor less, I trust,
To them I may have owed another gift,
Of aspect more sublime; that blessed mood
In which the burthen of the mystery,
In which the heavy and the weary weight
Of all this unintelligible world,
Is lightened:—that serene and blessed mood,
In which the affections gently lead us on,—
Until, the breath of this corporeal frame
And even the motion of our human blood
Almost suspended, we are laid asleep
In body, and become a living soul:
While with an eye made quiet by the power
Of harmony, and the deep power of joy,
We see into the life of things.
                                        If this
Be but a vain belief, yet, oh! how oft—
In darkness and amid the many shapes
Of joyless daylight; when the fretful stir
Unprofitable, and the fever of the world,
Have hung upon the beatings of my heart—
How oft, in spirit, have I turned to thee,
O sylvan Wye! thou wanderer thro' the woods,
How often has my spirit turned to thee!
   And now, with gleams of half-extinguished thought,
With many recognitions dim and faint,

And somewhat of a sad perplexity,
The picture of the mind revives again:
While here I stand, not only with the sense
Of present pleasure, but with pleasing thoughts
That in this moment there is life and food
For future years. And so I dare to hope,
Though changed, no doubt, from what I was when first
I came among these hills; when like a roe
I bounded o'er the mountains, by the sides
Of the deep rivers, and the lonely streams,
Wherever nature led: more like a man
Flying from something that he dreads than one
Who sought the thing he loved. For nature then
(The coarser pleasures of my boyish days,
And their glad animal movements all gone by)
To me was all in all.—I cannot paint
What then I was. The sounding cataract
Haunted me like a passion: the tall rock,
The mountain, and the deep and gloomy wood,
Their colours and their forms, were then to me
An appetite; a feeling and a love,
That had no need of a remoter charm,
By thought supplied, nor any interest
Unborrowed from the eye.—That time is past,
And all its aching joys are now no more,
And all its dizzy raptures. Not for this
Faint I, nor mourn nor murmur; other gifts
Have followed; for such loss, I would believe,
Abundant recompense. For I have learned
To look on nature, not as in the hour
Of thoughtless youth; but hearing oftentimes
The still, sad music of humanity,
Nor harsh nor grating, though of ample power
To chasten and subdue. And I have felt
A presence that disturbs me with the joy
Of elevated thoughts; a sense sublime
Of something far more deeply interfused,
Whose dwelling is the light of setting suns,
And the round ocean and the living air,
And the blue sky, and in the mind of man:
A motion and a spirit, that impels
All thinking things, all objects of all thought,
And rolls through all things. Therefore am I still

A lover of the meadows and the woods,
And mountains; and of all that we behold
From this green earth; of all the mighty world
Of eye, and ear,—both what they half create,
And what perceive; well pleased to recognize
In nature and the language of the sense
The anchor of my purest thoughts, the nurse,
The guide, the guardian of my heart, and soul
Of all my moral being.

                Nor perchance,
If I were not thus taught, should I the more
Suffer my genial spirits to decay:
For thou art with me here upon the banks
Of this fair river; thou my dearest Friend,
My dear, dear Friend; and in thy voice I catch
The language of my former heart, and read
My former pleasures in the shooting lights
Of thy wild eyes. Oh! yet a little while
May I behold in thee what I was once,
My dear, dear Sister! and this prayer I make,
Knowing that Nature never did betray
The heart that loved her; 'tis her privilege,
Through all the years of this our life, to lead
From joy to joy: for she can so inform
The mind that is within us, so impress
With quietness and beauty, and so feed
With lofty thoughts, that neither evil tongues,
Rash judgments, nor the sneers of selfish men,
Nor greetings where no kindness is, nor all
The dreary intercourse of daily life,
Shall e'er prevail against us, or disturb
Our cheerful faith, that all which we behold
Is full of blessings. Therefore let the moon
Shine on thee in thy solitary walk;
And let the misty mountain-winds be free
To blow against thee: and, in after years,
When these wild ecstasies shall be matured
Into a sober pleasure; when thy mind
Shall be a mansion for all lovely forms,
Thy memory be as a dwelling-place
For all sweet sounds and harmonies; oh! then,
If solitude, or fear, or pain, or grief,
Should be thy portion, with what healing thoughts

Of tender joy wilt thou remember me,
And these my exhortations! Nor, perchance—
If I should be where I no more can hear
Thy voice, nor catch from thy wild eyes these gleams
Of past existence—wilt thou then forget
That on the banks of this delightful stream
We stood together; and that I, so long
A worshipper of Nature, hither came
Unwearied in that service: rather say
With warmer love—oh! with far deeper zeal
Of holier love. Nor wilt thou then forget,
That after many wanderings, many years
Of absence, these steep woods and lofty cliffs,
And this green pastoral landscape, were to me
More dear, both for themselves and for thy sake!

                                    William Wordswo

177   The Hushing of the Wye

The Danube to the Severn gave
    The darkened heart that beat no more;
    They laid him by the pleasant shore,
And in the hearing of the wave.

There twice a day the Severn fills;
    The salt sea-water passes by,
    And hushes half the babbling Wye,
And makes a silence in the hills.

The Wye is hushed nor moved along,
    And hushed my deepest grief of all,
    When filled with tears that cannot fall,
I brim with sorrow drowning song.

The tide flows down, the wave again
    Is vocal in its wooded walls;
    My deeper anguish also falls,
And I can speak a little then.

                                    Alfred Tenny

178   Fern Hill
(Llangain, Carmarthenshire)

ow as I was young and easy under the apple boughs
bout the lilting house and happy as the grass was green,
    The night above the dingle starry,
        Time let me hail and climb
    Golden in the heydays of his eyes,
nd honoured among wagons I was prince of the apple towns
nd once below a time I lordly had the trees and leaves
        Trail with daisies and barley
    Down the rivers of the windfall light.

nd as I was green and carefree, famous among the barns
bout the happy yard and singing as the farm was home,
    In the sun that is young once only,
        Time let me play and be
    Golden in the mercy of his means,
nd green and golden I was huntsman and herdsman, the calves
ng to my horn, the foxes on the hills barked clear and cold.
        And the sabbath rang slowly
    In the pebbles of the holy streams.

l the sun long it was running, it was lovely, the hay
lds high as the house, the tunes from the chimneys, it was air
    And playing, lovely and watery
        And fire green as grass.
    And nightly under the simple stars
 I rode to sleep the owls were bearing the farm away,
  the moon long I heard, blessed among stables, the night-jars
    Flying with the ricks, and the horses
        Flashing into the dark.

And then to awake, and the farm, like a wanderer white
With the dew, come back, the cock on his shoulder: it was all
   Shining, it was Adam and maiden,
     The sky gathered again
    And the sun grew round that very day.
So it must have been after the birth of the simple light
In the first, spinning place, the spellbound horses walking warm
   Out of the whinnying green stable
    On to the fields of praise.

And honoured among foxes and pheasants by the gay house
Under the new made clouds and happy as the heart was long,
   In the sun born over and over,
    I ran my heedless ways,
    My wishes raced through the house high hay
And nothing I cared, at my sky blue trades, that time allows
In all his tuneful turning so few and such morning songs
   Before the children green and golden
    Follow him out of grace,

Nothing I cared, in the lamb white days, that time would take me
Up to the swallow thronged loft by the shadow of my hand,
   In the moon that is always rising,
    Nor that riding to sleep
   I should hear him fly with the high fields
And wake to the farm forever fled from the childless land.
Oh as I was young and easy in the mercy of his means,
    Time held me green and dying
   Though I sang in my chains like the sea.

                            Dylan Thomas

179   On Malverne Hilles,
the Place of Piers Plowman's Vision
(Colwall?)

In a somer seson, whan softe was the sonne,
I shoop me into shroudes as I a sheep were,
In habite as an heremite unholy of werkes,
Wente wide in this world wondres to here.
Ac on a May morwenynge on Malverne hilles
Me bife a ferly, of Fairye me thoghte.
I was wery forwandred and wente me to reste
Under a brood bank by a bourne syde;
And as I lay and lenede and loked on the watres,
I slombred into a slepyng, it sweyed so murye.
      Thanne gan I meten a merveillous swevene—
That I was in a wildernesse, wiste I nevere where.
A[c] as I biheeld into the eest an heigh to the sonne,
I seigh a tour on a toft trieliche ymaked,
A deep dale bynethe, a dongeon therinne,
With depe diches and derke and dredfulle of sighte.
A fair feeld ful of folk fond I ther bitwene—
Of alle manere of men, the meene and the riche,
Werchynge and wandrynge as the world asketh.

                              William Langland

oop: dressed
roudes: clothes
 but
ly: wonder
ry forwandred: travel-weary
eyed so murye: (the bourn, the stream) sounded so sweet
evene: dream
ur: tower
t: hillock
liche: elegantly

180   Aurora Leigh Reaches Herefordshire from Italy*
(Colwall)
(i)

Then, land!—then, England! oh, the frosty cliffs
Looked cold upon me. Could I find a home
Among those mean red houses through the fog?
And when I heard my father's language first
From alien lips which had no kiss for mine
I wept aloud, then laughed, then wept, then wept,
And some one near me said the child was mad
Through much sea-sickness. The train swept us on:
Was this my father's England? the great isle?
The ground seemed cut up from the fellowship
Of verdure, field from field, as man from man;
The skies themselves looked low and positive,
As almost you could touch them with a hand,
And dared to do it they were so far off
From God's celestial crystals; all things blurred
And dull and vague. Did Shakspeare and his mates
Absorb the light here?—not a hill or stone
With heart to strike a radiant colour up
Or active outline on the indifferent air.

(ii)

I had a little chamber in the house,
As green as any privet-hedge a bird
Might choose to build in, though the nest itself
Could show but dead-brown sticks and straws; the walls
Were green, the carpet was pure green, the straight
Small bed was curtained greenly, and the folds
Hung green about the window which let in
The out-door world with all its greenery.
You could not push your head out and escape
A dash of dawn-dew from the honeysuckle,
But so you were baptized into the grace
And privilege of seeing...

                         First, the lime,
(I had enough there, of the lime, be sure,—
My morning-dream was often hummed away

* For her return to Italy see page 354.

By the bees in it;) past the lime, the lawn,
Which, after sweeping broadly round the house,
Went trickling through the shrubberies in a stream
Of tender turf, and wore and lost itself
Among the acacias, over which you saw
The irregular line of elms by the deep lane
Which stopped the grounds and dammed the overflow
Of arbutus and laurel. Out of sight
The lane was; sunk so deep, no foreign tramp
Nor drover of wild ponies out of Wales
Could guess if lady's hall or tenant's lodge
Dispensed such odours,—though his stick well-crooked
Might reach the lowest trail of blossoming briar
Which dipped upon the wall. Behind the elms,
And through their tops, you saw the folded hills
Striped up and down with hedges, (burly oaks
Projecting from the line to show themselves)
Through which my cousin Romney's chimneys smoked
As still as when a silent mouth in frost
Breathes, showing where the woodlands hid Leigh Hall;
While, far above, a jut of table-land,
A promontory without water, stretched,—
You could not catch it if the days were thick,
Or took it for a cloud; but, otherwise,
The vigorous sun would catch it up at eve
And use it for an anvil till he had filled
The shelves of heaven with burning thunderbolts,
Protesting against night and darkness:—then,
When all his setting trouble was resolved
To a trance of passive glory, you might see
In apparition on the golden sky
(Alas, my Giotto's background!) the sheep run
Along the fine clear outline, small as mice
That run along a witch's scarlet thread.

Not a grand nature. Not my chesnut-woods
Of Vallombrosa, cleaving by the spurs
To the precipices. Not my headlong leaps
Of waters, that cry out for joy or fear
In leaping through the palpitating pines,
Like a white soul tossed out to eternity
With thrills of time upon it. Not indeed
My multitudinous mountains, sitting in

The magic circle, with the mutual touch
Electric, panting from their full deep hearts
Beneath the influent heavens, and waiting for
Communion and commission. Italy
Is one thing, England one.
                              On English ground
You understand the letter,—ere the fall
How Adam lived in a garden. All the fields
Are tied up fast with hedges, nosegay-like;
The hills are crumpled plains, the plains parterres,
The trees, round, woolly, ready to be clipped,
And if you seek for any wilderness
You find, at best, a park. A nature tamed
And grown domestic like a barn-door fowl,
Which does not awe you with its claws and beak
Nor tempt you to an eyrie too high up,
But which, in cackling, sets you thinking of
Your eggs to-morrow at breakfast, in the pause
Of finer meditation.

Elizabeth Barrett Browning

181   Acton Beauchamp, Herefordshire

Acton Beauchamp, the poorest place in all the nation,
A lousy parson, a nitty clerk, and a shabby congregation.

A

182   Wenlock Edge
(Shropshire)

'Tis time, I think, by Wenlock town
    The golden broom should blow;
The hawthorn sprinkled up and down
    Should charge the land with snow.

Spring will not wait the loiterer's time
    Who keeps so long away;
So others wear the broom and climb
    The hedgerows heaped with may.

Oh tarnish late on Wenlock Edge,
    Gold that I never see;
Lie long, high snowdrifts in the hedge
    That will not shower on me.

A. E. Housman

183   Hughley Steeple
        (Shropshire)

The vane on Hughley steeple
  Veers bright, a far-known sign,
And there lie Hughley people,
  And there lie friends of mine.
Tall in their midst the tower
  Divides the shade and sun,
And the clock strikes the hour
  And tells the time to none.

To south the headstones cluster,
  The sunny mounds lie thick;
The dead are more in muster
  At Hughley than the quick.
North, for a soon-told number,
  Chill graves the sexton delves,
And steeple-shadowed slumber
  The slayers of themselves.

To north, to south, lie parted,
  With Hughley tower above,
The kind, the single-hearted,
  The lads I used to love.
And, south or north, 'tis only
  A choice of friends one knows,
And I shall ne'er be lonely
  Asleep with these or those.

                                        A. E. Housman

184   The Churchyard on the Sands
        (Cheshire: the Wirrall)

My love lies in the gates of foam,
  The last dear wreck of shore;
The naked sea-marsh binds her home,
  The sand her chamber door.

The grey gull flaps the written stones,
  The ox-birds chase the tide;
And near that narrow field of bones
  Great ships at anchor ride.

Black piers with crust of dripping green,
  One foreland, like a hand,
O'er intervals of grass between
  Dim lonely dunes of sand.

A church of silent weathered looks,
  A breezy reddish tower,
A yard whose mounded resting-nooks
  Are tinged with sorrel flower.

In peace the swallow's eggs are laid
  Along the belfry walls;
The tempest does not reach her shade,
  The rain her silent halls.

But sails are sweet in summer sky,
  The lark throws down a lay;
The long salt levels steam and dry,
  The cloud-heart melts away.

But patches of the sea-pink shine,
  The pied crows poise and come;
The mallow hangs, the bindweeds twine,
  Where her sweet lips are dumb.

The passion of the wave is mute;
  No sound or ocean shock;
No music save the trilling flute
  That marks the curlew flock.

But yonder when the wind is keen,
  And rainy air is clear,
The merchant city's spires are seen,
  The toil of men grows near.

Along the coast-way grind the wheels
  Of endless carts of coal;
And on the sides of giant keels
  The shipyard hammers roll.

The world creeps here upon the shout,
  And stirs my heart in pain;
The mist descends and blots it out,
  And I am strong again.

Strong and alone, my dove, with thee;
 And, tho' mine eyes be wet,
There's nothing in the world to me
 So dear as my regret.

I would not change my sorrow, sweet,
 For others' nuptial hours;
I love the daisies at thy feet
 More than their orange flowers.

My hand alone shall tend thy tomb
 From leaf-bud to leaf-fall,
And wreathe around each season's bloom
 Till autumn ruins all.

Let snowdrops, early in the year,
 Droop o'er her silent breast;
And bid the later cowslip rear
 The amber of its crest.

Come hither, linnets tufted-red,
 Drift by, O wailing tern;
Set pure vale lilies at her head,
 At her feet lady-fern.

Grow, samphire, at the tidal brink,
 Wave, pansies of the shore,
To whisper how alone I think
 Of her for evermore.

Bring blue sea-hollies thorny, keen,
 Long lavender in flower;
Grey wormwood like a hoary queen,
 Stanch mullein like a tower.

O sea-wall mounded long and low,
 Let iron bounds be thine;
Nor let the salt wave overflow
 That breast I held divine.

Nor float its sea-weed to her hair,
 Nor dim her eyes with sands:
No fluted cockle burrow where
 Sleep folds her patient hands.

Tho' thy crest feel the wild sea's breath,
　Tho' tide-weight tear thy root,
Oh, guard the treasure house, where Death
　Has bound my darling mute.

Tho' cold her pale lips to reward
　With Love's own mysteries,
Ah, rob no daisy from her sward,
　Rough gale of eastern seas!

Ah, render sere no silken bent,
　That by her head-stone waves;
Let noon and golden summer blent
　Pervade these ocean graves.

And, ah, dear heart, in thy still nest,
　Resign this earth of woes,
Forget the ardours of the west,
　Neglect the morning glows.

Sleep, and forget all things but one,
　Heard in each wave of sea,—
How lonely all the years will run
　Until I rest by thee.

Lord de Table

185　The Sands of Dee
(Cheshire)

'O Mary, go and call the cattle home,
　And call the cattle home,
　And call the cattle home
　Across the sands of Dee;'
The western wind was wild and dank with foam,
　And all alone went she.

The western tide crept up along the sand,
　And o'er and o'er the sand,
　And round and round the sand,
　As far as eye could see.
The rolling mist came down and hid the land:
　And never home came she.

'Oh! is it weed, or fish, or floating hair—
    A tress of golden hair,
    A drownèd maiden's hair
  Above the nets at sea?
Was never salmon yet that shone so fair
  Among the stakes on Dee.'

They rowed her in across the rolling foam,
    The cruel crawling foam,
    The cruel hungry foam,
  To her grave beside the sea:
But still the boatmen hear her call the cattle home
  Across the sands of Dee.

                              Charles Kingsley

        186   Braddan Vicarage
              (Isle of Man)

I wonder if in that far isle,
    Some child is growing now, like me
When I was child: care-pricked, yet healed the while
    With balm of rock and sea.

I wonder if beyond the verge
    He dim conjectures England's coast:
The land of Edwards and of Henries, scourge
    Of insolent foemen, at the most
Faint caught where Cumbria looms a geographic ghost.

I wonder if to him the sycamore
    Is full of green and tender light;
If the gnarled ash stands stunted at the door,
    By salt sea-blast defrauded of its right;
If budding larches feed the hunger of his sight.

I wonder if to him the dewy globes
    Like mercury nestle in the caper leaf;
If, when the white narcissus dons its robes,
    It soothes his childish grief;
If silver plates the birch, gold rustles in the sheaf.

I wonder if to him the heath-clad mountain
    With crimson pigment fills the sensuous cells;
If like full bubbles from an emerald fountain
    Gorse-bloom luxuriant wells;
If God with trenchant forms the insolent lushness quells.

I wonder if the hills are long and lonely
    That North from South divide;
I wonder if he thinks that it is only
    The hither slope where men abide,
Unto all mortal homes refused the other side.

I wonder if some day he, chance-conducted,
    Attains the vantage of the utmost height,
And, by his own discovery instructed,
    Sees grassy plain and cottage white,
Each human sign and pledge that feeds him with delight.

At eventide, when lads with lasses dally,
    And milking Pei sits singing at the pail,
I wonder if he hears along the valley
    The wind's sad sough, half credulous of the tale
How from Slieu-whallian moans the murdered witches'
    wail.

I wonder if to him 'the Boat,' descending
    From the proud East, his spirit fills
With a strange joy, adventurous ardour lending
    To the mute soul that thrills
As booms the herald gun, and westward wakes the hills.

I wonder if he loves that Captain bold
    Who has the horny hand,
Who swears the mighty oath, who well can hold,
    Half-drunk, serene command,
And guide his straining bark to refuge of the land.

I wonder if he thinks the world has aught
    Of strong, or nobly wise,
Like him by whom the invisible land is caught
    With instinct true, nor storms, nor midnight skies
Avert the settled aim, or daunt the keen emprise.

I wonder if he deems the English men
  A higher type beyond his reach,
Imperial blood, by Heaven ordained with pen
  And sword the populous world to teach;
If awed he hears the tones as of an alien speech;

Or, older grown, suspects a braggart race,
  Ignores phlegmatic claim
Of privileged assumption, holding base
  Their technic skill and aim,
And all the prosperous fraud that binds their social frame.

Young rebel! how he pants, who knows not what
  He hates, yet hates: all one to him
If Guelph, or Buonaparte, or sans-culotte,
  If Strafford or if Pym
Usurp the clumsy helm—if England sink or swim!

Ah! crude, undisciplined, when thou shalt know
  What good is in this England, still of joys
The chiefest count it thou wast nurtured so
  That thou may'st keep the larger equipoise,
And stand outside these nations and their noise.

                                    T. E. Brown

8 The Lakes and the North

187   On the Solitary Fells around Hawkshead

Fair seed-time had my soul, and I grew up
Foster'd alike by beauty and by fear;
Much favour'd in my birthplace, and no less
In that beloved Vale to which, erelong,
I was transplanted. Well I call to mind
('Twas at an early age, ere I had seen
Nine summers) when upon the mountain slope
The frost and breath of frosty wind had snapp'd
The last autumnal crocus, 'twas my joy
To wander half the night among the Cliffs
And the smooth Hollows, where the woodcocks ran
Along the open turf. In thought and wish
That time, my shoulder all with springes hung,
I was a fell destroyer. On the heights
Scudding away from snare to snare, I plied
My anxious visitation, hurrying on,
Still hurrying, hurrying onward; moon and stars
Were shining o'er my head; I was alone,
And seem'd to be a trouble to the peace
That was among them. Sometimes it befel
In these night-wanderings, that a strong desire
O'erpower'd my better reason, and the bird
Which was the captive of another's toils
Became my prey; and, when the deed was done
I heard among the solitary hills
Low breathings coming after me, and sounds
Of undistinguishable motion, steps
Almost as silent as the turf they trod.
Nor less in springtime when on southern banks
The shining sun had from his knot of leaves
Decoy'd the primrose flower, and when the Vales

And woods were warm, was I a plunderer then
In the high places, on the lonesome peaks
Where'er, among the mountains and the winds,
The Mother Bird had built her lodge. Though mean
My object, and inglorious, yet the end
Was not ignoble. Oh! when I have hung
Above the raven's nest, by knots of grass
And half-inch fissures in the slippery rock
But ill sustain'd, and almost, as it seem'd,
Suspended by the blast which blew amain,
Shouldering the naked crag; Oh! at that time,
While on the perilous ridge I hung alone,
With what strange utterance did the loud dry wind
Blow through my ears! the sky seem'd not a sky
Of earth, and with what motion mov'd the clouds!

                                   William Wordsworth

    188   Wordsworth Skates on Esthwaite Water

    Nor was this fellowship vouchsaf'd to me
With stinted kindness. In November days,
When vapours, rolling down the valleys, made
A lonely scene more lonesome; among woods
At noon, and 'mid the calm of summer nights,
When, by the margin of the trembling Lake,
Beneath the gloomy hills I homeward went
In solitude, such intercourse was mine;
'Twas mine among the fields both day and night,
And by the waters all the summer long.

    And in the frosty season, when the sun
Was set, and visible for many a mile
The cottage windows through the twilight blaz'd,
I heeded not the summons:—happy time
It was, indeed, for all of us; to me
It was a time of rapture: clear and loud
The village clock toll'd six; I wheel'd about,
Proud and exulting, like an untired horse,
That cares not for his home.—All shod with steel,
We hiss'd along the polish'd ice, in games
Confederate, imitative of the chace
And woodland pleasures, the resounding horn,
The Pack loud bellowing, and the hunted hare.

So through the darkness and the cold we flew,
And not a voice was idle; with the din,
Meanwhile, the precipices rang aloud,
The leafless trees, and every icy crag
Tinkled like iron, while the distant hills
Into the tumult sent an alien sound
Of melancholy, not unnoticed, while the stars,
Eastward, were sparkling clear, and in the west
The orange sky of evening died away.

  Not seldom from the uproar I retired
Into a silent bay, or sportively
Glanced sideway, leaving the tumultuous throng,
To cut across the image of a star
That gleam'd upon the ice: and oftentimes
When we had given our bodies to the wind,
And all the shadowy banks, on either side,
Came sweeping through the darkness, spinning still
The rapid line of motion; then at once
Have I, reclining back upon my heels,
Stopp'd short, yet still the solitary Cliffs
Wheeled by me, even as if the earth had roll'd
With visible motion her diurnal round;
Behind me did they stretch in solemn train
Feebler and feebler, and I stood and watch'd
Till all was tranquil as a dreamless sleep.

                                    William Wordswo

189   It was an April Morning
(Easedale)

It was an April morning: fresh and clear
The Rivulet, delighting in its strength,
Ran with a young man's speed; and yet the voice
Of waters which the winter had supplied
Was softened down into a vernal tone.
The spirit of enjoyment and desire,
And hopes and wishes, from all living things
Went circling, like a multitude of sounds.
The budding groves seemed eager to urge on
The steps of June; as if their various hues
Were only hindrances that stood between
Them and their object: but, meanwhile, prevailed

Such an entire contentment in the air
That every naked ash, and tardy tree
Yet leafless, showed as if the countenance
With which it looked on this delightful day
Were native to the summer.—Up the brook
I roamed in the confusion of my heart,
Alive to all things and forgetting all.
At length I to a sudden turning came
In this continuous glen, where down a rock
The Stream, so ardent in its course before,
Sent forth such sallies of glad sound, that all
Which I till then had heard appeared the voice
Of common pleasure: beast and bird, the lamb,
The shepherd's dog, the linnet and the thrush
Vied with this waterfall, and made a song,
Which, while I listened, seemed like the wild
     growth
Or like some natural produce of the air,
That could not cease to be. Green leaves were here;
But 'twas the foliage of the rocks—the birch,
The yew, the holly, and the bright green thorn,
With hanging islands of resplendent furze:
And, on a summit, distant a short space,
By any who should look beyond the dell
A single mountain-cottage might be seen.
I gazed and gazed, and to myself I said,
'Our thoughts at least are ours; and this wild nook,
My EMMA, I will dedicate to thee.'
—Soon did the spot become my other home,
My dwelling, and my out-of-doors abode.
And, of the Shepherds who have seen me there,
To whom I sometimes in our idle talk
Have told this fancy, two or three, perhaps,
Years after we are gone and in our graves,
When they have cause to speak of this wild place,
May call it by the name of EMMA'S DELL.

                              William Wordsworth

190   On Windermere: Bowness Bay and Belle Isle

Upon the Eastern Shore of Windermere,
Above the crescent of a pleasant Bay,
There stood an Inn, no homely-featured Shed,
Brother of the surrounding Cottages,
But 'twas a splendid place, the door beset
With Chaises, Grooms, and Liveries, and within
Decanters, Glasses, and the blood-red Wine.
In ancient times, or ere the Hall was built
On the large Island, had this Dwelling been
More worthy of a Poet's love, a Hut,
Proud of its one bright fire, and sycamore shade.
But though the rhymes were gone which once inscribed
The threshold, and large golden characters
On the blue-frosted Signboard had usurp'd
The place of the old Lion, in contempt
And mockery of the rustic painter's hand,
Yet to this hour the spot to me is dear
With all its foolish pomp. The garden lay
Upon a slope surmounted by the plain
Of a small Bowling-green; beneath us stood
A grove; with gleams of water through the trees
And over the tree-tops; nor did we want
Refreshment, strawberries and mellow cream.
And there, through half an afternoon, we play'd
On the smooth platform, and the shouts we sent
Made all the mountains ring. But ere the fall
Of night, when in our pinnace we return'd
Over the dusky Lake, and to the beach
Of some small Island steer'd our course with one,
The Minstrel of our troop, and left him there,
And row'd off gently, while he blew his flute
Alone upon the rock; Oh! then the calm
And dead still water lay upon my mind
Even with a weight of pleasure, and the sky
Never before so beautiful, sank down
Into my heart, and held me like a dream.

William Wordswort

191   On Ullswater

One evening (surely I was led by her)
I went alone into a Shepherd's Boat,
A Skiff that to a Willow tree was tied
Within a rocky Cave, its usual home.
'Twas by the shores of Patterdale, a Vale
Wherein I was a Stranger, thither come
A School-boy Traveller, at the Holidays.
Forth rambled from the Village Inn alone
No sooner had I sight of this small Skiff,
Discover'd thus by unexpected chance,
Than I unloos'd her tether and embark'd.
The moon was up, the Lake was shining clear
Among the hoary mountains; from the Shore
I push'd, and struck the oars and struck again
In cadence, and my little Boat mov'd on
Even like a Man who walks with stately step
Though bent on speed. It was an act of stealth
And troubled pleasure; not without the voice
Of mountain-echoes did my Boat move on,
Leaving behind her still on either side
Small circles glittering idly in the moon,
Until they melted all into one track
Of sparkling light. A rocky Steep uprose
Above the Cavern of the Willow tree
And now, as suited one who proudly row'd
With his best skill, I fix'd a steady view
Upon the top of that same craggy ridge,
The bound of the horizon, for behind
Was nothing but the stars and the grey sky.
She was an elfin Pinnace; lustily
I dipp'd my oars into the silent Lake,
And, as I rose upon the stroke, my Boat
Went heaving through the water, like a Swan;
When from behind that craggy Steep, till then
The bound of the horizon, a huge Cliff,
As if with voluntary power instinct,
Uprear'd its head. I struck, and struck again,
And, growing still in stature, the huge Cliff
Rose up between me and the stars, and still,
With measur'd motion, like a living thing,
Strode after me. With trembling hands I turn'd,

And through the silent water stole my way
Back to the Cavern of the Willow tree.
There, in her mooring-place, I left my Bark,
And, through the meadows homeward went, with
    grave
And serious thoughts; and after I had seen
That spectacle, for many days, my brain
Work'd with a dim and undetermin'd sense
Of unknown modes of being; in my thoughts
There was a darkness, call it solitude,
Or blank desertion, no familiar shapes
Of hourly objects, images of trees,
Of sea or sky, no colours of green fields;
But huge and mighty Forms that do not live
Like living men mov'd slowly through the mind
By day and were the trouble of my dreams.

                        William Wordsworth

192   I Wandered Lonely as a Cloud
        (Ullswater)

    I wandered lonely as a cloud
    That floats on high o'er vales and hills,
    When all at once I saw a crowd,
    A host, of golden daffodils;
    Beside the lake, beneath the trees,
    Fluttering and dancing in the breeze.

    Continuous as the stars that shine
    And twinkle on the milky way,
    They stretched in never-ending line
    Along the margin of a bay:
    Ten thousand saw I at a glance,
    Tossing their heads in sprightly dance.

    The waves beside them danced; but they
    Out-did the sparkling waves in glee:
    A poet could not but be gay,
    In such a jocund company:
    I gazed—and gazed—but little thought
    What wealth the show to me had brought:

For oft, when on my couch I lie
In vacant or in pensive mood,
They flash upon that inward eye
Which is the bliss of solitude;
And then my heart with pleasure fills,
And dances with the daffodils.

William Wordsworth

193   The Voice of the Derwent

Yet once again do I behold the forms
Of these huge mountains, and yet once again,
Standing beneath these elms, I hear thy voice,
Beloved Derwent, that peculiar voice
Heard in the stillness of the evening air,
Half-heard and half-created.

William Wordsworth

194   The Fair below Helvellyn

What sounds are those, Helvellyn, which are heard
Up to thy summit? Through the depth of air
Ascending, as if distance had the power
To make the sounds more audible: what Crowd
Is yon, assembled in the gay green Field?
Crowd seems it, solitary Hill! to thee,
Though but a little Family of Men,
Twice twenty, with their Children and their Wives,
And here and there a Stranger interspers'd.
It is a summer festival, a Fair,
Such as, on this side now, and now on that,
Repeated through his tributary Vales,
Helvellyn, in the silence of his rest,
Sees annually, if storms be not abroad,
And mists have left him an unshrouded head.
Delightful day it is for all who dwell
In this secluded Glen, and eagerly
They give it welcome. Long ere heat of noon
Behold the cattle are driven down; the sheep
That have for traffic been cull'd out are penn'd
In cotes that stand together on the Plain
Ranged side by side; the chaffering is begun.
The Heifer lows uneasy at the voice

Of a new Master, bleat the Flocks aloud;
Booths are there none; a Stall or two is here,
A lame Man, or a blind, the one to beg,
The other to make music; hither, too,
From far, with Basket, slung upon her arm,
Of Hawker's Wares, books, pictures, combs, and pins,
Some aged Woman finds her way again,
Year after year a punctual visitant!
The Showman with his Freight upon his Back,
And once, perchance, in lapse of many years
Prouder Itinerant, Mountebank, or He
Whose Wonders in a cover'd Wain lie hid.
But One is here, the loveliest of them all,
Some sweet Lass of the Valley, looking out
For gains, and who that sees her would not buy?
Fruits of her Father's Orchard, apples, pears,
(On that day only to such office stooping)
She carries in her Basket, and walks round
Among the crowd, half pleas'd with, half ashamed
Of her new calling, blushing restlessly.
The Children now are rich, the old Man now
Is generous; so gaiety prevails
Which all partake of, Young and Old. Immense
Is the Recess, the circumambient World
Magnificent, by which they are embraced.
They move about upon the soft green field:
How little They, they and their doings seem,
Their herds and flocks about them, they themselves,
And all that they can further or obstruct!
Through utter weakness pitiably dear
As tender Infants are: and yet how great!
For all things serve them; them the Morning light
Loves as it glistens on the silent rocks,
And them the silent Rocks, which now from high
Look down upon them; the reposing Clouds,
The lurking Brooks from their invisible haunts,
And Old Helvellyn, conscious of the stir,
And the blue Sky that roofs their calm abode.

                                        William Wordswort

195   A Recollection of the Stone Circle near Keswick

Scarce images of life, one here, one there,
Lay vast and edgeways; like a dismal cirque
Of Druid stones, upon a forlorn moor,
When the chill rain begins at shut of eve,
In dull November, and their chancel vault,
The Heaven itself, is blinded throughout night.
Each one kept shroud, nor to his neighbour gave
Or word, or look, or action of despair.

John Keats

196   Southey Looks out of the Window at Greta Hall

Twas at that sober hour when the light of day is receding,
And from surrounding things the hues wherewith day has adorn'd
them
fade, like the hopes of youth, till the beauty of earth is departed:
Pensive, though not in thought, I stood at the window, beholding
Mountain and lake and vale; the valley disrobed of its verdure;
Derwent retaining yet from eve a glassy reflection
Where his expanded breast, then still and smooth as a mirror,
Under the woods reposed; the hills that, calm and majestic,
Lifted their heads in the silent sky, from far Glaramara
Bleacrag, and Maidenmawr, to Grizdal and westermost Withop.
Dark and distinct they rose. The clouds have gather'd above them
High in the middle air, huge, purple, pillowy masses,
While in the west beyond was the last pale tint of the twilight:
Green as a stream in the glen whose pure and chrysolite waters
flow o'er a schistous bed, and serene as the age of the righteous.
Earth was hush'd and still; all motion and sound were suspended:
Neither man was heard, bird, beast, nor humming of insect,
Only the voice of the Greta, heard only when all is in stillness.
Pensive I stood and alone, the hour and the scene had subdued me,
And as I gazed in the west, where Infinity seem'd to be open,
Yearn'd to be free from time, and felt that this life is a thraldom.

Robert Southey

197   Elegiac Stanzas Suggested by a Picture of Peele Castle, in
Storm, Painted by Sir George Beaumont
(Lancashire)

I was thy neighbour once, thou rugged Pile!
Four summer weeks I dwelt in sight of thee:
I saw thee every day; and all the while
Thy Form was sleeping on a glassy sea.

So pure the sky, so quiet was the air!
So like, so very like, was day to day!
Whene'er I looked, thy Image still was there;
It trembled, but it never passed away.

How perfect was the calm! it seemed no sleep;
No mood, which season takes away, or brings:
I could have fancied that the mighty Deep
Was even the gentlest of all gentle Things.

Ah! Then, if mine had been the Painter's hand,
To express what then I saw; and add the gleam,
The light that never was, on sea or land,
The consecration, and the Poet's dream;

I would have planted thee, thou hoary Pile,
Amid a world how different from this!
Beside a sea that could not cease to smile;
On tranquil land, beneath a sky of bliss.

Thou shouldst have seemed a treasure-house divine
Of peaceful years; a chronicle of heaven;—
Of all the sunbeams that did ever shine
The very sweetest had to thee been given.

A Picture had it been of lasting ease,
Elysian quiet, without toil or strife;
No motion but the moving tide, a breeze,
Or merely silent Nature's breathing life.

Such, in the fond illusion of my heart,
Such Picture would I at that time have made:
And seen the soul of truth in every part,
A stedfast peace that might not be betrayed.

So once it would have been,—'tis so no more;
I have submitted to a new control:
A power is gone, which nothing can restore;
A deep distress hath humanized my Soul.*

Not for a moment could I now behold
A smiling sea, and be what I have been:
The feeling of my loss will ne'er be old;
This, which I know, I speak with mind serene.

Then, Beaumont, Friend! who would have been the Friend,
If he had lived, of Him whom I deplore,
This work of thine I blame not, but commend;
This sea in anger, and that dismal shore.

O 'tis a passionate Work!—yet wise and well,
Well chosen is the spirit that is here;
That Hulk which labours in the deadly swell,
This rueful sky, this pageantry of fear!

And this huge Castle, standing here sublime,
I love to see the look with which it braves,
Cased in the unfeeling armour of old time,
The lightning, the fierce wind, and trampling waves.

Farewell, farewell the heart that lives alone,
Housed in a dream, at distance from the Kind!
Such happiness, wherever it be known,
Is to be pitied, for 'tis surely blind.

But welcome fortitude, and patient cheer,
And frequent sights of what is to be borne!
Such sights, or worse, as are before me here.—
Not without hope we suffer and we mourn.

William Wordsworth

The loss at sea of Wordsworth's brother John in 1805.]

198   To the River Duddon: After-thought

I thought of Thee, my partner and my guide,
As being past away.—Vain sympathies!
For, backward, Duddon! as I cast my eyes,
I see what was, and is, and will abide;
Still glides the Stream, and shall for ever glide;
The Form remains, the Function never dies;
While we, the brave, the mighty, and the wise,
We Men, who in our morn of youth defied
The elements, must vanish;—be it so!
Enough, if something from our hands have power
To live, and act, and serve the future hour;
And if, as toward the silent tomb we go,
Through love, through hope, and faith's transcendent dower,
We feel that we are greater than we know.

William Wordswo

199   The Youth of Nature: Wordsworth's Country

Raised are the dripping oars,
Silent the boat! the lake,
Lovely and soft as a dream,
Swims in the sheen of the moon.
The mountains stand at its head
Clear in the pure June-night,
But the valleys are flooded with haze.
Rydal and Fairfield are there;
In the shadow Wordsworth lies dead.
So it is, so it will be for aye.
Nature is fresh as of old,
Is lovely; a mortal is dead.

The spots which recall him survive,
For he lent a new life to these hills.
The Pillar still broods o'er the fields
Which border Ennerdale Lake,
And Egremont sleeps by the sea.
The gleam of The Evening Star
Twinkles on Grasmere no more,
But ruined and solemn and grey
The sheepfold of Michael survives;
And, far to the south, the heath

Still blows in the Quantock coombs,
By the favourite waters of Ruth.
These survive!—yet not without pain,
Pain and dejection to-night,
Can I feel that their poet is gone.

He grew old in an age he condemned.
He looked on the rushing decay
Of the times which had sheltered his youth;
Felt the dissolving throes
Of a social order he loved;
Outlived his brethren, his peers,
And, like the Theban seer,
Died in his enemies' day.

Cold bubbled the spring of Tilphusa,
Copais lay bright in the moon,
Helicon glassed in the lake
Its firs, and afar rose the peaks
Of Parnassus, snowily clear;
Thebes was behind him in flames,
And the clang of arms in his ear,
When his awe-struck captors led
The Theban seer to the spring.
Tiresias drank and died.
Nor did reviving Thebes
See such a prophet again.

Well may we mourn, when the head
Of a sacred poet lies low
In an age which can rear them no more!
The complaining millions of men
Darken in labour and pain;
But he was a priest to us all
Of the wonder and bloom of the world,
Which we saw with his eyes, and were glad.
He is dead, and the fruit-bearing day
Of his race is past on the earth;
And darkness returns to our eyes.

                                        Matthew Arnold

200   Wordsworth's Grave

Keep fresh the grass upon his grave,
O Rotha, with thy living wave!
Sing him thy best! for few or none
Hears thy voice right, now he is gone.

                                    Matthew Arnol

201   Hayeswater

A region desolate and wild.
Black, chafing water: and afloat,
And lonely as a truant child
In a waste wood, a single boat:
No mast, no sails are set thereon;
It moves, but never moveth on:
And welters like a human thing
Amid the wild waves weltering.

Behind, a buried vale doth sleep,
Far down the torrent cleaves its way:
In front the dumb rock rises steep,
A fretted wall of blue and grey;
Of shooting cliff and crumbled stone
With many a wild weed overgrown:
All else, black water: and afloat,
One rood from shore, that single boat.

                                    Matthew Arno

202   After Floods on the Wharfe
(Yorkshire, West Riding)

How safe, methinks, and strong, behind
These trees have I encamped my mind;
Where beauty, aiming at the heart,
Bends in some tree its useless dart;
And where the world no certain shot
Can make, or me it toucheth not.
But I on it securely play,
And gall its horsemen all the day.

Bind me, ye woodbines, in your twines,
Curl me about, ye gadding vines,

And, oh, so close your circles lace,
That I may never leave this place:
But lest your fetters prove too weak,
Ere I your silken bondage break,
Do you, O brambles, chain me too,
And, courteous briars, nail me through.

Here in the morning tie my chain,
Where the two woods have made a lane,
While, like a guard on either side,
The trees before their Lord divide;
This, like a long and equal thread,
Betwixt two labyrinths does lead.
But where the floods did lately drown,
There at the evening stake me down.

For now the waves are fall'n and dried,
And now the meadows fresher dyed,
Whose grass, with moister colour dashed,
Seems as green silks but newly washed.
No serpent new nor crocodile
Remains behind our little Nile,
Unless itself you will mistake,
Among these meads the only snake.

See in what wanton harmless folds
It everywhere the meadow holds;
And its yet muddy back doth lick,
Till as a crystal mirror slick,
Where all things gaze themselves, and doubt
If they be in it or without.
And for his shade which therein shines,
Narcissus-like, the sun too pines.

Oh what a pleasure 'tis to hedge
My temples here with heavy sedge,
Abandoning my lazy side,
Stretched as a bank unto the tide,
Or to suspend my sliding foot
On th' osier's underminèd root,
And in its branches tough to hang,
While at my lines the fishes twang!

Andrew Marvell

203   In Teesdale
(Yorkshire, North Riding)

No, not tonight,
Not by this fading light,
Not by those high fells where the forces
Fall from the mist like the white tails of
    horses.

From that dark slack
Where peat-hags gape too black
I turn to where the lighted farm
Holds out through the open door a golden
    arm.

No, not tonight,
Tomorrow by daylight;
Tonight I fear the fabulous horses
Whose white tails flash down the steep
    water-courses.

Andrew Yo

204   Haworth Churchyard
(after the death in 1855 of Charlotte Brontë:
Yorkshire, West Riding)

Where, behind Keighley, the road
Up to the heart of the moors
Between heath-clad showery hills
Runs, and colliers' carts
Poach the deep ways coming down,
And a rough, grimed race have their homes—
There on its slope is built
The moorland town. But the church
Stands on the crest of the hill,
Lonely and bleak; at its side
The parsonage-house and the graves.

Strew with laurel the grave
Of the early-dying! Alas,
Early she goes on the path
To the silent country, and leaves
Half her laurels unwon,

Dying too soon!—yet green
Laurels she had, and a course
Short, but redoubled by fame.

And not friendless, and not
Only with strangers to meet,
Faces ungreeting and cold,
Thou, O mourned one, to-day
Enterest the house of the grave!
Those of thy blood, whom thou lov'dst,
Have preceded thee—young,
Loving, a sisterly band;
Some in art, some in gift
Inferior—all in fame.
They, like friends, shall receive
This comer, greet her with joy;
Welcome the sister, the friend;
Hear with delight of thy fame!

Round thee they lie—the grass
Blows from their graves to thy own!
She, whose genius, though not
Puissant like thine, was yet
Sweet and graceful; and she
(How shall I sing her?) whose soul
Knew no fellow for might,
Passion, vehemence, grief,
Daring, since Byron died,
That world-famed son of fire—she, who sank
Baffled, unknown, self-consumed;
Whose too bold dying song
Stirred, like a clarion-blast, my soul.

Of one, too, I have heard,
A brother—sleeps he here?
Of all that gifted race
Not the least gifted; young,
Unhappy, eloquent—the child
Of many hopes, of many tears.
O boy, if here thou sleep'st, sleep well!
On thee too did the Muse
Bright in thy cradle smile;
But some dark shadow came
(I know not what) and interposed.

Sleep, O cluster of friends,
Sleep!—or only when May,
Brought by the west-wind, returns
Back to your native heaths,
And the plover is heard on the moors,
Yearly awake to behold
The opening summer, the sky,
The shining moorland—to hear
The drowsy bee, as of old,
Hum o'er the thyme, the grouse
Call from the heather in bloom!
Sleep, or only for this
Break your united repose!

Matthew Ar[

205   Ilkla Moor
(Ilkley, Yorkshire, West Riding)

Wheear 'as tha been sin' ah saw thee?
   On Ilkla Moor baht 'at.
Wheear 'as tha been sin' ah saw thee?
Wheear 'as tha been sin' ah saw thee?
   On Ilkla Moor baht 'at,
   On Ilkla Moor baht 'at,
   On Ilkla Moor baht 'at.

Tha's been a-coortin' Mary Jane,
   On Ilkla Moor baht 'at.
Tha's been a-coortin' Mary Jane,
Tha's been a-coortin' Mary Jane,
   On Ilkla Moor baht 'at,
   On Ilkla Moor baht 'at,
   On Ilkla Moor baht 'at.

Tha'll go an get thi deeath o'cold
   On Ilkla Moor baht 'at.
Tha'll go an get thi deeath o'cold,
Tha'll go an get thi deeath o'cold
   On Ilkla Moor baht 'at,
   On Ilkla Moor baht 'at,
   On Ilkla Moor baht 'at.

Then we shall ha' to bury thee
   On Ilkla Moor baht 'at.
Then we shall ha' to bury thee,
Then we shall ha' to bury thee
   On Ilkla Moor baht 'at,
   On Ilkla Moor baht 'at,
   On Ilkla Moor baht 'at.

Then th' worms'll come an ate thee up,
   On Ilkla Moor baht 'at.
Then th' worms'll come an ate thee up,
Then th' worms'll come an ate thee up
   On Ilkla Moor baht 'at,
   On Ilkla Moor baht 'at,
   On Ilkla Moor baht 'at.

Then t'ducks'll come an ate t'worms
   On Ilkla Moor baht 'at,
Then t'ducks'll come an ate t'worms,
Then t'ducks'll come an ate t'worms
   On Ilkla Moor baht 'at,
   On Ilkla Moor baht 'at,
   On Ilkla Moor baht 'at.

Then we shall go an ate the ducks,
   On Ilkla Moor baht 'at,
Then we shall go an ate the ducks,
Then we shall go an ate the ducks
   On Ilkla Moor baht 'at,
   On Ilkla Moor baht 'at,
   On Ilkla Moor baht 'at.

That's how we get our oahn ones back,
   On Ilkla Moor baht 'at,
That's how we get our oahn ones back,
That's how we get our oahn ones back
   On Ilkla Moor baht 'at,
   On Ilkla Moor baht 'at,
   On Ilkla Moor baht 'at.

                                        Anon

206   The Wensleydale Lad
(a visit to Leeds)

When I were at home wi' my fayther an' mother, I niver had n
    fun;
They kept me goin' frae morn to neet, so I thowt frae them I'd
    run.
Leeds Fair were coomin' on, an' I thowt I'd have a spree,
So I put on my Sunday cooat an' went right merrily.

First thing I saw were t' factory, I niver seed one afore;
There were threads an' tapes, an' tapes an' silks, to sell by
    monny a score.
Owd Ned turn'd iv'ry wheel, an' iv'ry wheel a strap;
'Begor!' says I to t' maister-man, 'Owd Ned's a rare strong
    chap.'

Next I went to Leeds Owd Church—I were niver i' one i' my
    days,
An' I were maistly ashamed o' misel, for I didn't knaw their
    ways;
There were thirty or forty folk, i' tubs an' boxes sat,
When up cooms a saucy owd fellow. Says he, 'Noo, lad, tak of
    thy hat.'

Then in there cooms a great Lord Mayor, an' over his shooder
    a club,
An' he gat into a white sack-poke, an gat into t' topmost tub.
An' then there cooms anither chap, I thinks they call'd him
    Ned,
An' he gat into t' bottommost tub, an' mock'd all t' other chap
    said.

So they began to preach an' pray, they prayed for George, oor
    King;
When up jumps t' chap i' t' bottommost tub. Says he, 'Good
    folks, let's sing.'
I thowt some sang varra weel, while others did grunt an' groa
Ivery man sang what he wad, so I sang 'Darby an' Joan.'

sack-poke: corn sack

When preachin' an' prayin' were over, an' folks were gangin'
    away,
went to t' chap i' t' topmost tub. Says I, 'Lad, what's to pay?'
'Why, nowt,' says he, 'my lad.' Begor! I were right fain,
So I click'd hod o' my gret club stick an' went whistlin' oot
    again.

Anon

click'd hod: caught hold

207   Inside the Cave
(Chapel-le-Dale, Yorkshire, West Riding)

(i)

What if outside the dying pine trees sing in the clearing gale,
The frail rose petals blush towards their death,
The curlew curves and whimpers to the ground,
The sky goes clean and lights the greenness and the grey
    around?

What if I know that rose-root and the soft-clumped saxifrage,
Where this black-ended mountain checks one dove-grey cloud,
Make gardens richly on its dribbling shale,
With their wet flowers no longer shaking in the lunch-hour
    gale?

The limestone plateaus shine, the sheep walls curve and climb,
Soft is the turf, the red-knee'd walkers trail down to the inn—
What if all this miscellany, this dale of Norse-named farms,
    for a period softer than a girl with unfelt breasts and
    small-haired arms?

(ii)

What if beyond bleak Whernside's shoulders flutter
    thousand feet above the speckled hay-fields and the
    grey-walled barns,
Like breeze-blown petals, gulls above the dark-waved tarns?

Or where the gamboge flowers draw down the stream the
    widest band
Of yellow, and the stream drops from day, below its
    wet-domed nest
The hunting dipper feels the fast heavy water on its whitened
    breast?

The red-knee'd walkers trail through flowers above
The hollow structure of this wold. The turf and round-breast hills
Conceal the frigid windings and the enormous falls.

(iii)

Wanders a man I know, old now and here content
With trout-flies in his cap and easy tread
Creeping the dale around with all the indifference of the dead.

Wander the sheep above the shining clint,
And just as if some life had painfully bled,
A plant spreads on the warm stone its flattened flowers of red

Beyond the farm, trees in a wood much bent
Grow up through rock, and on the rock is flatly, quietly spread
A mat of moss, a carpet for the creepings of the dead.

(iv)

No one or six inch map details
This landscape of the unrestricted heart,
Or keeps on lead
Its wild, or shrieking, mild or quiet-toned art.

No guide-book, and no coloured card,
No black vasculum can yet contain
Its plants, and no romantic panel
Order its great disorder in a gesso frame,

And so in the pine and orchid-scented hollow
The flaring heart I force into its grave,
And the pale parting in the grass
Leads me to this leaf-fringed cave.

(v)

Green leaves: and in the cold entry of the cave
Green light which turns to a darkness:
Green water from the bellowing dark, here still;
Yet forward flows to turn no green-wheeled mill.

It sinks under its antique pebble-studded bed,
And carves rock shiningly and cleanly into curves:
Gives back no eyes but mine, no shiver of sun, or stars,
Floats down no seedling from the gamboge-throated flowers.

Yet pulled, I push inside the ivy-hanging screen,
Adjust my eyesight to the delicate green,
And press sharp footmarks on its pale-ribbed sand
And feel this classic water's cruelness with my hand.

Geoffrey Grigson

208   Ma Canny Hinny
(a search in Newcastle-upon-Tyne)

Where hast 'te been, ma' canny hinny?
An' where hast 'te been, ma' bonny bairn?
Aw was up and down seekin ma' hinny,
Aw was thro' the town, seekin for my bairn;
Aw went up the Butcher Bank and down Grundin
         Chare,
Call'd at the Dun Cow, but aw cuddent find thee
         there.
         Where hast 'te been, etc.

Then aw went t' th' Cassel Garth, and caw'd on
         Johnny Fife.
The beer drawer tell'd me she ne'er saw thee in her
         life.
         Where hast 'te been, etc.

Then aw went into the Three Bulls Heads, and down
         the Lang Stairs,
And a' the way alang the Close, as far as Mr Mayor's.
         Where hast 'te been, etc.

Fra there aw went alang the brig, an up t' Jackson's
         Chare,
Then back again t' the Cross Keys, but cuddent find
         thee there.
         Where hast 'te been, etc.

nny: honey

Then comin out o' Pipergate, aw met wi' Willy Rigg,
Whe tell'd me that he saw thee stannin pissin on the
        brig.
        Where hast 'te been, etc.

Comin alang the brig again, aw met wi' Cristy Gee,
He tell'd me et he saw thee gannin down Humeses
        entery.
        Where hast 'te been, etc.

Where hev aw been! aw sune can tell ye that:
Comin up the Key, aw met wi' Peter Pratt,
Meeting Peter Pratt, we met wi' Tommy Wear,
And went t' Humeses t' get a gill o' beer.

That's where a've been, ma' canny hinny,
That's where a've been, ma' bonny lamb!
Wast 'tu up and down seekin for yur hinny?
Wast 'tu up an down seekin for yur lamb?

Then aw met yur Ben, an we were like to fight,
An when we cam to Sandgate it was pick night;
Crossin the road, aw met wi' Bobby Swinny:
Hing on the girdle, let's hev a singin hinny.

Aw my sorrow's ower now, a've fund my hinny,
Aw my sorrow's ower now, a've fund my bairn;
Lang may aw shout, ma' canny hinny!
Lang may aw shout, ma' canny bairn!

                                                        Anoi

pick night: pitch dark
girdle: griddle
singin hinny: 'singing honey', a sizzling griddle cake

209   At Elsdon
(Northumberland)

Hae ye ivver been at Elsdon?—
  The world's unfinish'd neuk;
It stands amang the hungry hills
  An' wears a frozen leuk.
The Elsdon folks like diein' stegs
  At ivvery stranger stare;
An' hather broth an' curlew eggs
  Ye'll get for supper there.

Yen neet aw cam tiv Elsdon,
  Sair tired efter dark;
Aw'd travell'd mony a leynsome meyle
  Wet through the varra sark.
Maw legs were warkin' fit ta brik,
  An' empty was me kite,
But nowther love nor money could
  Get owther bed or bite.

At ivvery hoose iv Elsdon
  Aw teld me desperate need,
But nivver a corner had the churls
  Where aw might lay me heed;
Sae at the public-hoose aw boos'd.
  Till aw was sent away;
Then tiv a steyble-loft aw crept,
  An' coil'd amang the hay.

Should the Frenchers land iv England,
  Just gie them Elsdon fare;
By George! they'll sharply hook it back,
  An' nivver cum ne mair.
For a hungry hole like Elsdon,
  Aw nivver yit did see;
An' if aw gan back tiv Elsdon,
  'The de'il may carry me.'

                              George Chatt

210   Elsdon
(Northumberland)

All day the irises have draped blue velvets
In the window, but now dusk turns blind,
They blacken and stand off with nocturnal trees
As if to say colour is a matter of the mind.

And mind, yielding to the darkness of this place,
Would hang the window with a more pungent flower,
For now I think the gallows creaks the hill,
The castle shrugs off its green pelt, the Peel Tower

Withstands nothing, and the significance
Of three long skulls cannot be re-interred.
Now I know the red dwarf of the hills survives—
Comes spitting meanness in his bloody beard,

Angry as a side-show deformity; comes ready
To pinch my heart blue-black as these
Arranged flowers growing indistinguishable
From the coldness of nocturnal trees.

Freda Downie

211   Tweed and Till

Says Tweed to Till,
What gars ye rin sae still?
Says Till to Tweed,
Though ye rin wi' speed
And I rin slaw,
For ae man that ye droun
I droun twa.

Anon

9 Scotland and Ireland

212 O Caledonia!

O Caledonia! stern and wild,
Meet nurse for a poetic child!
Land of brown heath and shaggy wood,
Land of the mountain and the flood,
Land of my sires! what mortal hand
Can e'er untie the filial band,
That knits me to thy rugged strand!
Still, as I view each well known scene,
Think what is now, and what hath been,
Seems as, to me, of all bereft,
Sole friends thy woods and streams were left;
And thus I love them better still,
Even in extremity of ill.
By Yarrow's stream still let me stray,
Though none should guide my feeble way;
Still feel the breeze down Ettricke break,
Although it chill my withered cheek;
Still lay my head by Teviot Stone,
Though there, forgotten and alone,
The Bard may draw his parting groan.

Sir Walter Scott

213 Arran

Arran of the many stags,
the sea reaches to its shoulder;
island where companies are fed,
ridges whereon blue spears are reddened.

Wanton deer upon its peaks,
Mellow blaeberries on its heaths,
cold water in its streams,
mast upon its brown oaks.

Hunting dogs there, and hounds,
blackberries and sloes of the dark blackthorn,
dense thorn-bushes in its woods,
stags astray among its oak-groves.

Gathering of purple lichen on its rocks,
grass without blemish on its slopes;
over its fair shapely crags
gambolling of dappled fawns leaping.

Smooth is its lowland, fat are its swine,
pleasant its fields, a tale to be believed;
its nuts on the boughs of its hazel-wood,
sailing of long galleys past it.

It is delightful when fine weather comes,
trout under the banks of its streams,
seagulls answer each other round its white clif
delightful at all times is Arran.

                    Anon, translated from the Iris
                        by Kenneth Jacksc

214   The Quiet Tide near Ardrossan
        (Ayrshire)

On to the beach the quiet waters crept:
But, though I stood not far within the land,
No tidal murmur reach'd me from the strand.
The mirror'd clouds beneath old Arran slept.
I look'd again across the watery waste:
The shores were full, the tide was near its height,
Though scarcely heard: the reefs were drowning fas
And an imperial whisper told the might
Of the outer floods, that press'd into the bay,
Though all besides was silent. I delight
In the rough billows, and the foam-ball's flight:
I love the shore upon a stormy day;
But yet more stately were the power and ease
That with a whisper deepen'd all the seas.

                        Charles Tennyson Turn

215   To the Merchantis of Edinburgh

Quhy will ye, merchantis of renoun,
Lat Edinburgh, your nobill toun,
For laik of reformatioun
The commone proffeitt tyine and fame?
    Think ye not schame,
That onie uther regioun
Sall with dishonour hurt your name!

May nane pas throw your principall gaittis
For stink of haddockis and of scattis,
For cryis of carlingis and debaittis,
For fensum flyttingis of defame:
    Think ye not schame,
Befoir strangeris of all estaittis
That sic dishonour hurt your name!

Your stinkand Scull, that standis dirk,
Haldis the lycht fra your parroche kirk;
Your foirstairis makis your housis mirk,
Lyk na cuntray bot heir at hame:
    Think ye not schame,
Sa litill polesie to wirk
In hurt and sklander of your name!

At your hie Croce, quhar gold and silk
Sould be, thair is bot crudis and milk;
And at your Trone bot cokill and wilk,
Pansches, pudingis of Jok and Jame:
    Think ye not schame,
Sen as the world sayis that ilk
In hurt and sclander of your name!

Your commone menstrallis hes no tone
Bot 'Now the day dawis,' and 'Into Joun';
Cunningar men man serve Sanct Cloun,
And nevir to uther craftis clame:
    Think ye not schame,
To hald sic mowaris on the moyne,
In hurt and sclander of your name!

yine: lose   mowaris: jesters
ensum: offensive   moyne: moon
ansches: tripe

Tailyouris, soutteris, and craftis vyll,
The fairest of your streitis dois fyll;
And merchandis at the Stinkand Styll
Ar hamperit in ane hony came:
　　Think ye not schame,
That ye have nether witt nor wyll
To win yourselff ane bettir name!

Your burgh of beggeris is ane nest,
To schout thai swentyouris will not rest;
All honest folk they do molest,
Sa piteuslie thai cry and rame:
　　Think ye not schame,
That for the poore hes nothing drest,
In hurt and sclander of your name!

Your proffeit daylie dois incres,
Your godlie workis les and les;
Through streittis nane may mak progres
For cry of cruikit, blind, and lame:
　　Think ye not schame,
That ye sic substance dois posses,
And will nocht win ane bettir name!

Sen for the Court and the Sessioun,
The great repair of this regioun
Is in your burgh, thairfoir be boun
To mend all faultis that ar to blame,
　　And eschew schame;
Gif thai pas to ane uther toun
Ye will decay, and your great name!

Thairfoir strangeris and leigis treit,
Tak not ouer meikle for thair meit,
And gar your merchandis be discreit,
That na extortiounes be proclame
　　All fraud and schame:
Keip ordour, and poore nighbouris beit,
That ye may gett ane bettir name!

soutteris: cobblers   leigis: lieges
rame: scream   beit: (bate) supply
sen: since

Singular proffeit so dois yow blind,
The common proffeit gois behind:
I pray that Lord remeid to fynd,
That deit into Jerusalem,
    And gar yow schame!
That sum tyme ressoun may yow bind,
For to [   ] yow guid name.

                                        William Dunbar

216   Edinburgh from the Pentland Hills

Still on the spot Lord Marmion stay'd,
For fairer scene he ne'er survey'd.
    When sated with the martial show
    That peopled all the plain below,
    The wandering eye could o'er it go,
    And mark the distant city glow
        With gloomy splendour red;
    For on the smoke-wreaths, huge and slow,
    That round her sable turrets flow,
        The morning beams were shed,
    And ting'd them with a lustre proud,
    Like that which streaks a thunder-cloud.
Such dusky grandeur cloth'd the height,
Where the huge Castle holds its state,
    And all the steep slope down,
Whose ridgy back heaves to the sky,
Pil'd deep and massy, close and high,
    Mine own romantic town!
But northward far, with purer blaze,
On Ochil mountains fell the rays,
And as each heathy top they kiss'd,
It gleam'd a purple amethyst.
Yonder the shores of Fife you saw;
Here Preston-Bay and Berwick-Law:
    And, broad between them roll'd,
The gallant Frith the eye might note,
Whose islands on its bosom float,
    Like emeralds chas'd in gold.

                                        Sir Walter Scott

217   Melrose Abbey
(Roxburghshire)

If thou would'st view fair Melrose aright,
Go visit it by the pale moonlight;
For the gay beams of lightsome day
Gild, but to flout, the ruins grey.
When the broken arches are black in night,
And each shafted oriel glimmers white;
When the cold light's uncertain shower
Streams on the ruin'd central tower;
When buttress and buttress, alternately,
Seem fram'd of ebon and ivory;
When silver edges the imagery,
And the scrolls that teach thee to live and die;
When distant Tweed is heard to rave,
And the owlet to hoot o'er the dead man's grave,
Then go—but go alone the while—
Then view St. David's ruin'd pile;
And, home returning, soothly swear,
Was never scene so sad and fair!

Sir Walter Sc

218   The Dreary Change
(Selkirkshire)

The sun upon the Weirdlaw Hill,
  In Ettrick's vale, is sinking sweet;
The westland wind is hush and still,
  The lake lies sleeping at my feet.
Yet not the landscape to mine eye
  Bears those bright hues that once it bore;
Though evening, with her richest dye,
  Flames o'er the hills of Ettrick's shore.

With listless look along the plain
  I see Tweed's silver current glide,
And coldly mark the holy fane
  Of Melrose rise in ruin'd pride.
The quiet lake, the balmy air,
  The hill, the stream, the tower, the tree,—
Are they still such as once they were,
  Or is the dreary change in me?

Alas, the warp'd and broken board,
　How can it bear the painter's dye!
The harp of strain'd and tuneless chord,
　How to the minstrel's skill reply!
To aching eyes each landscape lowers,
　To feverish pulse each gale blows chill;
And Araby's or Eden's bowers
　Were barren as this moorland hill.

Sir Walter Scott

219　To S. R. Crockett
(the Pentland Hills)

Blows the wind to-day, and the sun and the rain are
　　flying,
　Blows the wind on the moors to-day and now,
Where about the graves of the martyrs the whaups are
　　crying,
　My heart remembers how!

Grey recumbent tombs of the dead in desert places,
　Standing stones on the vacant wine-red moor,
Hills of sheep, and the homes of the silent vanquished
　　races,
　And winds, austere and pure:

Be it granted me to behold you again in dying,
　Hills of home! and to hear again the call;
Hear about the graves of the martyrs the peewees crying,
　And hear no more at all.

Robert Louis Stevenson

ups: curlews

220　Ettrick Forest in November
(Selkirkshire)

November's sky is chill and drear,
November's leaf is red and sear:
Late, gazing down the steepy linn,
That hems our little garden in,
Low in its dark and narrow glen
You scarce the rivulet might ken,

So thick the tangled greenwood grew,
So feeble trill'd the streamlet through:
Now, murmuring hoarse, and frequent seen
Through bush and brier, no longer green,
An angry brook, it sweeps the glade,
Brawls over rock and wild cascade,
And, foaming brown with doubled speed,
Hurries its waters to the Tweed.

No longer Autumn's glowing red
Upon our Forest hills is shed;
No more beneath the evening beam
Fair Tweed reflects their purple gleam;
Away hath pass'd the heather-bell
That bloom'd so rich on Needpathfell;
Sallow his brow; and russet bare
Are now the sister-heights of Yair.
The sheep, before the pinching heaven,
To shelter'd dale and down are driven,
Where yet some faded herbage pines,
And yet a watery sunbeam shines:
In meek despondency they eye
The wither'd sward and wintry sky,
And far beneath their summer hill,
Stray sadly by Glenkinnon's rill:
The shepherd shifts his mantle's fold,
And wraps him closer from the cold;
His dogs no merry circles wheel,
But shivering follow at his heel;
A cowering glance they often cast,
As deeper moans the gathering blast.

Sir Walter Sc

221   The Village of Balmaquhapple

NORTH: Stop, stop, Beelzebub, and read aloud that bit of paper
have in your fist.

BEELZEBUB: Yes, sir.

SHEPHERD: Lord sauf us, what a voice! They're my ain verses, t
Whisht, whisht!

BEELZEBUB *sings 'The Great Muckle Village of Balmaquhapple', to
tune of 'The Sodger Laddie'.*

D'ye ken the big village of Balmaquhapple,
The great muckle village of Balmaquhapple?
Tis steep'd in iniquity up to the thrapple,
An' what's to become o' poor Balmaquhapple?
Fling a' aff your bannets, an' kneel for your life, fo'ks,
And pray to St Andrew, the god o' the Fife fo'ks;
Gar a' the hills yout wi' sheer vociferation,
And thus you may cry on sic needfu' occasion:

O, blessed St Andrew, if e'er ye could pity fo'k,
Men fo'k or women fo'k, country or city fo'k,
Come for this aince wi' the auld thief to grapple,
An' save the great village of Balmaquhapple
Frae drinking an' leeing, an' flyting an' swearing,
An' sins that ye wad be affrontit at hearing,
An' cheating an' stealing; O, grant them redemption,
All save an' except the few after to mention:

There's Johnny the elder, wha hopes ne'er to need ye
Sae pawkie, sae holy, sae gruff, an' sae greedy;
Wha prays every hour as the wayfarer passes,
But aye at a hole where he watches the lasses;
He's cheated a thousand, an' e'en to this day yet,
Can cheat a young lass, or they're leears that say it;
Then gie him his gate; he's sae slee an' sae civil,
Perhaps in the end he may wheedle the devil.

There's Cappie the cobbler, an' Tammie the tinman,
An Dickie the brewer, an' Peter the skinman,
An' Geordie our deacon, for want of a better,
An' Bess, wha delights in the sins that beset her.
O, worthy St Andrew, we canna compel ye,
But ye ken as weel as a body can tell ye,
If these gang to heaven, we'll a' be sae shockit,
Your garret o' blue will but thinly be stockit.

But for a' the rest, for the women's sake, save them,
Their bodies at least, an' their sauls, if they have them;
But it puzzles Jock Lesly, an' sma' it avails,
If they dwell in their stamocks, their heads, or their tails.
An' save, without word of confession auricular,
The clerk's bonny daughters, an' Bell in particular;
For ye ken that their beauty's the pride an' the staple
Of the great wicked village of Balmaquhapple!'

James Hogg

222   Afton Water
(SE. Ayrshire)

Flow gently, sweet Afton, among thy green braes,
Flow gently, I'll sing thee a song in thy praise;
My Mary's asleep by thy murmuring stream,
Flow gently, sweet Afton, disturb not her dream.

Thou stock dove whose echo resounds thro' the glen,
Ye wild whistling blackbirds in yon thorny den,
Thou green crested lapwing thy screaming forbear,
I charge you disturb not my slumbering Fair.

How lofty, sweet Afton, thy neighbouring hills,
Far marked with the courses of clear, winding rills;
There daily I wander as noon rises high,
My flocks and my Mary's sweet cot in my eye.

How pleasant thy banks and green valleys below,
Where wild in the woodlands the primroses blow;
There oft as mild ev'ning weeps over the lea,
The sweet scented birk shades my Mary and me.

Thy chrystal stream, Afton, how lovely it glides,
And winds by the cot where my Mary resides;
How wanton thy waters her snowy feet lave,
As gathering sweet flowerets she stems thy clear wave.

Flow gently, sweet Afton, among thy green braes,
Flow gently, sweet River, the theme of my lays;
My Mary's asleep by thy murmuring stream,
Flow gently, sweet Afton, disturb not her dream.

                                        Robert Burns

223   To Aberdein

Blyth Aberdeane, thow beriall of all tounis,
   The lamp of bewtie, bountie, and blythnes;
Unto the heaven [ascendit] thy renoun is
   Off vertew, wisdome, and of worthines;
   He nottit is thy name of nobilnes,
Into the cuming of oure lustie Quein,
   The wall of welth, guid cheir, and mirrines:
Be blyth and blisfull, burgh of Aberdein.

And first hir mett the burges of the toun
   Richelie arrayit, as become thame to be,
Of quhom they cheset four men of renoun,
   In gounes of velvot, young, abill, and lustie,
   To beir the paill of velves cramase
Abone hir heid, as the custome hes bein;
   Gryt was the sound of the artelyie:
Be blyth and blisfull, burgh of Aberdein.

Ane fair processioun mett hir at the Port,
   In a cap of gold and silk, full pleasantlie,
Syne at hir entrie, with many fair disport,
   Ressaveit hir on streittis lustilie;
   Quhair first the Salutatioun honorabilly
Of the sweitt Virgin guidlie mycht be seine;
   The sound of menstrallis blawing to the sky:
Be blyth and blisfull, burgh of Aberdein.

And syne thow gart the orient kingis thrie
   Offer to Chryst, with benyng reverence,
Gold, sence, and mir, with all humilitie,
   Schawand him king with most magnificence;
   Syne quhow the angill, with sword of violence,
Furth of the joy of paradice putt clein
   Adame and Ev for innobedience:
Be blyth and blisfull, burcht of Aberdein.

eriall: beryl   velves cramase: crimson velvet
e: high   gart: dost, makest

And syne the Bruce, that evir was bold in sto[u]r,
　　Thow gart as roy cum rydand under croun,
Richt awfull, strang, and large of portratour,
　　As nobill, dreidfull, michtie campioun:
　　The [nobill Stewarts] syne, of great renoun,
Thow gart upspring, with branches new and greine,
　　Sa gloriouslie, quhill glaidid all the toun:
Be blyth and blisfull, burcht of Aberdein.

Syne come thair four and tuentie madinis ying,
　　All claid in greine of mervelous bewtie,
With hair detressit, as threidis of gold did hing,
　　With quhyt hattis all browderit rycht brav[elie,]
　　Playand on timberallis and svngand rycht sweitlie;
That seimlie sort, in ordour weill besein,
　　Did meit the Quein, hir [saluand] reverentlie:
Be blyth and blisfull, burcht of Aberdein.

The streittis war all hung with tapestrie,
　　Great was the pres of peopill dwelt about,
And pleasant padgeanes playit prattelie;
　　The legeis all did to thair Lady loutt,
　　Quha was convoyed with ane royall routt
Off gryt barrounes and lustie ladyis [schene];
　　Welcum, our Quein! the commones gaif ane schou
Be blyth and blisfull, burcht of Aberdein.

At hir cuming great was the mirth and joy,
　　For at thair croce aboundantlie rane wyne;
Untill hir ludgeing the toun did hir convoy;
　　Hir for to treit thai sett thair haill ingyne,
　　Ane riche present thai did till hir propyne,
Ane costlie coup that large thing wald contene,
　　Coverit and full of cunyeitt gold rycht fyne:
Be blyth and blisfull, burcht of Aberdein.

stour: combat	schene: bright
roy: monarch	haill: whole
portratour: Figure	ingyne: mind
legeis: lieges	propyne: present
loutt: bow down	cunyeitt: coined

O potent princes, pleasant and preclair,
  Great caus thow hes to thank this nobill toun,
That, for to do the honnour, did not spair
  Thair geir, riches, substance, and persoun,
  The to ressave on maist fair fasoun;
The for to pleis thay socht all way and mein;
  Thairfoir, sa lang as Quein thow beiris croun,
Be thankfull to this burcht of Aberdein.

William Dunbar

224   On an Aberdeen Favourite

Here lies the body of Elizabeth Charlotte,
Who was born a virgin and died a harlot.
She was aye a virgin till seventeen—
An extraordinary thing for Aberdeen.

Anon

225   My Heart's in the Highlands

My heart's in the Highlands, my heart is not here;
My heart's in the Highlands a chasing the deer;
Chasing the wild deer, and following the roe;
My heart's in the Highlands, wherever I go.—

Farewell to the Highlands, farewell to the North;
The birth-place of valour, the country of worth:
Wherever I wander, wherever I rove,
The hills of the Highlands for ever I love.—

Farewell to the mountains high cover'd with snow;
Farewell to the Straths and green valleys below:
Farewell to the forests and wild-hanging woods;
Farewell to the torrents and loud-pouring floods.—

My heart's in the Highlands, my heart is not here,
My heart's in the Highlands a chasing the deer:
Chasing the wild deer, and following the roe;
My heart's in the Highlands, wherever I go.—

Robert Burns

226　A Highland Glen near Loch Ericht
(Inverness-shire)

There is a stream, I name not its name, lest inquisitive tourist
Hunt it, and make it a lion, and get it at last into guide-books,
Springing far off from a loch unexplored in the folds of great
　　mountains,
Falling two miles through rowan and stunted alder, enveloped
Then for four more in a forest of pine, where broad and ample
Spreads, to convey it, the glen with heathery slopes on both sides:
Broad and fair the stream, with occasional falls and narrows;
But, where the glen of its course approaches the vale of the river,
Met and blocked by a huge interposing mass of granite,
Scarce by a channel deep-cut, raging up, and raging onward,
Forces its flood through a passage so narrow a lady would step it.
There, across the great rocky wharves, a wooden bridge goes,
Carrying a path to the forest; below, three hundred yards, say,
Lower in level some twenty-five feet, through flats of shingle,
Stepping-stones and a cart-track cross in the open valley.
　　But in the interval here the boiling, pent-up water
Frees itself by a final descent, attaining a bason,
Ten feet wide and eighteen long, with whiteness and fury
Occupied partly, but mostly pellucid, pure, a mirror;
Beautiful there for the colour derived from green rocks under;
Beautiful, most of all, where beads of foam uprising
Mingle their clouds of white with the delicate hue of the stillness.
Cliff over cliff for its sides, with rowan and pendent birch boughs,
Here it lies, unthought of above at the bridge and pathway,
Still more enclosed from below by wood and rocky projection.
You are shut in, left alone with yourself and perfection of water,
Hid on all sides, left alone with yourself and the goddess of bathing.
　　Here, the pride of the plunger, you stride the fall and clear it;
Here, the delight of the bather, you roll in beaded sparklings,
Here into pure green depth drop down from lofty ledges.
　　Hither, a month agone, they had come, and discovered it; hither
(Long a design, but long unaccountably left unaccomplished,)
Leaving the well-known bridge and pathway above to the forest,
Turning below from the track of the carts over stone and shingle,
Piercing a wood, and skirting a narrow and natural causeway
Under the rocky wall that hedges the bed of the streamlet,
Rounded a craggy point, and saw on a sudden before them
Slabs of rock, and a tiny beach, and perfection of water,
Picture-like beauty, seclusion sublime, and the goddess of bathing.

Arthur Hugh Clough

227   Inversnaid
(Stirlingshire)

This darksome burn, horseback brown,
His rollrock highroad roaring down,
In coop and in comb the fleece of his foam
Flutes and low to the lake falls home.

A windpuff-bonnet of fáwn-fróth
Turns and twindles over the broth
Of a pool so pitchblack, féll-fró́wning,
It rounds and rounds Despair to drowning.

Degged with dew, dappled with dew
Are the groins of the braes that the brook treads
        through,
Wiry heathpacks, flitches of fern,
And the beadbonny ash that sits over the burn.

What would the world be, once bereft
Of wet and of wildness? Let them be left,
O let them be left, wildness and wet;
Long live the weeds and the wilderness yet.

                          Gerard Manley Hopkins

228   Rannoch, by Glen Coe
(Argyllshire)

Here the crow starves, here the patient stag
Breeds for the rifle. Between the soft moor
And the soft sky, scarcely room
To leap or soar. Substance crumbles, in the thin air
Moon cold or moon hot. The road winds in
Listlessness of ancient war,
Languor of broken steel,
Clamour of confused wrong, apt
In silence. Memory is strong
Beyond the bone. Pride snapped,
Shadow of pride is long, in the long pass
No concurrence of bone.

                          T. S. Eliot

229   The Fair Hills of Ireland
(Old Irish song)

A plenteous place is Ireland for hospitable cheer,
    Uileacan dubh O!
Where the wholesome fruit is bursting from the yellow barley
    ear;
    Uileacan dubh O!
There is honey in the trees where her misty vales expand,
And her forest paths, in summer, are by falling waters fann'd,
There is dew at high noontide there, and springs i'the yellow
    sand,
    On the fair hills of holy Ireland.

Curl'd he is and ringletted, and plaited to the knee,
    Uileacan dubh O!
Each captain who comes sailing across the Irish sea;
    Uileacan dubh O!
And I will make my journey, if life and health but stand,
Unto that pleasant country, that fresh and fragrant strand,
And leave your boasted braveries, your wealth and high
    command,
    For the fair hills of holy Ireland.

Large and profitable are the stacks upon the ground,
    Uileacan dubh O!
The butter and the cream do wondrously abound,
    Uileacan dubh O!
The cresses on the water and the sorrels are at hand,
And the cuckoo's calling daily his note of mimic bland,
And the bold thrush sings so bravely his song i'the forests
    grand,
    On the fair hills of holy Ireland.

Sir Samuel Ferguson

Uileacan dubh O: O black lament

230   The Dead at Clonmacnois
(From the Irish of Angus O'Gillan)

In a quiet-water'd land, a land of roses,
    Stands Saint Kieran's city fair,
And the warriors of Erinn in their famous generation
    Slumber there.

There beneath the dewy hillside sleep the noblest
      Of the Clan of Conn,
Each below his stone; his name in branching Ogham
      And the sacred knot thereon.

There they laid to rest the Seven Kings of Tara,
      There the sons of Cairbrè sleep—
Battle-banners of the Gael, that in Kieran's plain of crosses
      Now their final hosting keep.

And in Clonmacnois they laid the men of Teffia
      And right many a lord of Breagh;
Deep the sod above Clan Creidè and Clan Connall,
      Kind in hall and fierce in fray.

Many and many a son of Conn the Hundred-Fighter
      In the red earth lies at rest;
Many a blue eye of Clan Colman the turf covers,
      Many a swan-white breast.

                              Thomas William Rolleston

231   He Hears the Bugle at Killarney

The splendour falls on castle walls
   And snowy summits old in story:
The long light shakes across the lakes,
   And the wild cataract leaps in glory.
Blow, bugle, blow, set the wild echoes flying,
Blow, bugle; answer, echoes, dying, dying, dying.

O hark, O hear! how thin and clear,
   And thinner, clearer, farther going!
O sweet and far from cliff and scar
   The horns of Elfland faintly blowing!
Blow, let us hear the purple glens replying:
Blow, bugle; answer, echoes, dying, dying, dying.

O love, they die in yon rich sky,
   They faint on hill or field or river:
Our echoes roll from soul to soul,
   And grow for ever and for ever.
Blow, bugle, blow, set the wild echoes flying,
And answer, echoes, answer, dying, dying, dying.

                              Alfred Tennyson

232   Mountown! Thou Sweet Retreat
(Dublin)

Mountown! thou sweet retreat from Dublin cares,
Be famous for thy apples and thy pears;
For turnips, carrots, lettuce, beans, and pease;
For Peggy's butter, and for Peggy's cheese.
May clouds of pigeons round about thee fly!
But condescend sometimes to make a pie.
May fat geese gaggle with melodious voice,
And ne'er want gooseberries or apple-sauce!
Ducks in thy ponds, and chicken in thy pens,
And be thy turkeys numerous as thy hens!
May thy black pigs lie warm in little sty,
And have no thought to grieve them till they die!
Mountown! the Muses' most delicious theme;
Oh! may thy codlins ever swim in cream!
Thy rasp-and-straw-berries in Bourdeaux drown,
To add a redder tincture to their own!
Thy white-wine, sugar, milk, together club,
To make that gentle viand syllabub.
Thy tarts to tarts, cheese-cakes to cheese-cakes join,
To spoil the relish of the flowing wine.
But to the fading palate bring relief,
By thy Westphalian ham, or Belgic beef;
And, to complete thy blessings, in a word,
May still thy soil be generous as its lord!

William Ki

233   At Ballyshannon, Co. Donegal

The Boy from his bedroom-window
   Look'd over the little town,
And away to the bleak black upland
   Under a clouded moon.

The moon came forth from her cavern
   He saw the sudden gleam
Of a tarn in the swarthy moorland;
   Or perhaps the whole was a dream.

For I never could find that water
   In all my walks and rides:
Far-off, in the Land of Memory,
   That midnight pool abides.

Many fine things had I glimpse of,
   And said, 'I shall find them one day.'
Whether within or without me
   They were, I cannot say.

                     William Allingham

234   The Fairies
(Co. Donegal)

Up the airy mountain,
   Down the rushy glen,
We daren't go a-hunting
   For fear of little men;
Wee folk, good folk,
   Trooping all together;
Green jacket, red cap,
   And white owl's feather!

Down along the rocky shore
   Some make their home,
They live on crispy pancakes
   Of yellow tide-foam;
Some in the reeds
   Of the black mountain lake,
With frogs for their watch-dogs,
   All night awake.

High on the hill-top
   The old King sits;
He is now so old and gray
   He's nigh lost his wits.
With a bridge of white mist
   Columbkill he crosses,
On his stately journeys
   From Slieveleague to Rosses;
Or going up with music
   On cold starry nights,
To sup with the Queen
   Of the gay Northern Lights.

They stole little Bridget
  For seven years long;
When she came down again
  Her friends were all gone.
They took her lightly back,
  Between the night and morrow,
They thought that she was fast asleep,
  But she was dead with sorrow.
They have kept her ever since
  Deep within the lake,
On a bed of flag-leaves,
  Watching till she wake.

By the craggy hill-side,
  Through the mosses bare,
They have planted thorn-trees
  For pleasure here and there.
Is any man so daring
  As dig them up in spite,
He shall find their sharpest thorns
  In his bed at night.

Up the airy mountain,
  Down the rushy glen,
We daren't go a-hunting
  For fear of little men;
Wee folk, good folk,
  Trooping all together;
Green jacket, red cap,
  And white owl's feather!

William Allingh...

235   The Groves of Blarney
(Blarney Castle, Co. Cork)

The Groves of Blarney
They look so charming
Down by the purling,
  Of sweet silent streams.
Being banked with posies
That spontaneous grow there,
Planted in order
  By the sweet 'Rock Close'.

'Tis there the daisy
And the sweet carnation,
The blooming pink
  And the rose so fair.
The daffodowndilly,
Likewise the lily,
All flowers that scent
  The sweet, fragrant air.

'Tis Lady Jeffers
That owns this station;
Like Alexander,
  Or Queen Helen fair,
There's no commander
In all the nation,
For emulation,
  Can with her compare.
Such walls surround her,
That no nine-pounder
Could dare to plunder
  Her place of strength;
But Oliver Cromwell
Her he did pommell,
And made a breach
  In her battlement.

There's gravel walks there
For speculation
And conversation
  In sweet solitude.
'Tis there the lover
May hear the dove, or
The gentle plover
  In the afternoon;
And if a lady
Would be so engaging
As to walk alone in
  Those shady bowers,
'Tis there the courtier
He may transport her
Into some fort, or
  All underground.

For 'tis there's a cave where
No daylight enters,
But cats and badgers
   Are for ever bred;
Being mossed by nature,
That makes it sweeter
Than a coach-and-six or
   A feather bed.
'Tis there the lake is,
Well stored with perches,
And comely eels in
   The verdant mud;
Besides the leeches,
And groves of beeches,
Standing in order
   For to guard the flood.

There's statues gracing
This noble place in—
All heathen gods
   And nymphs so fair;
Bold Neptune, Plutarch,
And Nicodemus,
All standing naked
   In the open air!
So now to finish
This brave narration,
Which my poor genii
   Could not entwine;
But were I Homer,
Or Nebuchadnezzar,
'Tis in every feature
   I would make it shine.

Richard Alfred Mill

236   Castle Hyde
(Fermoy, Co. Cork)

As I roved out on a summer's morning
    Down by the banks of Blackwater side,
To view the groves and the meadows charming,
    The pleasant gardens of Castle Hyde;
'Tis there I heard the thrushes warbling,
    The dove and partridge I now describe;
The lambkins sporting on ev'ry morning,
    All to adorn sweet Castle Hyde.

The richest groves throughout this nation
    And fine plantations you will see there;
The rose, the tulip, the rich carnation,
    All vying with the lily fair.
The buck, the doe, the fox, the eagle,
    They skip and play by the river side;
The trout and salmon are always sporting
    In the clear streams of sweet Castle Hyde.

There are fine walks in these pleasant gardens,
    And seats most charming in shady bowers.
The gladiators both bold and darling
    Each night and morning do watch the flowers.
There's a church for service in this fine arbour
    Where nobles often in coaches ride
To view the groves and the meadow charming,
    The pleasant gardens of Castle Hyde.

There are fine horses and stall-fed oxes,
    And dens for foxes to play and hide;
Fine mares for breeding and foreign sheep there
    With snowy fleeces in Castle Hyde.
The grand improvements they would amuse you,
    The trees are drooping with fruit of all kind;
The bees perfuming the fields with music,
    Which yields more beauty to Castle Hyde.

If noble princes from foreign nations
   Should chance to sail to this Irish shore,
'Tis in this valley they would be feasted
   As often heroes have been before.
The wholesome air of this habitation
   Would recreate your heart with pride.
There is no valley throughout this nation
   In beauty equal to Castle Hyde.

I rode from Blarney to Castlebarnet,
   To Thomastown, and sweet Doneraile,
To Kilshannick that joins Rathcormack,
   Besides Killarney and Abbeyfeale;
The flowing Nore and the rapid Boyne,
   The river Shannon and pleasant Clyde;
In all my ranging and serenading
   I met no equal to Castle Hyde.

An

237   The Attractions of a Fashionable Irish Watering-Place
         (Passage West, Co. Cork)

The town of Passage
Is both large and spacious,
And situated
   Upon the say.
'Tis nate and dacent
And quite adjacent
To come from Cork
   On a summer's day:
There you may slip in
To take a dipping,
Fornent the shipping
   That at anchor ride.
Or in a wherry
Come o'er the ferry,
To Carrigaloe,
   On the other side.

Mud cabins swarm in
This place so charming,
With sailor garments
   Hung out to dry;
And each abode is
Snug and commodious.
With pigs melodious
   In their straw-built sty.
It's there the turf is,
And lots of murphies,
Dead sprats and herrings
   And oyster-shells;
Nor any lack, O!
Of good tobacco—
Though what is smuggled
   By far excels.

There are ships from Cadiz,
And from Barbadoes,
But the leading trade is
   In whisky-punch;
And you may go in
Where one Molly Bowen
Keeps a nate hotel
   For a quiet lunch.
But land or deck on,
You may safely reckon,
Whatever country
   You came hither from,
On an invitation
To a jollification,
With a parish priest
   That's called 'Father Tom.'

Of ships there's one fixed
For lodging convicts
A floating 'stone jug'
   Of amazing bulk;
The hake and salmon,
Playing at backgammon,
Swim for divarsion
   All round this 'hulk';

There 'Saxon' jailors
Keep brave repailors
Who soon with sailors
   Must anchor weigh
From the em'rald island
Ne'er to see dry land
Until they spy land
   In sweet Bot'ny Bay.

                              Francis Sylvester Mahon

238   By the Pool at the Third Rosses
           (Co. Donegal)

I heard the sighing of the reeds
In the grey pool in the green land,
The sea-wind in the long reeds sighing
Between the green hill and the sand.

I heard the sighing of the reeds
Day after day, night after night;
I heard the whirring wild ducks flying,
I saw the sea-gulls' wheeling flight.

I heard the sighing of the reeds
Night after night, day after day,
And I forgot old age, and dying,
And youth that loves, and love's decay.

I heard the sighing of the reeds
At noontide and at evening,
And some old dream I had forgotten
I seemed to be remembering.

I hear the sighing of the reeds:
Is it in vain, is it in vain
That some old peace I had forgotten
Is crying to come back again?

                              Arthur Symo

239   The Wild Swans at Coole
      (Coole Park, Galway)

The trees are in their autumn beauty,
The woodland paths are dry,
Under the October twilight the water
Mirrors a still sky;
Upon the brimming water among the stones
Are nine-and-fifty swans.

The nineteenth autumn has come upon me
Since I first made my count;
I saw, before I had well finished,
All suddenly mount
And scatter wheeling in great broken rings
Upon their clamorous wings.

I have looked upon those brilliant creatures,
And now my heart is sore.
All's changed since I, hearing at twilight,
The first time on this shore,
The bell-beat of their wings above my head,
Trod with a lighter tread.

Unwearied still, lover by lover,
They paddle in the cold
Companionable streams or climb the air;
Their hearts have not grown old;
Passion or conquest, wander where they will,
Attend upon them still.

But now they drift on the still water,
Mysterious, beautiful;
Among what rushes will they build,
By what lake's edge or pool
Delight men's eyes when I awake some day
To find they have flown away?

                              W. B. Yeats

240   The Lake Isle of Innisfree
(Lough Gill, Sligo)

I will arise and go now, and go to Innisfree,
And a small cabin build there, of clay and wattles made:
Nine bean-rows will I have there, a hive for the
        honey-bee,
And live alone in the bee-loud glade.

And I shall have some peace there, for peace comes
        dropping slow,
Dropping from the veils of the morning to where the
        cricket sings;
There midnight's all a glimmer, and noon a purple glow
And evening full of the linnet's wings.

I will arise and go now, for always night and day
I hear lake water lapping with low sounds by the shore;
While I stand on the roadway, or on the pavements grey
I hear it in the deep heart's core.

                                        W. B. Yeat

241   In Kerry

We heard the thrushes by the shore and sea,
And saw the golden stars' nativity,
Then round we went the lane by Thomas Flynn,
Across the church where bones lie out and in;
And there I asked beneath a lonely cloud
Of strange delight, with one bird singing loud,
What change you'd wrought in graveyard, rock and
        sea,
This new wild paradise to wake for me. . . .
Yet knew no more than knew these merry sins
Had built this stack of thigh-bones, jaws and shins.

                                        J. M. Syng

242   Prelude
(Wicklow)

Still south I went and west and south again,
Through Wicklow from the morning till the night,
And far from cities, and the sites of men,
Lived with the sunshine and the moon's delight.

I knew the stars, the flowers, and the birds,
The grey and wintry sides of many glens,
And did but half remember human words,
In converse with the mountains, moors, and fens.

J. M. Synge

243   Carrickfergus

I was born in Belfast between the mountain and the gantries
  To the hooting of lost sirens and the clang of trams:
Thence to Smoky Carrick in County Antrim
  Where the bottle-neck harbour collects the mud which jams

The little boats beneath the Norman castle,
  The pier shining with lumps of crystal salt;
The Scotch Quarter was a line of residential houses
  But the Irish Quarter was a slum for the blind and halt.

The brook ran yellow from the factory stinking of chlorine,
  The yarn-mill called its funeral cry at noon;
Our lights looked over the lough to the lights of Bangor
  Under the peacock aura of a drowning moon.

The Norman walled this town against the country
  To stop his ears to the yelping of his slave
And built a church in the form of a cross but denoting
  The list of Christ on the cross in the angle of the nave.

I was the rector's son, born to the anglican order,
  Banned for ever from the candles of the Irish poor;
The Chichesters knelt in marble at the end of a transept
  With ruffs about their necks, their portion sure.

The war came and a huge camp of soldiers
  Grew from the ground in sight of our house with long
Dummies hanging from gibbets for bayonet practice
  And the sentry's challenge echoing all day long;

A Yorkshire terrier ran in and out by the gate-lodge
  Barred to civilians, yapping as if taking affront:
Marching at ease and singing 'Who Killed Cock Robin?'
  The troops went out by the lodge and off to the Front.

The steamer was camouflaged that took me to England—
  Sweat and khaki in the Carlisle train;
I thought that the war would last for ever and sugar
  Be always rationed and that never again

Would the weekly papers not have photos of sandbags
  And my governess not make bandages from moss
And people not have maps above the fireplace
  With flags on pins moving across and across—

Across the hawthorn hedge the noise of bugles,
  Flares across the night,
Somewhere on the lough was a prison ship for Germans,
  A cage across their sight.

I went to school in Dorset, the world of parents
  Contracted into a puppet world of sons
Far from the mill girls, the smell of porter, the salt-mines
  And the soldiers with their guns.

                                        Louis MacNeice

244   Dublin

        Grey brick upon brick,
        Declamatory bronze
        On sombre pedestals—
        O'Connell, Grattan, Moore—
        And the brewery tugs and the swans
        On the balustraded stream
        And the bare bones of a fanlight
        Over a hungry door
        And the air soft on the cheek
        And porter running from the taps
        With a head of yellow cream
        And Nelson on his pillar
        Watching his world collapse.

        This was never my town,
        I was not born nor bred
        Nor schooled here and she will not
        Have me alive or dead
        But yet she holds my mind
        With her seedy elegance,

With her gentle veils of rain
And all her ghosts that walk
And all that hide behind
Her Georgian façades—
The catcalls and the pain,
The glamour of her squalor,
The bravado of her talk.

The lights jig in the river
With a concertina movement
And the sun comes up in the morning
Like barley-sugar on the water
And the mist on the Wicklow hills
Is close, as close
As the peasantry were to the landlord,
As the Irish to the Anglo-Irish,
As the killer is close one moment
To the man he kills,
Or as the moment itself
Is close to the next moment.

She is not an Irish town
And she is not English,
Historic with guns and vermin
And the cold renown
Of a fragment of Church latin,
Of an oratorical phrase.
But oh the days are soft,
Soft enough to forget
The lesson better learnt,
The bullet on the wet
Streets, the crooked deal,
The steel behind the laugh,
The Four Courts burnt.

Fort of the Dane,
Garrison of the Saxon,
Augustan capital
Of a Gaelic nation,
Appropriating all
The alien brought,
You give me time for thought
And by a juggler's trick

You poise the toppling hour—
O greyness run to flower,
Grey stone, grey water,
And brick upon grey brick.

                                    Louis MacNeice

245   Glen Lough
(Co. Donegal)

'We are the dead,' we shouted up in fun,
Standing between the brown lake and the falling sun—
We are the dead; then, frightened at the sound
As the three times echo in the mountains rolled it
      round
And round, the Dead, the Dead, the Dead—
And the wide sunset turned the Atlantic red
And the light below us yellowed from the farm,
With hair on end we stumbled through the fern
Down to the red-quilted bed,
Low stools, and richly carbon'd roof,
And powdery-glowing, scented fire of turf,
That never has been out, the farmer said,
A hundred years;
And company, and warmth, replaced our pointless
      fears,
And Dan Ward's awkward, Irish-speaking, silent wife
In the close warmth, pale light, and sudden life,
Was setting spuds in a bowl, and trout we'd taken in
      the lake,
And milk, and eggs, and a hot orange cake
Of maize, and the lifting ears
Of the lazing dog
Accepted us. Two signs of God,
A niche of holy water with a tiny light,
A pale cross of rushes up in the thatch's night,
Told us once more the country we were in;
And sitting in the past, we waited for the farmer to
      begin
His tales of Maoris, seals, and poteen-making in the
      fog,
And murdered men:
He warmed his brown feet in the silent glow, and
      then,

Free and happy, under the black thatch, or in the next
    day's
Gilded air, how little thought we of the curious ways
And fears our world was turning to; out in the glen
Corn-marigold and loose-strife mixed into a flame,
The mountains that had cried the dead were not the
    same,
But pink and blue above the blue unrippled lake:
We lay on the warm and gentle turf, watching the easy
    gannets make
Splashes of white in the deep sea, then,
In the summer morning of that day,
Upon the bar of skull-like stones we sat and sang,
Until the immense cliffs rang,
And curious seals pushed out their whiskered heads
    and came
Closer and closer to us, neither wild nor tame,
To see who made those ringing noises in that summer
    bay.

                                  Geoffrey Grigson

246   Sligo and Mayo

In Sligo the country was soft; there were turkeys
    Gobbling under sycamore trees
And the shadows of clouds on the mountains moving
    Like browsing cattle at ease.

And little distant fields were sprigged with haycocks
    And splashed against a white
Roadside cottage a welter of nasturtium
    Deluging the sight,

And pullets pecking the flies from around the eyes of
    heifers
    Sitting in farmyard mud
Among hydrangeas and the falling ear-rings
    Of fuchsias red as blood.

But in Mayo the tumbledown walls went leap-frog
    Over the moors,
The sugar and salt in the pubs were damp in the casters
    And the water was brown as beer upon the shores

Of desolate loughs, and stumps of hoary bog-oak
   Stuck up here and there
And as the twilight filtered on the heather
   Water-music filled the air,

And when the night came down upon the bogland
   With all-enveloping wings
The coal-black turfstacks rose against the darkness
   Like the tombs of nameless kings.

Louis MacNeice

247   Ireland

We Irish pride ourselves as patriots
and tell the beadroll of the valiant ones
since Clontarf's sunset saw the Norsemen
     broken . . .
Aye, and before that too we had our heroes:
but they were mighty fighters and victorious.
The later men got nothing save defeat,
hard transatlantic sidewalks or the scaffold . . .

We Irish, vainer than tense Lucifer,
are yet content with half-a-dozen turf,
and cry our adoration for a bog,
rejoicing in the rain that never ceases,
and happy to stride over the sterile acres,
or stony hills that scarcely feed a sheep.
But we are fools, I say, are ignorant fools
to waste the spirit's warmth in this cold air,
to spend our wit and love and poetry
on half-a-dozen peat and a black bog.

We are not native here or anywhere.
We were the keltic wave that broke over Europe,
and ran up this bleak beach among these stones:
but when the tide ebbed, were left stranded here
in crevices, and ledge-protected pools
that have grown salter with the drying up
of the great common flow that kept us sweet
with fresh cold draughts from deep down in the
     ocean.

So we are bitter, and are dying out
in terrible harshness in this lonely place,
and what we think is love for usual rock,
or old affection for our customary ledge,
is but forgotten longing for the sea
that cries far out and calls us to partake
in his great tidal movements round the earth.

John Hewitt

10 France

248   Heureux qui, comme Ulysse
(Liré, Maine-et-Loire)

Heureux qui, comme Ulysse, a fait un beau voyage,
Ou comme celui-là qui conquit la toison,
Et puis est retourné, plein d'usage et raison,
Vivre entre ses parents le reste de son âge!

Quand reverrai-je, hélas, de mon petit village
Fumer la cheminée, et en quelle saison
Reverrai-je le clos de ma pauvre maison,
Qui m'est une province, et beaucoup davantage?

Plus me plaît le séjour qu'ont bâti mes aïeux
Que des palais romains le front audacieux,
Plus que le marbre dur me plaît l'ardoise fine,

Plus mon Loire gaulois que le Tibre latin,
Plus mon petit Liré que le mont Palatin,
Et plus que l'air marin la douceur angevine.

Joachim du Bellay

249   Ode: Les Louanges de Vandomois
(the Vendômois, Loir-et-Cher)

Des-Autels, qui redore'
Le langage François,
Oy ce vers qui honore
Mon terroir Vandomois.

O terre fortunée,
Des Muses le sejour,
Que le cours de l'année
Seréne d'un beau jour!

En toy le Ciel non chiche
Prodiguant son bonheur
A de la corne riche
Renversé tout l'honneur.

Deux longs tertres te ceignent,
Qui de leur flanc hardi
Les Aquilons contraignent
Et les vents du Midi.

Sur l'un Gastine sainte,
Mere des demi-Dieux,
Sa teste de verd peinte
Envoye jusqu'aux Cieux;

Et sur l'autre prend vie
Maint beau cep dont le vin
Porte bien peu d'envie
Au vignoble Angevin.

Le Loir tard à la fuite,
En soy s'esbanoyant,
D'eau lentement conduite
Tes champs va tournoyant,

Et rend en prez fertile
Le païs traversé
Par l'humeur qui distile
De son limon versé.

Bien qu'on n'y vienne querre
Par flots injurieux
De quelque estrange terre
L'or tant laborieux,

Et la gemme, peschée
En l'Orient si cher,
Chez toy ne soit cherchée
Par l'avare nocher,

L'Inde pourtant ne pense
Te veincre, car les Dieux
D'une autre recompense
Te fortunent bien mieux.

La Justice grand'erre
S'enfuyant d'ici-bas
Imprima sur ta terre
Le dernier de ses pas,

Et s'encore à ceste heure
De l'antique saison
Quelque vertu demeure,
Tu es bien sa maison.

Bref, quelque part que j'erre,
Tant le Ciel m'y soit dous,
Ce petit coin de terre
Me rira par-sus tous.

Là je veux que la Parque
Tranche mon fatal fil,
Et m'envoye en la barque
De perdurable exil;

Là te faudra respandre
Maintes larmes parmi
Les ombres et la cendre
De Ronsard ton ami.

                                        Pierre de Ronsa

250   Ode à la Fontaine Bellerie
        (Couture, Loir-et-Cher)

O fontaine Bellerie,
Belle fontaine, cherie
De nos Nymphes, quand ton eau
Les cache au creux de ta source,
Fuyantes le Satyreau,
Qui les pourchasse à la course
Jusqu'au bord de ton ruisseau,

Tu es la Nymphe eternelle
De ma terre paternelle.
Pource, en ce pré verdelet,
Voy ton Poëte qui t'orne
D'un petit chevreau de lait,
A qui l'une et l'autre corne
Sortent du front nouvelet.

L'Esté, je dors ou repose
Sus ton herbe, où je compose,
Caché sous tes saules vers,
Je ne sçay quoy, qui ta gloire
Envoira par l'univers,
Commandant à la Memoire
Que tu vives par mes vers.

L'ardeur de la Canicule
Ton verd rivage ne brule,
Tellement qu'en toutes pars
Ton ombre est espaisse et drue
Aux pasteurs venans des parcs,
Aux bœufs las de la charrue,
Et au bestial espars.

Iô, tu seras sans cesse
Des fontaines la princesse
Moy celebrant le conduit
Du rocher percé, qui darde
Avec un enroué bruit
L'eau de ta source jazarde
Qui trepillante se suit.

                                        Pierre de Ronsard

251   Élégie sur la forêt de Gastine
       (the Vendômois, Loir-et-Cher)

Quiconque aura premier la main embesongnée
A te couper, forest, d'une dure congnée,
Qu'il puisse s'enferrer de son propre baston,
Et sente en l'estomac la faim d'Erisichthon,
Qui coupa de Cerès le Chesne venerable,
Et qui gourmand de tout, de tout insatiable,
Les bœufs et les moutons de sa mere esgorgea,
Puis pressé de la faim soy-mesme se mangea:
Ainsi puisse engloutir ses rentes et sa terre
Et se devore apres par les dents de la guerre!
Qu'il puisse, pour venger le sang de nos forests,
Tousjours nouveaux emprunts sur nouveaux interests
Devoir à l'usurier, et qu'enfin il consomme
Tout son bien à payer la principale somme!
Que tousjours sans repos ne face en son cerveau
Que tramer pour-neant quelque dessein nouveau,

Porté d'impatience et de fureur diverse,
Et de mauvais conseil qui les hommes renverse!
 Escoute, bucheron, arreste un peu le bras:
Ce ne sont pas des bois que tu jettes à bas;
Ne vois-tu pas le sang, lequel degout te à force
Des Nymphes qui vivoient dessous la dure escorce?
Sacrilege meurtrier, si on pend un voleur
Pour piller un butin de bien peu de valeur,
Combien de feux, de fers, de morts et de destresses
Merites-tu, meschant, pour tuer des Deesses?
 Forest, haute maison des oiseaux bocagers,
Plus le cerf solitaire et les chevreuls legers
Ne paistront sous ton ombre et ta verte criniere
Plus du soleil d'Esté ne rompra la lumiere.
Plus l'amoureux pasteur sur un tronq adossé,
Enflant son flageolet à quatre trous percé,
Son mastin à ses pieds, à son flanc la houlette,
Ne dira plus l'ardeur de sa belle Janette.
Tout deviendra muet, Echo sera sans voix,
Tu deviendras campagne, et en lieu de tes bois,
Dont l'ombrage incertain lentement se remue,
Tu sentiras le soc, le coutre et la charrue,
Tu perdras ton silence, et haletans d'effroy
Ny satyres ny Pans ne viendront plus chez toy.
 Adieu, vieille forest, le jouët de Zephyre,
Où premier j'accorday les langues de ma lyre,
Où premier j'entendi les fleches resonner
D'Apollon, qui me vint tout le cœur estonner,
Où premier, admirant la belle Calliope,
Je devins amoureux de sa neuvaine trope,
Quand sa main sur le front cent roses me jetta
Et de son propre laict Euterpe m'allaita.
 Adieu, vieille forest, adieu testes sacrées,
De tableaux et de fleurs autrefois honorées,
Maintenant le desdain des passans alterez,
Qui bruslez en Esté des rayons etherez,
Sans plus trouver le frais de tes douces verdures,
Accusent vos meurtriers, et leur disent injures.
 Adieu, chesnes, couronne aux vaillans citoyens,
Arbres de Jupiter, germes Dodonéens,
Qui premiers aux humains donnastes à repaistre,
Peuples vraiment ingrats, qui n'ont sceu recognoistre
Les biens receus de vous, peuples vraiment grossiers,
De massacrer ainsi nos peres nourriciers.

Que l'homme est malheureux qui au monde se fie!
O Dieux, que veritable est la philosophie,
Qui dit que toute chose à la fin perira.
Et qu'en changeant de forme une autre vestira!
De Tempé la vallée un jour sera montagne,
Et la cyme d'Athos une large campagne,
Neptune quelquefois de blé sera couvert:
La matiere demeure et la forme se perd.

Pierre de Ronsard

252　Blois

Ville de Blois, naissance de ma Dame,
Sejour des Roys et de ma volonté,
Où jeune d'ans je me vy surmonté
Par un œil brun qui m'outre-perça l'ame:

Chez toy je pris ceste premiere flame,
Chez toy j'apris que peut la cruauté,
Chez toy je vy ceste fiere beauté,
Dont la memoire encore me r'enflame.

Habite Amour en ta ville à jamais,
Et son carquois, ses lampes et ses trais
Pendent en toy, le temple de sa gloire:

Puisse-il tousjours ses murailles couver
Dessous son aile, et nud tousjours laver
Son chef crespu dans les eaux de ton Loire.

Pierre de Ronsard

253　Gastine and the Loir
(the Vendômois, Loir-et-Cher)

Saincte Gastine, ô douce secretaire
De mes ennuis, qui respons en ton bois,
Ores en haute ores en basse voix,
Aux longs souspirs que mon cœur ne peut taire;

Loir, qui refreins la course volontaire
Des flots roulans par nostre Vandomois,
Quand accuser ceste beauté tu m'ois,
De qui tousjours je m'affame et m'altere;

Si dextrement l'augure j'ay receu,
Et si mon œil ne fut hier deceu
Des doux regards de ma douce Thalie,

Maugré la mort Poëte me ferez,
Et par la France appellez vous serez
L'un mon Laurier, l'autre ma Castalie.

                                   Pierre de Ronsar

254   Ode de l'election de son sepulcre
       (Couture, Loir-et-Cher)

       Antres, et vous fontaines,
       De ces roches hautaines
       Qui tombez contre-bas
              D'un glissant pas;

       Et vous forests, et ondes
       Par ces prez vagabondes,
       Et vous rives et bois,
              Oyez ma vois.

       Quand le ciel et mon heure
       Jugeront que je meure,
       Ravy du beau sejour
              Du commun jour,

       Je veil, j'enten, j'ordonne
       Qu'un sepulcre on me donne
       Non pres des Rois levé
              Ne d'or gravé,

       Mais en ceste isle verte
       Où la course entrouverte
       Du Loir autour coulant
              Est acollant',

       Là où Braie s'amie
       D'une eau non endormie
       Murmure à l'environ
              De son giron.

Je defens qu'on ne rompe
Le marbre pour la pompe
De vouloir mon tombeau
    Bastir plus beau;

Mais bien je veux qu'un arbre
M'ombrage en lieu d'un marbre,
Arbre qui soit couvert
    Tousjours de vert.

De moy puisse la terre
Engendrer un lierre,
M'embrassant en maint tour
    Tout à l'entour;

Et la vigne tortisse
Mon sepulcre embellisse,
Faisant de toutes pars
    Un ombre espars.

Là viendront chaque année
A ma feste ordonnée
Avecque leurs troupeaux
    Les pastoureaux;

Puis ayant fait l'office
De leur beau sacrifice
Parlans à l'isle ainsi,
    Diront ceci:

«Que tu es renommée
D'estre tombeau nommée
D'un, de qui l'univers
    Chante les vers!

Et qui onc en sa vie
Ne fut bruslé d'envie,
Mendiant les honneurs
    Des grands Seigneurs!

Ny ne r'apprist l'usage
De l'amoureux breuvage,
Ny l'art des anciens
    Magiciens,

Mais bien à nos campagnes
Fist voir les Sœurs compagnes,
Foulantes l'herbe aux sons
    De ses chansons;

Car il fist à sa Lyre
Si bons accords eslire,
Qu'il orna de ses chants
    Nous et noz champs.

La douce manne tombe
A jamais sur sa tombe,
Et l'humeur que produit
    En May la nuit.

Tout à l'entour l'emmure
L'herbe et l'eau qui murmure,
L'un tousjours verdoyant,
    L'autre ondoyant.

Et nous, ayans memoire
Du renom de sa gloire,
Luy ferons, comme à Pan,
    Honneur chaque an.»

Ainsi dira la troupe,
Versant de mainte coupe
Le sang d'un agnelet
    Avec du laict,

Desur moy, qui à l'heure
Seray par la demeure
Où les heureux espris
    Ont leur pourpris.

La gresle ne la neige
N'ont tels lieux pour leur siege,
Ne la foudre oncque là
    Ne devala;

Mais bien constante y dure
L'immortelle verdure,
Et constant en tout temps
    Le beau Printemps.

Le soin qui sollicite
Les Rois, ne les incite
Le monde ruiner
     Pour dominer,

Ains comme freres vivent,
Et morts encore suivent
Les mestiers qu'ils avoient
     Quand ils vivoient.

Là là j'oirray d'Alcée
La lyre courroucée,
Et Sapphon qui sur tous
     Sonne plus dous.

Combien ceux qui entendent
Les chansons qu'ils respandent
Se doivent resjouir
     De les ouïr,

Quand la peine receue
Du rocher est deceue,
Et quand le vieil Tantal
     N'endure mal!

La seule lyre douce
L'ennuy des cœurs repousse,
Et va l'esprit flatant
     De l'escoutant.

                                   Pierre de Ronsard

255   Midsummer Day in France
              (i)
         The Morning

The golden globe incontinent,
Sets up his shining head,
And ou'r the earth and firmament,
Displayes his beims abroad.

For joy the birds with boulden throts,
Agains his visage shein,
Takes up their kindelie musicke nots,
In woods and gardens grein.

Up braids the carefull husbandman,
His cornes and vines to see,
And everie tymous artisan,
In buith worke busilie.

The pastor quits the slouthfull sleepe,
And passis forth with speede,
His little camow-nosed sheepe,
And rowtting kie to feede.

The passenger from perrels sure,
Gangs gladly foorth the way:
Briefe, everie living creature,
Takes comfort of the day.

The subtile mottie rayons light,
At rifts thay are in wonne,
The glansing phains and vitre bright,
Resplends against the sunne.

The dew upon the tender crops,
Lyke pearles white and round,
Or like to melted silver drops,
Refreshes all the ground.

The mystie rocke, the clouds of raine,
From tops of mountaines skails,
Cleare are the highest hils and plaine,
The vapors takes the vails.

Begaried is the saphire pend,
With spraings of skarlet hew,
And preciously from end till end,
Damasked white and blew.

boulden: swollen	mottie: full of motes	skails: clears
up braids: springs up	rifts: cracks	vails: valleys
tymous: early	in wonne: got into	begaried: decorated
camow-nosed: flat-nosed	phains: vanes	pend: vault of heaven
rowtting: lowing	vitre: window glass	spraings: streaks

The ample heaven of fabrik sure,
In cleannes dois surpas,
The chrystall and the silver pure,
Or clearest poleist glas.

The time sa tranquill is and still,
That na where sall ye find,
Saif on ane high and barren hill,
Ane aire of peeping wind.

All trees and simples great and small,
That balmie leife do beir,
Nor thay were painted on a wall,
Na mair they move or steir.

Calme is the deepe and purpour se,
Yee smuther nor the sand,
The wals that woltring wont to be,
Are stable like the land.

Sa silent is the cessile air,
That every cry and call,
The hils, and dails, and forrest fair,
Againe repeates them all.

The rivers fresh, the callor streames,
Ou'r rockes can softlie rin,
The water cleare like chrystall seames,
And makes a pleasant din.

The fields and earthly superfice,
With verdure greene is spread,
And naturallie but artifice,
In partie coulors cled.

The flurishes and fragrant flowres,
Throw Phoebus fostring heit,
Refresht with dew and silver showres,
Casts up ane odor sweit.

muther: smoother   callor: cool
vals: waves   but artifice: without human work
voltring: rolling   partie: motley
cessile: at rest   flurishes: buds

The clogged busie humming beis,
That never thinks to drowne,
On flowers and flourishes of treis,
Collects their liquor browne.

The sunne maist like a speedie post,
With ardent course ascends,
The beautie of the heavenly host,
Up to our zenith tends.

Nocht guided be na Phaeton,
Nor trained in a chyre,
Bot be the high and haly On,
Quhilk dois all where impire.

The burning beims downe from his face,
Sa fervently can beat:
That man and beast now seekes a place
To save them fra the heat.

The brethles flocks drawes to the shade,
And frechure of their fald,
The startling nolt as they were made,
Runnes to the rivers cald.

The heards beneath some leaffie trie,
Amids the flowers they lie,
The stabill ships upon the sey,
Tends up their sails to drie.

The hart, the hynd and fallow deare,
Are tapisht at their rest,
The foules and birdes that made the beare,
Prepares their prettie nest.

The rayons dures descending downe,
All kindlis in a gleid,
In cittie nor in borroughstowne,
May nane set foorth their heid.

post: post-rider, postboy	tapisht: crouched
trained in a chyre: drawn in a chariot	beare: noise
impire: empire, rule (verb)	dures: endures, continues
nolt: cattle	gleid: flame
tends up: stretches up	

Back from the blew paymented whun,
And from ilk plaister wall:
The hote reflexing of the sun,
Inflams the aire and all.

The labourers that timellie raise
All wearie faint and weake:
For heate downe to their houses gaise,
Noone-meate and sleepe to take.

The callour wine in cave is sought,
Mens brothing breists to cule:
The water cald and cleare is brought,
And sallets steipt in ule.

Sume plucks the honie plowm and peare,
The cherrie and the pesche,
Sume likes the reamand London beare,
The bodie to refresh.

(ii)

Now noone is went, gaine is mid-day,
The heat dois slake at last,
The sunne descends downe west away,
Fra three of clock be past.

A little cule of braithing wind,
Now softly can arise,
The warks throw heate that lay behind,
Now men may enterprise.

Furth fairis the flocks to seeke their fude,
On everie hill and plaine,
Ilk labourer as he thinks gude,
Steppes to his turne againe.

The rayons of the sunne we see,
Diminish in their strength,
The schad of everie towre and tree,
Extended is in length.

ymented whun: paved whinstone   honie plowm: greengage
thing: sweating   reamand: foaming
: (olive) oil

Great is the calme for everie quhair,
The wind is sitten downe,
The reik thrawes right up in the air,
From everie towre and towne.

Their firdoning the bony birds,
In banks they do begin,
With pipes of reides the jolie hirds,
Halds up the mirrie din.

The maveis and the philomeen,
The stirling whissilles loud,
The cuschetts on the branches green,
Full quietly they crowd.

The gloming comes, the day is spent,
The sun goes out of sight,
And painted is the occident,
With pourpour sanguine bright.

The skarlet nor the golden threid,
Who would their beautie trie,
Are nathing like the colour reid,
And beutie of the sky.

Our west horizon circuler,
Fra time the sunne be set,
Is all with rubies (as it wer)
Or rosis reid ou'rfret.

What pleasour were to walke and see,
Endlang a river cleare,
The perfite forme of everie tree,
Within the deepe appeare?

The salmon out of cruifs and creils
Up hailed into skowts,
The bels and circles on the weills,
Throw lowpping of the trouts.

reik: smoke
firdoning: piping
crowd: coo
pourpour sanguine: blood–red purple

cruifs: cruives, wicker fish-traps
skowts: punts
bels: bubbles
weills: pools

O! then it were a seemely thing,
While all is still and calme,
The praise of God to play and sing,
With cornet and with shalme.

                                        Alexander Hume

halme: shawm

256   Stances
(St–Paterne–Racan, Indre-et-Loire)

Tircis, il faut penser à faire la retraite;
La course de nos jours est plus qu'à demi faite;
L'âge insensiblement nous conduit à la mort:
Nous avons assez vu sur la mer de ce monde
Errer au gré des flots notre nef vagabonde;
Il est temps de jouir des délices du port.

Le bien de la fortune est un bien périssable;
Quand on bâtit sur elle, on bâtit sur le sable;
Plus on est élevé, plus on court de dangers;
Les grands pins sont en butte aux coups de la tempête,
Et la rage des vents brise plutôt le faîte
Des maisons de nos rois que les toits des bergers.

O bienheureux celui qui peut de sa mémoire
Effacer pour jamais ce vain espoir de gloire,
Dont l'inutile soin traverse nos plaisirs;
Et qui, loin retiré de la foule importune,
Vivant dans sa maison, content de sa fortune,
A, selon son pouvoir, mesuré ses désirs!

Il laboure le champ que labourait son père;
Il ne s'informe point de ce qu'on délibère
Dans ces graves conseils d'affaires accablés;
Il voit sans intérêt la mer grosse d'orages,
Et n'observe des vents les sinistres présages,
Que pour le soin qu'il a du salut de ses blés.

Roi de ses passions, il a ce qu'il désire.
Son fertile domaine est son petit empire,
Sa cabane est son Louvre et son Fontainebleau;
Ses champs et ses jardins sont autant de provinces,
Et sans porter envie à la pompe des princes
Se contente chez lui de les voir en tableau.

Il voit de toutes parts combler d'heur sa famille,
La javelle à plein poing tomber sous sa faucille,
Le vendangeur ployer sous le faix des paniers;
Et semble qu'à l'envi les fertiles montagnes,
Les humides vallons, et les grasses campagnes
S'efforcent à remplir sa cave et ses greniers.

Il suit aucune fois un cerf par les foulées,
Dans ces vieilles forêts du peuple reculées,
Et qui même du jour ignorent le flambeau;
Aucune fois des chiens il suit les voix confuses,
Et voit enfin le lièvre, après toutes ses ruses,
Du lieu de sa naissance en faire son tombeau.

Tantôt il se promène au long de ses fontaines,
De qui les petits flots font luire dans les plaines
L'argent de leurs ruisseaux parmi l'or des moissons;
Tantôt il se repose, avecque les bergères,
Sur des lits naturels de mousse et de fougères,
Qui n'ont d'autres rideaux que l'ombre des buissons.

Il soupire en repos l'ennui de sa vieillesse,
Dans ce même foyer où sa tendre jeunesse
A vu dans le berceau ses bras emmaillotés;
Il tient par les moissons registre des années,
Et voit de temps en temps leurs courses enchaînées
Vieillir avecque lui les bois qu'il a plantés.

Il ne va point fouiller aux terres inconnues,
A la merci des vents et des ondes chenues,
Ce que nature avare a caché de trésors;
Et ne recherche point, pour honorer sa vie
De plus illustre mort, ni plus digne d'envie,
Que de mourir au lit où ses pères sont morts.

Il contemple, du port, les insolentes rages
Des vents de la faveur, auteurs de nos orages,
Allumer des mutins les desseins factieux;
Et voit en un clin d'œil, par un contraire échange,
L'un déchiré du peuple au milieu de la fange
Et l'autre à même temps élevé dans les cieux.

S'il ne possède point ces maisons magnifiques,
Ces tours, ces chapiteaux, ces superbes portiques
Où la magnificence étale ses attraits,
Il jouit des beautés qu'ont les saisons nouvelles;
Il voit de la verdure et des fleurs naturelles,
Qu'en ces riches lambris l'on ne voit qu'en portraits.

Crois-moi, retirons-nous hors de la multitude,
Et vivons désormais loin de la servitude
De ces palais dorés où tout le monde accourt:
Sous un chêne élevé les arbrisseaux s'ennuient,
Et devant le soleil tous les astres s'enfuient,
De peur d'être obligés de lui faire la cour.

Après qu'on a suivi sans aucune assurance
Cette vaine faveur qui nous paît d'espérance,
L'envie en un moment tous nos desseins détruit;
Ce n'est qu'une fumée; il n'est rien de si frêle;
Sa plus belle moisson est sujette à la grêle,
Et souvent elle n'a que des fleurs pour du fruit.

Agréables déserts, séjour de l'innocence,
Où loin des vanités, de la magnificence,
Commence mon repos et finit mon tourment,
Vallons, fleuves, rochers, plaisante solitude,
Si vous fûtes témoins de mon inquiétude,
Soyez-le désormais de mon contentement!

                                   Honorat de Racan

257   It is a Beauteous Evening, Calm and Free
         (on the beach at Calais)

   It is a beauteous evening, calm and free,
   The holy time is quiet as a Nun
   Breathless with adoration; the broad sun
   Is sinking down in its tranquillity;
   The gentleness of heaven broods o'er the Sea:
   Listen! the mighty Being is awake,
   And doth with his eternal motion make
   A sound like thunder—everlastingly.
   Dear Child! dear Girl! that walkest with me here,
   If thou appear untouched by solemn thought,

Thy nature is not therefore less divine:
Thou liest in Abraham's bosom all the year;
And worship'st at the Temple's inner shrine,
God being with thee when we know it not.

William Wordswo

258   To the Seine

Des vallons de Bourgogne, ô toi fille limpide,
Qui pare de raisins ton front pur et liquide,
Belle Seine, à pas lents de ton berceau sacré
Descends, tandis qu'assise en cet antre azuré,
D'un vers syracusain la Muse de Mantoue
Fait résonner ton onde où le cygne se joue.

André Ché

259   Près d'Avranches
(Manche)

La nuit morne tombait sur la morne étendue.

Le vent du soir soufflait, et, d'une aile éperdue,
Faisait fuir, à travers les écueils de granit,
Quelques voiles au port, quelques oiseaux au nid.

Triste jusqu'à la mort, je contemplais le monde.
Oh! que la mer est vaste et que l'âme est profonde!

Saint-Michel surgissait, seul sur les flots amers,
Chéops de l'occident, pyramide des mers.

Je songeais à l'Égypte aux plis infranchissables,
A la grande isolée éternelle des sables,
Noire tente des rois, ce tas d'ombres qui dort
Dans le camp immobile et sombre de la mort.

Hélas! dans ces déserts, qu'emplit d'un souffle
        immense
Dieu, seul dans sa colère et seul dans sa clémence,
Ce que l'homme a dressé debout sur l'horizon,
Là-bas, c'est le sépulcre, ici, c'est la prison.

Mai 1843   Victor H

60   Le Retour à Tancarville après trente ans, septembre 1825
              (on the Seine, near Le Havre)

A mon émotion je sens que j'en approche.
Tancarville et ses tours, Pierre-Gante et sa roche
Sont là. J'ai reconnu cet air si vif des bois
Qu'avec tant de plaisir j'aspirais autrefois;
Le long frémissement qui court sous les ombrages,
Semblable au bruit sans fin qui montait des rivages,
Et cette odeur de mousse et de feuilles dans l'air,
Et les pommiers penchés par les vents de la mer.
Ne me conduisez pas, j'en sais toutes les routes;
Parmi ces bois grandis, je les retrouve toutes;
J'irai fermant les yeux, et, si rien n'est changé,
Au bout du chemin creux, de hêtres ombragé,
Le château va paraître. Oh! de quelle âme émue
J'ai revu, j'ai monté cette antique avenue
Qui s'élève, en tournant, sous ses larges noyers,
Jusqu'aux tours du portail, où nichaient les ramiers!
Arrêtons. Respirons. Presque tremblant, je sonne;
La cloche au son connu jusqu'en mon sein résonne.
La vaste porte, ouvrant ses battants vermoulus,
Me demande mon nom, et ne me connaît plus.

                                        Pierre Lebrun

261   Lettre
(from Champagne)

La Champagne est fort laide où je suis; mais qu'importe,
J'ai de l'air, un peu d'herbe, une vigne à ma porte;
D'ailleurs, je ne suis pas ici pour bien longtemps.
N'ayant pas mes petits près de moi, je prétends
Avoir droit à la fuite, et j'y songe à toute heure,
Et tous les jours je veux partir, et je demeure.
L'homme est ainsi.

                        Parfois tout s'efface à mes yeux
Sous la mauvaise humeur du nuage ennuyeux;
Il pleut. Triste pays. Moins de blé que d'ivraie.
Bientôt j'irai chercher la solitude vraie,
Où sont les fiers écueils, sombres, jamais vaincus,
La mer. En attendant, comme Horace à Fuscus,

Je t'envoie, ami cher, les paroles civiles
Que doit l'hôte des champs à l'habitant des villes;
Tu songes au milieu des tumultes hagards;
Et je salue, avec toutes sortes d'égards,
Moi qui vois les fourmis, toi qui vois les pygmées.
Parce que vous avez la forge aux renommées,
Aux vacarmes, aux faits tapageurs et soudains,
Ne croyez pas qu'à Bray-sur-Marne, ô citadins,
On soit des paysans au point d'être des brutes;
Non, on danse, on se cherche au bois, on fait des chut
On s'aime; on est toujours Estelle et Némorin;
Simone et Gros Thomas sautent au tambourin;
Et les grands vieux parents grondent quand, le
    dimanche,
Les filles vont tirer les garçons par la manche.
Le presbytère est là qui garde le troupeau.
Parfois j'entre à l'église et j'ôte mon chapeau
Quand monsieur le curé foudroie en pleine chaire
L'idylle d'un bouvier avec une vachère.

Mais je suis indulgent plus que lui; le ciel bleu,
Diable! et le doux printemps, tout cela trouble un peu
Et les petits oiseaux, quel détestable exemple!
Le jeune mois de mai, c'est toujours le vieux temple
Où, doucement raillés par les merles siffleurs,
Les gens qui s'aiment vont s'adorer dans les fleurs;
Jadis c'était Phyllis, aujourd'hui c'est Javotte;
Mais c'est toujours la femme au mois de mai dévote.

Moi, je suis spectateur, et je pardonne; ayant
L'âme très débonnaire et l'air très effrayant.
Car j'inquiète fort le village. On me nomme
Le sorcier; on m'évite; ils disent: C'est un homme
Qu'on entend parler haut dans sa chambre, le soir;
Or on ne parle seul qu'avec quelqu'un de noir.—
C'est pourquoi je fais peur.

                    La maison que j'habite,
Grotte dont j'ai fait choix pour être cénobite,
C'est l'auberge; on y boit dans la salle d'en bas;
Les filles du pays viennent, ôtent leurs bas,
Et salissent leurs pieds dans la mare voisine.
La soupe aux choux, c'est là toute notre cuisine;
Un lit et quatre murs, c'est là tout mon logis.

Je vis; les champs le soir sont largement rougis;
L'espace est, le matin, confusément sonore;
L'angélus se répand dans le ciel dès l'aurore,
Et j'ai le bercement des cloches en dormant.
Poésie: un roulier avec un jurement;
Des poules becquetant un vieux mur en décembre;
De lointains aboiements dialoguant dans l'ombre;
Parfois un vol d'oiseaux sauvages émigrant.
C'est petit, car c'est laid, et le beau seul est grand.
Cette campagne où l'aube à regret semble naître,
M'offre à perte de vue au loin sous ma fenêtre
Rien, la route, un sol âpre, usé, morne, inclément.
Quelques arbres sont là; j'écoute vaguement
Les conversations du vent avec les branches.
La plaine brune alterne avec les plaines blanches;
Pas un coteau, des prés maigres, peu de gazon;
Et j'ai pour tout plaisir de voir à l'horizon
Un groupe de toits bas d'où sort une fumée,
Le paysage étant plat comme Mérimée.

Victor Hugo

262   Un Peintre
(Brittany, baie de Douarnenez)

Il a compris la race antique aux yeux pensifs
Qui foule le sol dur de la terre bretonne,
La lande rase, rose et grise et monotone
Où croulent les manoirs sous le lierre et les ifs.

Des hauts talus plantés de hêtres convulsifs,
Il a vu, par les soirs tempétueux d'automne,
Sombrer le soleil rouge en la mer qui moutonne;
Sa lèvre s'est salée à l'embrun des récifs.

Il a peint l'Océan splendide, immense et triste,
Où le nuage laisse un reflet d'améthyste,
L'émeraude écumante et le calme saphir;

Et fixant l'eau, l'air, l'ombre et l'heure insaisissables,
Sur une toile étroite il a fait réfléchir
Le ciel occidental dans le miroir des sables.

José-Maria de Heredia

263   Scenes from Carnac

Far on its rocky knoll descried
Saint Michael's chapel cuts the sky.
I climbed; beneath me, bright and wide,
Lay the lone coast of Brittany.

Bright in the sunset, weird and still,
It lay beside the Atlantic wave,
As though the wizard Merlin's will
Yet charmed it from his forest-grave.

Behind me on their grassy sweep,
Bearded with lichen, scrawled and grey,
The giant stones of Carnac sleep,
In the mild evening of the May.

No priestly stern procession now
Moves through their rows of pillars old;
No victims bleed, no Druids bow—
Sheep make the daisied aisles their fold.

From bush to bush the cuckoo flies,
The orchis red gleams everywhere;
Gold furze with broom in blossom vies,
The blue-bells perfume all the air.

And o'er the glistening, lonely land,
Rise up, all round, the Christian spires;
The church of Carnac, by the strand,
Catches the westering sun's last fires.

And there, across the watery way,
See, low above the tide at flood,
The sickle-sweep of Quiberon Bay,
Whose beach once ran with loyal blood!

And beyond that, the Atlantic wide!
All round, no soul, no boat, no hail;
But, on the horizon's verge descried,
Hangs, touched with light, one snowy sail!

Ah! where is he, who should have come
Where that far sail is passing now,
Past the Loire's mouth, and by the foam
Of Finistère's unquiet brow,

Home, round into the English wave?
—He tarries where the Rock of Spain
Mediterranean waters lave;
He enters not the Atlantic main.

Oh, could he once have reached this air
Freshened by plunging tides, by showers!
Have felt this breath he loved, of fair
Cool northern fields, and grass, and flowers!

He longed for it—pressed on. In vain!
At the Straits failed that spirit brave.
The south was parent of his pain,
The south is mistress of his grave.

Matthew Arnold

264   Au Vieux Roscoff
Berceuse en Nord-Ouest Mineur

Trou de flibustiers, vieux nid
À corsaires!—dans la tourmente,
Dors ton bon somme de granit
Sur tes caves que le flot hante...

Ronfle à la mer, ronfle à la brise;
Ta corne dans la brume grise,
Ton pied marin dans les brisans...
—Dors: tu peux fermer ton œil borgne
Ouvert sur le large, et qui lorgne
Les Anglais, depuis trois cents ans.

—Dors, vieille coque bien ancrée;
Les margats et les cormorans
Les margats et les cormorans
Tes grands poètes d'ouragans
Viendront chanter à la marée...

—Dors, vieille fille-à-matelots;
Plus ne te soûleront ces flots
Qui te faisaient une ceinture
Dorée, aux nuits rouges de vin,
De sang, de feu!—Dors... Sur ton sein
L'or ne fondra plus en friture.

—Où sont les noms de tes amants...
—La mer et la gloire étaient folles!—
Noms de lascars! noms de géants!
Crachés des gueules d'espingoles...

Où battaient-ils, ces pavillons,
Écharpant ton ciel en haillons! . . .
—Dors au ciel de plomb sur tes dunes...
Dors: plus ne viendront ricocher
Les boulets morts, sur ton clocher
Criblé—comme un prunier—de prunes...

—Dors: sous les noires cheminées,
Écoute rêver tes enfants,
Mousses de quatre-vingt-dix ans,
Épaves des belles années...
               . . . .

Il dort ton bon canon de fer,
À plat-ventre aussi dans sa souille.
Grêlé par les lunes d'hyver...
Il dort son lourd sommeil de rouille,

—Va: ronfle au vent, vieux ronfleur,
Tiens toujours ta gueule enragée
Braquée à l'Anglais! . . . et chargée
De maigre jonc-marin en fleur

                              Tristan Corbièr

265   Paris aux Réverbères

Paris dort: avez-vous, nocturne sentinelle,
Gravi, minuit sonnant, le pont de la Tournelle,
C'est de là que l'on voit Paris de fange imbu;
Et comme un mendiant ivre près d'une cuve,
Le géant Est qui ronfle et qui râle, et qui cuve
        Le vin ou le sang qu'il a bu.

C'était donc aujourd'hui fête à la guillotine;
Un homme, ce matin, dressait une machine:
Sur la place où là-bas le sang est mal lavé,
Au peuple qui hurlait comme autour d'une orgie,
Le bourreau las jetait avec sa main rougie
      Une tête sur le pavé.

Et puis voici surgir la vieille cathédrale
Avec son front rugueux et son bourdon qui râle;
Comme un large vaisseau portant l'humanité,
Déployant ses deux mâts, avançant sa carène,
Elle semble être prête, en labourant l'arène,
      A partir pour l'éternité!

Entendez-vous dans l'ombre aboyer les cerbères?
J'aime à voir dans les flots briller les réverbères;
C'est un concert de nuit; c'est la grande cité,
Avec ses yeux de feu, qui de loin me regarde.
C'est la voix d'une ronde ou le fusil d'un garde
      Qui passe dans l'obscurité.

Pendant que je suis là, que de haine assouvie!
C'est le fils, du linceul couvrant sa mère en vie,
Le vieux magicien interrogeant l'enfer,
La veuve qui poursuit quelque passant qui rôde,
Et se vautre avec lui dans la couche encor chaude
      D'un époux qui vivait hier.

Mais, atome perdu dans la cité béante,
Je suis seul; pas de main à ma main suppliante
Ne s'unit; non, pour moi, pas de souffle embaumé,
Pas de regard de miel, pas une lèvre rose,
Pas de sein où mon front fatigué se repose,
      Et je mourrai sans être aimé!

                          Alphonse Esquiros

266   Nocturne Parisien

Roule, roule ton flot indolent, morne Seine.—
Sous tes ponts qu'environne une vapeur malsaine
Bien des corps ont passé, morts, horribles, pourris,
Dont les âmes avaient pour meurtrier Paris.
Mais tu n'en traînes pas, en tes ondes glacées,
Autant que ton aspect m'inspire de pensées!

Le Tibre a sur ses bords des ruines qui font
Monter le voyageur vers un passe profond,
Et qui, de lierre noir et de lichen couvertes,
Apparaissent, tas gris, parmi les herbes vertes.
Le gai Guadalquivir rit aux blonds orangers
Et reflète, les soirs, des boléros légers.
Le Pactole a son or, le Bosphore a sa rive
Où vient faire son kief l'odalisque lascive.
Le Rhin est un burgrave, et c'est un troubadour
Que le Lignon, et c'est un ruffian que l'Adour.
Le Nil, au bruit plaintif de ses eaux endormies,
Berce de rêves doux le sommeil des momies.
Le grand Meschascébé, fier de ses joncs sacrés,
Charrie augustement ses îlots mordorés,
Et soudain, beau d'éclairs, de fracas et de fastes,
Splendidement s'écroule en Niagaras vastes.
L'Eurotas, où l'essaim des cygnes familiers
Mêle sa grâce blanche au vert mat des lauriers,
Sous son ciel clair que raie un vol de gypaète,
Rhythmique et caressant, chante ainsi qu'un poëte.
Enfin, Ganga, parmi les hauts palmiers tremblants
Et les rouges padmas, marche à pas fiers et lents
En appareil royal, tandis qu'au loin la foule
Le long des temples va hurlant, vivante houle,
Au claquement massif des cymbales de bois,
Et qu'accroupi, filant ses notes de hautbois,
Du saut de l'antilope agile attendant l'heure,
Le tigre jaune au dos rayé s'étire et pleure.

—Toi, Seine, tu n'as rien. Deux quais, et voilà tout,
Deux quais crasseux, semés de l'un à l'autre bout
D'affreux bouquins moisis et d'une foule insigne
Qui fait dans l'eau des ronds et qui pêche à la ligne.
Oui, mais quand vient le soir, raréfiant enfin
Les passants alourdis de sommeil ou de faim,
Et que le couchant met au ciel des taches rouges,
Qu'il fait bon aux rêveurs descendre de leurs bouges
Et, s'accoudant au pont de la Cité, devant
Notre-Dame, songer, cœur et cheveux au vent!
Les nuages, chassés par la brise nocturne,
Courent, cuivreux et roux, dans l'azur taciturne.
Sur la tête d'un roi du portail, le soleil,
Au moment de mourir, pose un baiser vermeil.

L'hirondelle s'enfuit à l'approche de l'ombre,
Et l'on voit voleter la chauve-souris sombre.
Tout bruit s'apaise autour. À peine un vague son
Dit que la ville est là qui chante sa chanson,
Qui lèche ses tyrans et qui mord ses victimes;
Et c'est l'aube des vols, des amours et des crimes.
—Puis, tout à coup, ainsi qu'un ténor effaré
Lançant dans l'air bruni son cri désespéré,
Son cri qui se lamente et se prolonge, et crie,
Éclate en quelque coin l'orgue de Barbarie:
Il brame un de ces airs, romances ou polkas,
Qu'enfants nous tapotions sur nos harmonicas
Et qui font, lents ou vifs, réjouissants ou tristes,
Vibrer l'âme aux proscrits, aux femmes, aux artistes.
C'est écorché, c'est faux, c'est horrible, c'est dur,
Et donnerait la fièvre à Rossini, pour sûr;
Ces rires sont traînés, ces plaintes sont hachées;
Sur une clef de sol impossible juchées,
Les notes ont un rhume et les *do* sont des *la*,
Mais qu'importe! l'on pleure en entendant cela!
Mais l'esprit, transporté dans le pays des rêves,
Sent à ces vieux accords couler en lui des sèves;
La pitié monte au cœur et les larmes aux yeux,
Et l'on voudrait pouvoir goûter la paix des cieux,
Et dans une harmonie étrange et fantastique
Qui tient de la musique et tient de la plastique,
L'âme, les inondant de lumière et de chant,
Mêle les sons de l'orgue aux rayons du couchant!

—Et puis l'orgue s'éloigne, et puis c'est le silence,
Et la nuit terne arrive, et Vénus se balance
Sur une molle nue au fond des cieux obscurs;
On allume les becs de gaz le long des murs,
Et l'astre et les flambeaux font des zigzags fantasques
Dans le fleuve plus noir que le velours des masques;
Et le contemplateur sur le haut garde-fou
Par l'air et par les ans rouillé comme un vieux sou
Se penche, en proie aux vents néfastes de l'abîme.
Pensée, espoir serein, ambition sublime,
Tout, jusqu'au souvenir, tout s'envole, tout fuit,
Et l'on est seul avec Paris, l'Onde et la Nuit!

—Sinistre trinité! De l'ombre dures portes!
Mané-Thécel-Pharès des illusions mortes!
Vous êtes toutes trois, ô Goules de malheur,
Si terribles, que l'Homme, ivre de la douleur
Que lui font en perçant sa chair vos doigts de spectre,
L'Homme, espèce d'Oreste à qui manque une Électre,
Sous la fatalité de votre regard creux
Ne peut rien et va droit au précipice affreux;
Et vous êtes aussi toutes trois si jalouses
De tuer et d'offrir au grand Ver des épouses
Qu'on ne sait que choisir entre vos trois horreurs,
Et si l'on craindrait moins périr par les terreurs
Des Ténèbres que sous l'Eau sourde, l'Eau profonde,
Ou dans tes bras fardés, Paris, reine du monde!

—Et tu coules toujours, Seine, et, tout en rampant,
Tu traînes dans Paris ton cours de vieux serpent,
De vieux serpent boueux, emportant vers tes havres
Tes cargaisons de bois, de houille et de cadavres!

Paul Verlaine

267   At Dieppe: Green and Grey
to Walter Sickert

The grey-green stretch of sandy grass,
Indefinitely desolate;
A sea of lead, a sky of slate;
Already autumn in the air, alas!

One stark monotony of stone,
The long hotel, acutely white,
Against the after-sunset light
Withers grey-green, and takes the grass's tone.

Listless and endless it outlies,
And means, to you and me, no more
Than any pebble on the shore,
Or this indifferent moment as it dies.

Arthur Symons

268   Châteaux de Loire

Le long du coteau courbe et des nobles vallées
Les châteaux sont semés comme des reposoirs,
Et dans la majesté des matins et des soirs
La Loire et ses vassaux s'en vont par ces allées.

Cent vingt châteaux lui font une suite courtoise,
Plus nombreux, plus nerveux, plus fins que des palais.
Ils ont nom Valençay, Saint-Aignan et Langeais,
Chenonceaux et Chambord, Azay, le Lude, Amboise.

Et moi j'en connais un dans les châteaux de Loire
Qui s'élève plus haut que le château de Blois,
Plus haut que la terrasse où les derniers Valois
Regardaient le soleil se coucher dans sa gloire.

La moulure est plus fine et l'arceau plus léger.
La dentelle de pierre est plus dure et plus grave.
La décence et l'honneur et la mort qui s'y grave
Ont inscrit leur histoire au cœur de ce verger.

Et c'est le souvenir qu'a laissé sur ces bords
Une enfant qui menait son cheval vers le fleuve.
Son âme était récente et sa cotte était neuve.
Innocente elle allait vers le plus grand des sorts.

Car celle qui venait du pays tourangeau,
C'était la même enfant qui quelques jours plus tard,
Gouvernant d'un seul mot le rustre et le soudard,
Descendait devers Meung ou montait vers Jargeau.

                                        Paul Claudel

269   The Cathedral and the Plain
(Notre-Dame de Chartres and the Beauce)

(i)

Étoile de la mer voici la lourde nappe
Et la profonde houle et l'océan des blés
Et la mouvante écume et nos greniers comblés,
Voici votre regard sur cette immense chape

Et voici votre voix sur cette lourde plaine
Et nos amis absents et nos cœurs dépeuplés
Voici le long de nous nos poings désassemblés
Et notre lassitude et notre force pleine.

Étoile du matin, inaccessible reine,
Voici que nous marchons vers votre illustre cour,
Et voici le plateau de notre pauvre amour,
Et voici l'océan de notre immense peine.

Un sanglot rôde et court par-delà l'horizon.
A peine quelques toits font comme un archipel.
Du vieux clocher retombe une sorte d'appel.
L'épaisse église semble une basse maison.

Ainsi nous naviguons vers votre cathédrale.
De loin en loin surnage un chapelet de meules,
Rondes comme des tours, opulentes et seules
Comme un rang de châteaux sur la barque amirale.

Deux mille ans de labeur ont fait de cette terre
Un réservoir sans fin pour les âges nouveaux.
Mille ans de votre grâce ont fait de ces travaux
Un reposoir sans fin pour l'âme solitaire.

Vous nous voyez marcher sur cette route droite,
Tout poudreux, tout crottés, la pluie entre les dents
Sur ce large éventail ouvert à tous les vents
La route nationale est notre porte étroite.

Nous allons devant nous, les mains le long des
  poches,
Sans aucun appareil, sans fatras, sans discours,
D'un pas toujours égal, sans hâte ni recours,
Des champs les plus présents vers les champs les
  plus proches.

Vous nous voyez marcher, nous sommes la piétaille
Nous n'avançons jamais que d'un pas à la fois.
Mais vingt siècles de peuple et vingt siècles de rois,
Et toute leur séquelle et toute leur volaille

Et leurs chapeaux à plume avec leur valetaille
Ont appris ce que c'est que d'être familiers,
Et comme on peut marcher, les pieds dans ses
　　　souliers,
Vers un dernier carré le soir d'une bataille.

Nous sommes nés pour vous au bord de ce plateau,
Dans le recourbement de notre blonde Loire,
Et ce fleuve de sable et ce fleuve de gloire
N'est là que pour baiser votre auguste manteau.

Nous sommes nés au bord de ce vaste plateau,
Dans l'antique Orléans sévère et sérieuse,
Et la Loire coulante et souvent limoneuse
N'est là que pour laver les pieds de ce coteau.

Nous sommes nés au bord de votre plate Beauce
Et nous avons connu dès nos plus jeunes ans
Le portail de la ferme et les durs paysans
Et l'enclos dans le bourg et la bêche et la fosse.

Nous sommes nés au bord de votre Beauce plate
Et nous avons connu dès nos premiers regrets
Ce que peut recéler de désespoirs secrets
Un soleil qui descend dans un ciel écarlate

Et qui se couche au ras d'un sol inévitable
Dur comme une justice, égal comme une barre,
Juste comme une loi, fermé comme une mare,
Ouvert comme un beau socle et plan comme une
　　　table.

Un homme de chez nous, de la glèbe féconde
A fait jaillir ici d'un seul enlèvement,
Et d'une seule source et d'un seul portement,
Vers votre assomption la flèche unique au monde.

Tour de David voici votre tour beauceronne.
C'est l'épi le plus dur qui soit jamais monté
Vers un ciel de clémence et de sérénité,
Et le plus beau fleuron dedans votre couronne.

Un homme de chez nous a fait ici jaillir,
Depuis le ras du sol jusqu'au pied de la croix,
Plus haut que tous les saints, plus haut que tous les
    rois,
La flèche irréprochable et qui ne peut faillir.

C'est la gerbe et le blé qui ne périra point,
Qui ne fanera point au soleil de septembre,
Qui ne gèlera point aux rigueurs de décembre,
C'est votre serviteur et c'est votre témoin.

C'est la tige et le blé qui ne pourrira pas,
Qui ne flétrira point aux ardeurs de l'été,
Qui ne moisira point dans un hiver gâté,
Qui ne transira point dans le commun trépas.

C'est la pierre sans tache et la pierre sans faute,
La plus haute oraison qu'on ait jamais portée,
La plus droite raison qu'on ait jamais jetée,
Et vers un ciel sans bord la ligne la plus haute.

Celle qui ne mourra le jour d'aucunes morts,
Le gage et le portrait de nos arrachements,
L'image et le tracé de nos redressements,
La laine et le fuseau des plus modestes sorts.

(ii)

Nous arrivons vers vous de l'autre Notre Dame,
De celle qui s'élève au cœur de la cité,
Dans sa royale robe et dans sa majesté,
Dans sa magnificence et sa justesse d'âme.

Comme vous commandez un océan d'épis,
Là-bas vous commandez un océan de têtes,
Et la moisson des deuils et la moisson des fêtes
Se couche chaque soir devant votre parvis.

Nous arrivons vers vous du noble Hurepoix.
C'est un commencement de Beauce à notre usage,
Des fermes et des champs taillés à votre image,
Mais coupés plus souvent par des rideaux de bois,

Et coupés plus souvent par de creuses vallées
Pour l'Yvette et la Bièvre et leurs accroissements,
Et leurs savants détours et leurs dégagements,
Et par les beaux châteaux et les longues allées.

D'autres viendront vers vous du noble
        Vermandois,
Et des vallonnements de bouleaux et de saules.
D'autres viendront vers vous des palais et des
        geôles.
Et du pays picard et du vert Vendômois.

Mais c'est toujours la France, ou petite ou plus
        grande,
Le pays des beaux blés et des encadrements,
Le pays de la grappe et des ruissellements,
Le pays de genêts, de bruyère, de lande.

                                    Paul Claudel

        270   Le Pont Mirabeau
                (Paris)

Sous le pont Mirabeau coule la Seine
        Et nos amours
        Faut-il qu'il m'en souvienne
La joie venait toujours après la peine

        Vienne la nuit sonne l'heure
        Les jours s'en vont je demeure

Les mains dans les mains restons face à face
        Tandis que sous
        Le pont de nos bras passe
Des éternels regards l'onde si lasse

        Vienne la nuit sonne l'heure
        Les jours s'en vont je demeure

L'amour s'en va comme cette eau courante
        L'amour s'en va
        Comme la vie est lente
Et comme l'espérance est violente

Vienne la nuit sonne l'heure
Les jours s'en vont je demeure

Passent les jours et passent les semaines
Ni temps passé
Ni les amours reviennent
Sous le pont Mirabeau coule la Seine

Vienne la nuit sonne l'heure
Les jours s'en vont je demeure

Guillaume Apollina

271   Fishing Boats in Martigues

Around the quays, kicked off in twos
The Four Winds dry their wooden shoes.

Roy Campb

11 Italy

272 Satan's Legions and the Beech
Leaves of the Casentino

He stood and called
His legions, angel forms, who lay intranst
Thick as autumnal leaves that strow the brooks
In Vallombrosa, where th'Etrurian shades
High overarcht imbowr.

John Milton

273 Frater Ave atque Vale
(Sirmione, Lago di Garda)

Row us out from Desenzano, to your Sirmione row!
So they rowed, and there we landed—'O venusta Sirmio!'
There to me through all the groves of olive in the summer
    glow,
There beneath the Roman ruin where the purple flowers
    grow,
Came that 'Ave atque Vale' of the Poet's hopeless woe,
Tenderest of Roman poets nineteen-hundred years ago,
'Frater Ave atque Vale'—as we wandered to and fro
Gazing at the Lydian laughter of the Garda Lake below
Sweet Catullus's all-but-island, olive-silvery Sirmio!

Alfred Tennyson

274 Près des Bords où Venise

Près des bords où Venise est reine de la mer,
Le gondolier nocturne, au retour de Vesper,
D'un aviron léger bat la vague aplanie,
Chantant Renaud, Tancrède et la belle Erminie.
Il aime les chansons, il chante. Sans désir,
Sans gloire, sans projets, sans craindre l'avenir,
Il chante, et cheminant sur le liquide abîme,
Sait égayer ainsi sa route maritime.
. . . . comme lui je me plais à chanter.
Les rustiques chansons que j'aime à répéter
Adoucissent pour moi la route de la vie,
Route amère et souvent de naufrages suivie.

André Chén▮

275 On the Bridge of Sighs

I stood in Venice, on the Bridge of Sighs;
A palace and a prison on each hand:
I saw from out the wave her structures rise
As from the stroke of the enchanter's wand:
A thousand years their cloudy wings expand
Around me, and a dying Glory smiles
O'er the far times, when many a subject land
Look'd to the winged Lion's marble piles,
Where Venice sate in state, throned on her hundred
    isles!

She looks a sea Cybele, fresh from ocean,
Rising with her tiara of proud towers
At airy distance, with majestic motion,
A ruler of the waters and their powers:
And such she was;—her daughters had their dow▮
From spoils of nations, and the exhaustless East
Pour'd in her lap all gems in sparkling showers.
In purple was she robed, and of her feast
Monarchs partook, and deem'd their dignity increas▮

In Venice Tasso's echoes are no more,
And silent rows the songless gondolier;
Her palaces are crumbling to the shore,
And music meets not always now the ear:
Those days are gone—but Beauty still is here.
States fall, arts fade—but Nature doth not die,
Nor yet forget how Venice once was dear,
The pleasant place of all festivity,
The revel of the earth, the masque of Italy!

But unto us she hath a spell beyond
Her name in story, and her long array
Of mighty shadows, whose dim forms despond
Above the dogeless city's vanish'd sway;
Ours is a trophy which will not decay
With the Rialto; Shylock and the Moor,
And Pierre, cannot be swept or worn away—
The keystones of the arch! though all were o'er,
For us repeopled were the solitary shore.

George Gordon Noel,
Lord Byron

276   Ruins of Rome

(i)

Thou stranger, which for Rome in Rome here seekest,
And nought of Rome in Rome perceiv'st at all,
These same old walls, old arches, which thou see'st,
Old palaces, is that which Rome men call.
Behold what wreck, what ruin, and what waste,
And how that she, which with her mighty pow'r
Tamed all the world, hath tamed herself at last,
The prey of time, which all things doth devour.
Rome now of Rome is th' only funeral,
And only Rome of Rome hath victory;
Ne aught save Tiber hast'ning to his fall
Remains of all: O world's inconstancy!
That which is firm doth flit and fall away,
And that is flitting, doth abide and stay.

(ii)

Thou that at Rome astonished dost behold
The antique pride, which menaced the sky,
These haughty heaps, these palaces of old,
These walls, these arcs, these baths, these temples high,
    Judge by these ample ruins' view the rest
The which injurious time hath quite outworn,
Since of all workmen held in reck'ning best,
Yet these old fragments are for patterns born:
    Then also mark, how Rome from day to day,
Repairing her decayed fashion,
Renews herself with buildings rich and gay;
That one would judge that the Romaine Daemon
    Doth yet himself with fatal hand enforce,
    Again on foot to rear her poulder'd corse.

(iii)

He that hath seen a great oak dry and dead,
Yet clad with relics of some trophies old,
Lifting to heaven her aged hoary head,
Whose foot in ground hath left but feeble hold,
    But half disbowelled lies above the ground,
Shewing her wreathed roots, and naked arms,
And on her trunk all rotten and unsound
Only supports herself for meat of worms;
    And though she owe her fall to the first wind,
Yet of the devout people is adored,
And many young plants spring out of her rind;
Who such an oak hath seen let him record
    That such this city's honour was of yore,
    And mongst all cities flourished much more.

Joachim du Bellay
(translated by Edmund Spenser)

277   Rome
by Metella's Tomb

Perchance she died in age—surviving all,
Charms, kindred, children—with the silver gray
On her long tresses, which might yet recall,
It may be, still a something of the day
When they were braided, and her proud array
And lovely form were envied, praised, and eyed
By Rome—But whither would Conjecture stray?

Thus much alone we know—Metella died,
The wealthiest Roman's wife: Behold his love or pride!

I know not why—but standing thus by thee
It seems as if I had thine inmate known,
Thou Tomb! and other days come back on me
With recollected music, though the tone
Is changed and solemn, like the cloudy groan
Of dying thunder on the distant wind;
Yet could I seat me by this ivied stone
Till I had bodied, forth the heated mind,
Forms from the floating wreck which Ruin leaves behind;

And from the planks, far shatter'd o'er the rocks,
Built me a little bark of hope, once more
To battle with the ocean and the shocks
Of the loud breakers, and the ceaseless roar
Which rushes on the solitary shore
Where all lies founder'd that was ever dear:
But could I gather from the wave-worn store
Enough for my rude boat, where should I steer?
There woos no home, nor hope, nor life, save what is here.

Then let the winds howl on! their harmony
Shall henceforth be my music, and the night
The sound shall temper with the owlets' cry,
As I now hear them, in the fading light
Dim o'er the bird of darkness' native site,
Answering each other on the Palatine,
With their large eyes, all glistening gray and bright,
And sailing pinions.—Upon such a shrine
What are our petty griefs?—let me not number mine.

Cypress and ivy, weed and wallflower grown,
Matted and mass'd together, hillocks heap'd
On what were chambers, arch crush'd, column strown
In fragments, choked up vaults, and frescos steep'd
In subterranean damps, where the owl peep'd,
Deeming it midnight:—Temples, baths, or halls?
Pronounce who can; for all that Learning reap'd
From her research hath been, that these are walls—
Behold the Imperial Mount! 'tis thus the mighty falls.

George Gordon Noel,
Lord Byron

278   The Grave of Keats

Go thou to Rome,—at once the Paradise,
The grave, the city, and the wilderness;
And where its wrecks like shattered mountains rise,
And flowering weeds, and fragrant copses dress
The bones of Desolation's nakedness
Pass, till the spirit of the spot shall lead
Thy footsteps to a slope of green access
Where, like an infant's smile, over the dead
A light of laughing flowers along the grass is spread;

And gray walls moulder round, on which dull Time
Feeds, like slow fire upon a hoary brand;
And one keen pyramid with wedge sublime,
Pavilioning the dust of him who planned
This refuge for his memory, doth stand
Like flame transformed to marble; and beneath,
A field is spread, on which a newer band
Have pitched in Heaven's smile their camp of death,
Welcoming him we lose with scarce extinguished breath.

Here pause: these graves are all too young as yet
To have outgrown the sorrow which consigned
Its charge to each; and if the seal is set,
Here, on one fountain of a mourning mind,
Break it not thou! too surely shalt thou find
Thine own well full, if thou returnest home,
Of tears and gall. From the world's bitter wind
Seek shelter in the shadow of the tomb.
What Adonais is, why fear we to become?

The One remains, the many change and pass;
Heaven's light forever shines, Earth's shadows fly;
Life, like a dome of many-coloured glass,
Stains the white radiance of Eternity,
Until Death tramples it to fragments.—Die,
If thou wouldst be with that which thou dost seek!
Follow where all is fled!—Rome's azure sky,
Flowers, ruins, statues, music, words, are weak
The glory they transfuse with fitting truth to speak.

Why linger, why turn back, why shrink, my Heart?
Thy hopes are gone before: from all things here
They have departed; thou shouldst now depart!
A light is passed from the revolving year,
And man, and woman; and what still is dear
Attracts to crush, repels to make thee wither.
The soft sky smiles,—the low wind whispers near:
'Tis Adonais calls! oh, hasten thither,
No more let Life divide what Death can join together.

P. B. Shelley

279   At Pompeii

I stood within the City disinterred;
    And heard the autumnal leaves like light footfalls
Of spirits passing through the streets; and heard
    The Mountain's slumberous voice at intervals
        Thrill through those roofless halls;
The oracular thunder penetrating shook
    The listening soul in my suspended blood;
I felt that Earth out of her deep heart spoke—
    I felt, but heard not:—through white columns
        glowed
        The isle-sustaining ocean-flood,
A plane of light between two heavens of azure!
    Around me gleamed many a bright sepulchre
Of whose pure beauty, Time, as if his pleasure
Were to spare Death, had never made erasure;
    But every living lineament was clear
    As in the sculptor's thought; and there
The wreaths of stony myrtle, ivy, and pine,
    Like winter leaves o'ergrown by moulded snow,
    Seemed only not to move and grow
Because the crystal silence of the air
    Weighed on their life; even as the Power divine
    Which then lulled all things, brooded upon mine.

P. B. Shelley

280 Piano di Sorrento
(between the Gulfs of Naples and Salerno)

Time for rain! for your long hot dry Autumn
    Had net-worked with brown
The white skin of each grape on the bunches,
    Marked like a quail's crown,
Those creatures you make such account of,
    Whose heads,—speckled white
Over brown like a great spider's back,
    As I told you last night,—
Your mother bites off for her supper.
    Red-ripe as could be,
Pomegranates were chapping and splitting
    In halves on the tree:
And betwixt the loose walls of great flintstone,
    Or in the thick dust
On the path, or straight out of the rock-side,
    Wherever could thrust
Some burnt sprig of bold hardy rock-flower
    Its yellow face up,
For the prize were great butterflies fighting,
    Some five for one cup.
So, I guessed, ere I got up this morning,
    What change was in store,
By the quick rustle-down of the quail-nets
    Which woke me before
I could open my shutter, made fast
    With a bough and a stone,
And look thro' the twisted dead vine-twigs,
    Sole lattice that's known.
Quick and sharp rang the rings down the net-poles,
    While, busy beneath,
Your priest and his brother tugged at them,
    The rain in their teeth.
And out upon all the flat house-roofs
    Where split figs lay drying,
The girls took the frails under cover:
    Nor use seemed in trying
To get out the boats and go fishing,
    For, under the cliff,
Fierce the black water frothed o'er the blind-rock.
    No seeing our skiff

Arrive about noon from Amalfi,
      —Our fisher arrive,
And pitch down his basket before us,
      All trembling alive
With pink and grey jellies, your sea-fruit;
      You touch the strange lumps,
And mouths gape there, eyes open, all manner
      Of horns and of humps,
Which only the fisher looks grave at,
      While round him like imps
Cling screaming the children as naked
      And brown as his shrimps;
Himself too as bare to the middle
      —You see round his neck
The string and its brass coin suspended,
      That saves him from wreck.
But to-day not a boat reached Salerno,
      So back, to a man,
Came our friends, with whose help in the vineyards
      Grape-harvest began.
In the vat, halfway up in our house-side,
      Like blood the juice spins,
While your brother all bare-legged is dancing
      Till breathless he grins
Dead-beaten in effort on effort
      To keep the grapes under,
Since still when he seems all but master,
      In pours the fresh plunder
From girls who keep coming and going
      With basket on shoulder,
And eyes shut against the rain's driving;
      Your girls that are older,—
For under the hedges of aloe,
      And where, on its bed
Of the orchard's black mould, the love-apple
      Lies pulpy and red,
All the young ones are kneeling and filling
      Their laps with the snails
Tempted out by this first rainy weather,—
      Your best of regales,

As to-night will be proved to my sorrow,
  When, supping in state,
We shall feast our grape-gleaners (two dozen,
  Three over one plate)
With lasagne so tempting to swallow
  In slippery ropes,
And gourds fried in great purple slices,
  That colour of popes.
Meantime, see the grape bunch they've brought you:
  The rain-water slips
O'er the heavy blue bloom on each globe
  Which the wasp to your lips
Still follows with fretful persistence:
  Nay, taste, while awake,
This half of a curd-white smooth cheese-ball
  That peels, flake by flake,
Like an onion, each smoother and whiter;
  Next, sip this weak wine
From the thin green glass flask, with its stopper,
  A leaf of the vine;
And end with the prickly-pear's red flesh
  That leaves thro' its juice
The stony black seeds on your pearl-teeth.
  Scirocco is loose!
Hark, the quick, whistling pelt of the olives
  Which, thick in one's track,
Tempt the stranger to pick up and bite them,
  Tho' not yet half black!
How the old twisted olive trunks shudder,
  The medlars let fall
Their hard fruit, and the brittle great fig-trees
  Snap off, figs and all,
For here comes the whole of the tempest!
  No refuge, but creep
Back again to my side and my shoulder,
  And listen or sleep.

O how will your country show next week,
  When all the vine-boughs
Have been stripped of their foliage to pasture
  The mules and the cows?
Last eve, I rode over the mountains;
  Your brother, my guide,

Soon left me, to feast on the myrtles
    That offered, each side,
Their fruit-balls, black, glossy and luscious,—
    Or strip from the sorbs
A treasure, or, rosy and wondrous,
    Those hairy gold orbs!
But my mule picked his sure sober path out,
    Just stopping to neigh
When he recognized down in the valley
    His mates on their way
With the faggots and barrels of water;
    And soon we emerged
From the plain, where the woods could scarce follow;
    And still as we urged
Our way, the woods wondered, and left us,
    As up still we trudged
Though the wild path grew wilder each instant,
    And place was e'en grudged
'Mid the rock-chasms and piles of loose stones
    Like the loose broken teeth
Of some monster which climbed there to die
    From the ocean beneath—
Place was grudged to the silver-grey fume-weed
    That clung to the path,
And dark rosemary ever a-dying
    That, 'spite the wind's wrath,
So loves the salt rock's face to seaward,
    And lentisks as staunch
To the stone where they root and bear berries,
    And . . . what shows a branch
Coral-coloured, transparent, with circlets
    Of pale seagreen leaves;
Over all trod my mule with the caution
    Of gleaners o'er sheaves,
Still, foot after foot like a lady,
    Till, round after round,
He climbed to the top of Calvano,
    And God's own profound
Was above me, and round me the mountains,
    And under, the sea,
And within me my heart to bear witness
    What was and shall be.

Oh, heaven and the terrible crystal!
    No rampart excludes
Your eye from the life to be lived
    In the blue solitudes.
Oh, those mountains, their infinite movement!
    Still moving with you;
For, ever some new head and breast of them
    Thrusts into view
To observe the intruder; you see it
    If quickly you turn
And, before they escape you surprise them.
    They grudge you should learn
How the soft plains they look on, lean over
    And love (they pretend)
—Cower beneath them, the flat sea-pine crouches,
    The wild fruit-trees bend,
E'en the myrtle-leaves curl, shrink and shut:
    All is silent and grave:
'T is a sensual and timorous beauty,
    How fair! but a slave.
So, I turned to the sea; and there slumbered
    As greenly as ever
Those isles of the siren, your Galli;
    No ages can sever
The Three, nor enable their sister
    To join them,—halfway
On the voyage, she looked at Ulysses—
    No farther to-day,
Tho' the small one, just launched in the wave,
    Watches breast-high and steady
From under the rock, her bold sister
    Swum halfway already.
Fortù, shall we sail there together
    And see from the sides
Quite new rocks show their faces, new haunts
    Where the siren abides?
Shall we sail round and round them, close over
    The rocks, tho' unseen,
That ruffle the grey glassy water
    To glorious green?
Then scramble from splinter to splinter,
    Reach land and explore,
On the largest, the strange square black turret
    With never a door,

Just a loop to admit the quick lizards;
    Then, stand there and hear
The birds' quiet singing, that tells us
    What life is, so clear?
—The secret they sang to Ulysses
    When, ages ago,
He heard and he knew this life's secret
    I hear and I know.

Robert Browning

281   Italy of the South

What I love best in all the world
Is a castle, precipice-encurled,
In a gash of the wind-grieved Apennine.
Or look for me, old fellow of mine,
(If I get my head from out the mouth
O' the grave, and loose my spirit's bands,
And come again to the land of lands)—
In a sea-side house to the farther South,
Where the baked cicala die of drouth,
And one sharp tree—'tis a cypress—stands,
By the many hundred years red-rusted,
Rough iron-spiked, ripe fruit-o'ercrusted,
My sentinel to guard the sands
To the water's edge. For, what expands
Before the house, but the great opaque
Blue breadth of sea without a break?
While, in the house, for ever crumbles
Some fragment of the frescoed walls,
From blisters where a scorpion sprawls.
A girl bare-footed brings, and tumbles
Down on the pavement, green-flesh melons,
And says there's news to-day—the king
Was shot at, touched in the liver-wing,
Goes with his Bourbon arm in a sling:
—She hopes they have not caught the felons.
Italy, my Italy!
Queen Mary's saying serves for me—
    (When fortune's malice
    Lost her—Calais)—
Open my heart and you will see
Graved inside of it, 'Italy.'
Such lovers old are I and she:
So it always was, so shall ever be!

Robert Browning

282   Upon Apennine Slope

Yet to the wondrous St Peter's, and yet to the solemn
   Rotonda,
  Mingling with heroes and gods, yet to the Vatican walls,
Yet may we go, and recline, while a whole mighty world seem
   above us
  Gathered and fixed to all time into one roofing supreme;
Yet may we, thinking on these things, exclude what is meaner
   around us;
  Yet, at the worst of the worst, books and a chamber remain;
Yet may we think, and forget, and possess our souls in
   resistance.—
  Ah, but away from the stir, shouting, and gossip of war,
Where, upon Apennine slope, with the chestnut the oak-trees
   immingle,
  Where amid odorous copse bridle-paths wander and wind,
Where under mulberry-branches the diligent rivulet sparkles,
  Or amid cotton and maize peasants their water-works ply,
Where, over fig-tree and orange in tier upon tier still repeated,
  Garden on garden upreared, balconies step to the sky,—
Ah, that I were, far away from the crowd and the streets of the
   city,
  Under the vine-trellis laid, O my beloved, with thee!

Arthur Hugh Clough

283   Aurora Leigh's Return to Italy
(i)
Olives and Mountains

I felt the wind soft from the land of souls;
The old miraculous mountains heaved in sight,
One straining past another along the shore,
The way of grand dull Odyssean ghosts,
Athirst to drink the cool blue wine of seas
And stare on voyagers. Peak pushing peak
They stood: I watched, beyond that Tyrian belt
Of intense sea betwixt them and the ship,
Down all their sides the misty olive-woods
Dissolving in the weak congenial moon
And still disclosing some brown convent-tower
That seems as if it grew from some brown rock,
Or many a little lighted village, dropt

Like a fallen star upon so high a point,
You wonder what can keep it in its place
From sliding headlong with the waterfalls
Which powder all the myrtle and orange groves
With spray of silver. Thus my Italy
Was stealing on us. Genoa broke with day,
The Doria's long pale palace striking out,
From green hills in advance of the white town,
A marble finger dominant to ships,
Seen glimmering through the uncertain gray of
        dawn.

And then I did not think, 'my Italy,'
I thought, 'my father!' O my father's house,
Without his presence!—Places are too much
Or else too little, for immortal man,—
Too little, when love's May o'ergrows the ground,
Too much, when that luxuriant robe of green
Is rustling to our ankles in dead leaves.
'T is only good to be or here or there,
Because we had a dream on such a stone,
Or this or that,—but, once being wholly waked
And come back to the stone without the dream,
We trip upon 't,—alas, and hurt ourselves;
Or else it falls on us and grinds us flat,
The heaviest grave-stone on this burying earth.

(ii)
Florence

I found a house at Florence on the hill
Of Bellosguardo. 'T is a tower which keeps
A post of double-observation o'er
That valley of Arno (holding as a hand
The outspread city,) straight toward Fiesole
And Mount Morello and the setting sun,
The Vallombrosan mountains opposite,
Which sunrise fills as full as crystal cups
Turned red to the brim because their wine is red.
No sun could die nor yet be born unseen
By dwellers at my villa: morn and even
Were magnified before us in the pure
Illimitable space and pause of sky,

Intense as angels' garments blanched with God,
Less blue than radiant. From the outer wall
Of the garden, drops the mystic floating gray
Of olive-trees, (with interruptions green
From maize and vine) until 't is caught and torn
Upon the abrupt black line of cypresses
Which signs the way to Florence. Beautiful
The city lies along the ample vale,
Cathedral, tower and palace, piazza and street,
The river trailing like a silver cord
Through all, and curling loosely, both before
And after, over the whole stretch of land
Sown whitely up and down its opposite slopes
With farms and villas.

(iii)
Tuscan Life

The days went by. I took up the old days,
With all their Tuscan pleasures worn and spoiled,
Like some lost book we dropt in the long grass
On such a happy summer-afternoon
When last we read it with a loving friend,
And find in autumn when the friend is gone,
The grass cut short, the weather changed, too late
And stare at, as at something wonderful
For sorrow,—thinking how two hands before
Had held up what is left to only one,
And how we smiled when such a vehement nail
Impressed the tiny dint here which presents
This verse in fire for ever. Tenderly
And mournfully I lived. . . . I knew the birds
And insects,—which looked fathered by the flowers
And emulous of their hues: I recognised
The moths, with that great overpoise of wings
Which make a mystery of them how at all
They can stop flying: butterflies, that bear
Upon their blue wings such red embers round,
They seem to scorch the blue air into holes
Each flight they take: and fire-flies, that suspire
In short soft lapses of transported flame
Across the tingling Dark, while overhead
The constant and inviolable stars

Outburn those light-of-love: melodious owls,
(If music had but one note and was sad,
'T would sound just so); and all the silent swirl
Of bats that seem to follow in the air
Some grand circumference of a shadowy dome
To which we are blind: and then the nightingales,
Which pluck our heart across a garden-wall
(When walking in the town) and carry it
So high into the bowery almond-trees
We tremble and are afraid, and feel as if
The golden flood of moonlight unaware
Dissolved the pillars of the steady earth
And made it less substantial. And I knew
The harmless opal snakes, the large-mouthed frogs
(Those noisy vaunters of their shallow streams);
And lizards, the green lightnings of the wall,
Which, if you sit down quiet, nor sigh loud,
Will flatter you and take you for a stone,
And flash familiarly about your feet
With such prodigious eyes in such small heads!—
I knew them, (though they had somewhat
        dwindled from
My childish imagery,) and kept in mind
How last I sate among them equally,
In fellowship and mateship, as a child
Feels equal still toward insect, beast, and bird,
Before the Adam in him has foregone
All privilege of Eden,—making friends
And talk with such a bird or such a goat,
And buying many a two-inch-wide rush-cage
To let out the caged cricket on a tree,
Saying, 'Oh, my dear grillino, were you cramped?
And are you happy with the ilex-leaves?
And do you love me who have let you go?
Say *yes* in singing, and I'll understand.'

                        Elizabeth Barrett Browning

284   Up at a Villa—down in the City
(as distinguished by an Italian person of quality)

I

Had I but plenty of money, money enough and to spare,
The house for me, no doubt, were a house in the city-square;
Ah, such a life, such a life, as one leads at the window there!

II

Something to see, by Bacchus, something to hear, at least!
There, the whole day long, one's life is a perfect feast;
While up at a villa one lives, I maintain it, no more than a
        beast.

III

Well now, look at our villa! stuck like the horn of a bull
Just on a mountain-edge as bare as the creature's skull,
Save a mere shag of a bush with hardly a leaf to pull!
—I scratch my own, sometimes, to see if the hair's turned
        wool.

IV

But the city, oh the city—the square with the houses! Why?
They are stone-faced, white as a curd, there's something to
        take the eye!
Houses in four straight lines, not a single front awry;
You watch who crosses and gossips, who saunters, who
        hurries by;
Green blinds, as a matter of course, to draw when the sun
        gets high;
And the shops with fanciful signs which are painted properly.

V

What of a villa? Though winter be over in March by rights,
'T is May perhaps ere the snow shall have withered well off
        the heights:
You've the brown ploughed land before, where the oxen
        steam and wheeze,
And the hills over-smoked behind by the faint grey
        olive-trees.

VI

Is it better in May, I ask you? You've summer all at once;
In a day he leaps complete with a few strong April suns.
'Mid the sharp short emerald wheat, scarce risen three fingers
　　well,
The wild tulip, at end of its tube, blows out its great red
　　bell
Like a thin clear bubble of blood, for the children to pick and
　　sell.

VII

Is it ever hot in the square? There's a fountain to spout and
　　splash!
In the shade it sings and springs; in the shine such foam-bows
　　flash
On the horses with curling fish-tails, that prance and paddle
　　and pash
Round the lady atop in her conch—fifty gazers do not abash,
Though all that she wears is some weeds round her waist in a
　　sort of sash.

VIII

All the year long at the villa, nothing to see though you
　　linger,
Except yon cypress that points like death's lean lifted
　　forefinger.
Some think fireflies pretty, when they mix i' the corn and
　　mingle,
Or thrid the stinking hemp till the stalks of it seem a-tingle.
Late August or early September, the stunning cicala is shrill,
And the bees keep their tiresome whine round the resinous
　　firs on the hill.
Enough of the seasons,—I spare you the months of the fever
　　and chill.

IX

Ere you open your eyes in the city, the blessed church-bells
　　begin:
No sooner the bells leave off than the diligence rattles in:
You get the pick of the news, and it costs you never a pin.
By-and-by there's the travelling doctor gives pills, lets blood,
　　draws teeth;
Or the Pulcinello-trumpet breaks up the market beneath.

At the post-office such a scene-picture—the new play, piping
hot!

And a notice how, only this morning, three liberal thieves
were shot.

Above it, behold the Archbishop's most fatherly of rebukes,

And beneath, with his crown and his lion, some little new
law of the Duke's!

Or a sonnet with flowery marge, to the Reverend Don
So-and-so

Who is Dante, Boccaccio, Petrarca, Saint Jerome and Cicero,

'And moreover,' (the sonnet goes rhyming,) 'the skirts of
Saint Paul has reached,

'Having preached us those six Lent-lectures more unctuous
than ever he preached.'

Noon strikes,—here sweeps the procession! our Lady borne
smiling and smart

With a pink gauze gown all spangles, and seven swords stuck
in her heart!

Bang-whang-whang goes the drum, *tootle-te-tootle* the fife;

No keeping one's haunches still: it's the greatest pleasure in
life.

X

But bless you, it's dear—it's dear! fowls, wine, at double the
rate.

They have clapped a new tax upon salt, and what oil pays
passing the gate

It's a horror to think of. And so, the villa for me, not the
city!

Beggars can scarcely be choosers: but still—ah, the pity, the
pity!

Look, two and two go the priests, then the monks with cowl
and sandals,

And the penitents dressed in white shirts, a-holding the
yellow candles;

One, he carries a flag up straight, and another a cross with
handles,

And the Duke's guard brings up the rear, for the better
prevention of scandals:

Bang-whang-whang goes the drum, *tootle-te-tootle* the fife.

Oh, a day in the city-square, there is no such pleasure in life!

Robert Browning

285   Rome

(i)

Rome disappoints me much,—St. Peter's, perhaps, in especial;
Only the Arch of Titus and view from the Lateran please me:
This, however, perhaps, is the weather, which truly is horrid.
Greece must be better, surely; and yet I am feeling so spiteful,
That I could travel to Athens, to Delphi, and Troy, and Mount
      Sinai,
Though but to see with my eyes that these are vanity also.
   Rome disappoints me much; I hardly as yet understand, but
Rubbishy seems the word that most exactly would suit it.
All the foolish destructions, and all the sillier savings,
All the incongruous things of past incompatible ages,
Seem to be treasured up here to make fools of present and
      future.
Would to Heaven the old Goths had made a cleaner sweep of it!
Would to Heaven some new ones would come and destroy
      these churches!
However, one can live in Rome as also in London.
Rome is better than London, because it is other than London.

(ii)

Rome disappoints me still; but I shrink and adapt myself to it.
Somehow a tyrannous sense of a superincumbent oppression
Still, wherever I go, accompanies ever, and makes me
Feel like a tree (shall I say?) buried under a ruin of brickwork.
Rome, believe me, my friend, is like its own Monte Testaceo,
Merely a marvellous mass of broken and castaway wine-pots.
Ye gods! what do I want with this rubbish of ages departed,
Things that nature abhors, the experiments that she has failed in?
What do I find in the Forum? An archway and two or three
      pillars.
Well, but St. Peter's? Alas, Bernini has filled it with sculpture!
No one can cavil, I grant, at the size of the great Coliseum.
Doubtless the notion of grand and capacious and massive
      amusement,
This the old Romans had; but tell me, is this an idea?
Yet of solidity much, but of splendour little is extant:
'Brickwork I found thee, and marble I left thee!' their Emperor
      vaunted;
'Marble I thought thee, and brickwork I find thee!' the Tourist
      may answer.

                                        Arthur Hugh Clough

286　The Valley and Villa of Horace

Tibur is beautiful, too, and the orchard slopes, and the Anio
Falling, falling yet, to the ancient lyrical cadence;
Tibur and Anio's tide; and cool from Lucretilis ever,
With the Digentian stream, and with the Bandusian fountain,
Folded in Sabine recesses, the valley and villa of Horace:—
So not seeing I sang; so seeing and listening say I,
Here as I sit by the stream, as I gaze at the cell of the Sibyl,
Here with Albunea's home and the grove of Tiburnus beside
　　　me;*
Tivoli beautiful is, and musical, O Teverone,
Dashing from mountain to plain, thy parted impetuous
　　　waters!
Tivoli's waters and rocks; and fair under Monte Gennaro
(Haunt even yet, I must think, as I wander and gaze, of the
　　　shadows,
Faded and pale, yet immortal, of Faunus, the Nymphs, and
　　　the Graces),
Fair in itself, and yet fairer with human completing creations,
Folded in Sabine recesses the valley and villa of Horace:—
So not seeing I sang; so now—Nor seeing, nor hearing,
Neither by waterfall lulled, nor folded in sylvan embraces,
Neither by cell of the Sibyl, nor stepping the Monte Gennaro
Seated on Anio's bank, nor sipping Bandusian waters,
But on Montorio's height, looking down on the tile-clad
　　　streets, the
Cupolas, crosses, and domes, the bushes and kitchen-gardens,
Which, by the grace of the Tiber, proclaim themselves Rome
　　　of the Romans,—
But on Montorio's height, looking forth to the vapoury
　　　mountains,
Cheating the prisoner Hope with illusions of vision and
　　　fancy,—
But on Montorio's height, with these weary soldiers by me,
Waiting till Oudinot enter, to reinstate Pope and Tourist.

　　　　　　　　　　　　　　　　　Arthur Hugh Cloug

* —domus Albuneæ resonantis,
Et præceps Anio, et Tiburni lucus, et uda
　Mobilibus pomaria rivis.

287   Cypresses
(Fiesole)

Tuscan cypresses,
What is it?

Folded in like a dark thought,
For which the language is lost,
Tuscan cypresses,
Is there a great secret?
Are our words no good?

The undeliverable secret,
Dead with a dead race and a dead speech, and
      yet
Darkly monumental in you,
Etruscan cypresses.

Ah, how I admire your fidelity,
Dark cypresses!

Is it the secret of the long-nosed Etruscans?
The long-nosed, sensitive-footed, subtly-smiling
      Etruscans,
Who made so little noise outside the cypress
      groves?

Among the sinuous, flame-tall cypresses
That swayed their length of darkness all around
Etruscan-dusky, wavering men of old Etruria:
Naked except for fanciful long shoes,
Going with insidious, half-smiling quietness
And some of Africa's imperturbable sang-froid
About a forgotten business.

What business, then?
Nay, tongues are dead, and words are hollow as
      hollow seed-pods,
Having shed their sound and finished all their
      echoing
Etruscan syllables,
That had the telling.
Yet more I see you darkly concentrate,
Tuscan cypresses,

On one old thought:
On one old slim imperishable thought, while
    you remain
Etruscan cypresses;
Dusky, slim marrow-thought of slender,
    flickering men of Etruria,
Whom Rome called vicious.

Vicious, dark cypresses:
Vicious, you supple, brooding, softly-swaying
    pillars of dark flame.
Monumental to a dead, dead race
Embowered in you!

Were they then vicious, the slender,
    tender-footed
Long-nosed men of Etruria?
Or was their way only evasive and different,
    dark, like cypress-trees in a wind?

They are dead, with all their vices,
And all that is left
Is the shadowy monomania of some cypresses
And tombs.

The smile, the subtle Etruscan smile still lurking
Within the tombs,
Etruscan cypresses.

He laughs longest who laughs last;
Nay, Leonardo only bungled the pure Etruscan
    smile.

What would I not give
To bring back the rare and orchid-like
Evil-yclept Etruscan?
For as to the evil
We have only Roman word for it,
Which I, being a little weary of Roman virtue,
Don't hang much weight on.
For oh, I know, in the dust where we have
    buried
The silenced races and all their abominations,
We have buried so much of the delicate magic of
    life.

There in the deeps
That churn the frankincense and ooze the myrrh,
Cypress shadowy,
Such an aroma of lost human life!

They say the fit survive,
But I invoke the spirits of the lost.
Those that have not survived, the darkly lost,
To bring their meaning back into life again,
Which they have taken away
And wrapt inviolable in soft cypress-trees,
Etruscan cypresses.

Evil, what is evil?
There is only one evil, to deny life
As Rome denied Etruria
And mechanical America Montezuma still.

D. H. Lawrence

288   Bare Almond-Trees
(Taormina, Sicily)

Wet almond-trees, in the rain,
Like iron sticking grimly out of earth;
Black almond trunks, in the rain,
Like iron implements twisted, hideous, out of the
        earth,
Out of the deep, soft fledge of Sicilian winter-green,
Earth-grass uneatable,
Almond trunks curving blackly, iron-dark, climbing
        the slopes.

Almond-tree, beneath the terrace rail,
Black, rusted, iron trunk,
You have welded your thin stems finer,
Like steel, like sensitive steel in the air,
Grey, lavender, sensitive steel, curving thinly and
        brittly up in a parabola.
What are you doing in the December rain?
Have you a strange electric sensitiveness in your steel
        tips?
Do you feel the air for electric influences
Like some strange magnetic apparatus?
Do you take in messages, in some strange code,

From heaven's wolfish, wandering electricity, that
    prowls so constantly round Etna?
Do you take the whisper of sulphur from the air?
Do you hear the chemical accents of the sun?
Do you telephone the roar of the waters over the
    earth?
And from all this, do you make calculations?

Sicily, December's Sicily in a mass of rain
With iron branching blackly, rusted like old, twisted
    implements
And brandishing and stooping over earth's wintry
    fledge, climbing the slopes
Of uneatable soft green!

                              D. H. Lawrence

289   Almond Blossom
(Torrente Fontana Vecchia, Taormina)

Even iron can put forth,
Even iron.

This is the iron age,
But let us take heart
Seeing iron break and bud,
Seeing rusty iron puff with clouds of blossom.

The almond-tree,
December's bare iron hooks sticking out of earth.

The almond-tree,
That knows the deadliest poison, like a snake
In supreme bitterness.

Upon the iron, and upon the steel,
Odd flakes as if of snow, odd bits of snow,
Odd crumbs of melting snow.

But you mistake, it is not from the sky;
From out the iron, and from out the steel,
Flying not down from heaven, but storming up,
Strange storming up from the dense under-earth
Along the iron, to the living steel
In rose-hot tips, and flakes of rose-pale snow
Setting supreme annunciation to the world.

Nay, what a heart of delicate super-faith,
Iron-breaking,
The rusty swords of almond-trees.

Trees suffer, like races, down the long ages.
They wander and are exiled, they live in exile through long ages
Like drawn blades never sheathed, hacked and gone black,
The alien trees in alien lands: and yet
The heart of blossom,
The unquenchable heart of blossom!

Look at the many-cicatrised frail vine, none more scarred and frail,
Yet see him fling himself abroad in fresh abandon
From the small wound-stump.

Even the wilful, obstinate, gummy fig-tree
Can be kept down, but he'll burst like a polyp into prolixity.

And the almond-tree, in exile, in the iron age!

This is the ancient southern earth whence the vases were baked,
    amphoras, craters, cantharus œnochœ, and open-hearted cylix,
Bristling now with the iron of almond-trees

Iron, but unforgotten.
Iron, dawn-hearted,
Ever-beating dawn-heart, enveloped in iron against the exile, against
    the ages.

See it come forth in blossom
From the snow-remembering heart
In long-nighted January,
In the long dark nights of the evening star, and Sirius, and the Etna
    snow-wind through the long night.
Sweating his drops of blood through the long-nighted Gethsemane
Into blossom, into pride, into honey-triumph, into most exquisite
    splendour.
Oh, give me the tree of life in blossom
And the Cross sprouting its superb and fearless flowers!

Something must be reassuring to the almond, in the evening star,
    and the snow-wind, and the long, long nights,
Some memory of far, sun-gentler lands,
So that the faith in his heart smiles again

And his blood ripples with that untellable delight of once-mo
    vindicated faith,
And the Gethsemane blood at the iron pores unfolds, unfolds,
Pearls itself into tenderness of bud
And in a great and sacred forthcoming steps forth, steps out in on
    stride
A naked tree of blossom, like a bridegroom bathing in dew, dives
    of cover,
Frail-naked, utterly uncovered
To the green night-baying of the dog-star, Etna's snow-edged win
And January's loud-seeming sun.

Think of it, from the iron fastness
Suddenly to dare to come out naked, in perfection of blosso
    beyond the sword-rust.
Think, to stand there in full-unfolded nudity, smiling,
With all the snow-wind, and the sun-glare, and the dog-star bayi
    epithalamion.

Oh, honey-bodied beautiful one
Come forth from iron,
Red your heart is.
Fragile-tender, fragile-tender life-body,
More fearless than iron all the time,
And so much prouder, so disdainful of reluctances.

In the distance like hoar-frost, like silvery ghosts communing o
    green hill,
Hoar-frost-like and mysterious.
In the garden raying out
With a body like spray, dawn-tender, and looking about
With such insuperable, subtly-smiling assurance,
Sword-blade born.

Unpromised,
No bounds being set.
Flaked out and come unpromised,
The tree being life-divine,
Fearing nothing, life-blissful at the core
Within iron and earth.

Knots of pink, fish-silvery
In heaven, in blue, blue heaven,

Soundless, bliss-full, wide-rayed, honey-bodied,
Red at the core,
Red at the core,
Knotted in heaven upon the fine light.

Open,
Open,
Five times wide open,
Six times wide open,
And given, and perfect;
And red at the core with the last sore-heartedness,
Sore-hearted-looking.

D. H. Lawrence

290   Peace
(Taormina, below Etna)

Peace is written on the doorstep
In lava.

Peace, black peace congealed.
My heart will know no peace
Till the hill bursts.

Brilliant, intolerable lava,
Brilliant as a powerful burning-glass,
Walking like a royal snake down the mountain
          towards the sea.

Forests, cities, bridges
Gone again in the bright trail of lava.
Naxos thousands of feet below the olive-roots,
And now the olive leaves thousands of feet
          below the lava fire.

Peace congealed in black lava on the doorstep.
Within, white-hot lava, never at peace
Till it burst forth blinding, withering the earth;
To set again into rock,
Grey-black rock.

Call it Peace?

D. H. Lawrence

Acknowledgements

The following are thanked for their permission to include copyright poems:

John Murray (Publishers) Ltd for lines from Sir John Betjeman's *Summoned by Bells* and a poem from his *Collected Poems*.

The Bodley Head Ltd for a poem from Roy Campbell's *Collected Poems*, vol. II.

The executors of the W. H. Davies Estate and Jonathan Cape Ltd for a poem from *The Complete Poems of W. H. Davies*.

The Literary Trustees of Walter de la Mare and The Society of Authors as their representative for a poem from Walter de la Mare's *Complete Poems* published by Faber and Faber.

Freda Downie for her poem from *Man Dancing with the Moon* published by Mandeville Press.

Faber and Faber Ltd for a poem from *Collected Poems 1909–1962* by T. S. Eliot.

The Society of Authors as the literary representative of the Estate of John Meade Falkner for a poem from John Meade Falkner's *Poems*.

Geoffrey Grigson for four of his poems and Martin Secker and Warburg Ltd, publishers of 'Hardy's Plymouth' from *History of Him* by Geoffrey Grigson.

Poems by Ivor Gurney reprinted by permission of Oxford University Press: from their forthcoming *Selected Poems of Ivor Gurney*, edited by P. J. Kavanagh.

Granada Publishing Ltd for 'Ireland' from John Hewitt's *Collected Poems*.

The Society of Authors as the literary representative of the Estate of A. E. Housman and Jonathan Cape Ltd, publishers of A. E. Housman's *Collected Poems*, for three poems by A. E. Housman.

Editions Gallimard for three poems by Valery Larbaud from *Les poésies de A. O. Barnabooth,* © Editions Gallimard.

The Marvell Press Ltd for a poem from Philip Larkin's *The Less Deceived*.

The Society of Authors as the literary representative of the Estate of Richard le Gallienne for a poem from Richard le Gallienne's *Robert Louis Stevenson and Other Poems*.

Faber and Faber Ltd for three poems from *The Collected Poems of Louis MacNeice*.

John Crowe Ransom's 'Philomela', copyright 1924 by Alfred A. Knopf, Inc. Copyright 1952 by John Crowe Ransom. Reprinted from *Selected Poems*, third edition, revised and enlarged, by John Crowe Ransom, by permission of Alfred A. Knopf, Inc. and Laurence Pollinger Ltd.

London Magazine Editions for a poem by Bernard Spencer from his *Collected Poems* published by Alan Ross Ltd.

William Heinemann Ltd for three poems from *The Collected Poems of Arthur Symons*.

David Higham Associates Ltd, trustees for the copyrights of the late Dylan Thomas, for a poem from Dylan Thomas's *The Poems* published by J. M. Dent Ltd.

A. P. Watt Ltd as representative of Michael Yeats and Macmillan London Ltd for two poems from W. B. Yeats's *Collected Poems*.

Martin Secker and Warburg Ltd for four poems from Andrew Young's *Complete Poems*, edited by Leonard Clark.

Some Notes and References

1   *c.* 1500. Another version is printed in Celia Sisam's *Oxford Book of Medieval English Verse*.

2   *The Faerie Queene*, Book 4, Canto XI, 23–39. In the last two stanzas Spenser draws on Geoffrey of Monmouth's mythical *Historia Regum Britanniæ*. Humber, King of the Huns, kills Albanact, King of Albany, brother of Locrine, King of England. Locrine chases Humber, 'But when he had fled as far as the river, it chanced that he was drowned therein, and thus left his name to the stream.' (Sebastian Evans's tr. of Geoffrey of Monmouth, Book II, Chapter II.)

3   A fragment of Milton's childhood verse.

4   *Richard the Second*, II, i, 40–51.

5   Stanzas 21–3, 'Christ's Triumph after Dark', in *Christ's Victory and Triumph* (1610).

6   *Richard the Second*, III, iii, 47.

7   From Summer, in *The Seasons*, 1438–56.

8   (i) From 'Ode on the Departing Year'. (ii) From 'Fears in Solitude'.

9   *King Lear*, IV, vi, 11–24.

12 From 'Prologue to General Hamley'.

15 From *The Hop Garden*.

16 The successful opening of an unsuccessful poem, which will be found in *Samuel Palmer's Sketch-book 1824*, Trianon Press (1962).

17 From 'The Vales of the Medway' in *Vestigia Retrorsum* (1891). The Medway is seen from the Darland Heights above Chatham.

20 From 'Enoch Arden', 606–8, written while Tennyson was living on the Isle of Wight.

21 Swinburne describes the scenery of the famous landslip west of Bonchurch. It was there in the house called East Dene, with its long garden, above the sea and below St Boniface Down, that Swinburne spent much of his childhood.

22 Six of the twelve stanzas of 'To the Rev. F. D. Maurice', written in 1854, in the ferment which preceded the Crimean War.

24 Victor Hugo lived in exile in the Channel Islands from 1853 to 1870, first of all in Jersey. From 1856 until his return to Paris he lived on Guernsey in Hauteville House.

25 From 'The Garden of Cymodoce'. Swinburne visited the Channel Islands in May 1876, and was drunk with the combination of savagery

and colour on Sark: 'Everywhere the glory of flowers, and splendour of crags and cliffs and sea defy all words.'

26, 27 See note on No. 24.

29 Bodleian MSS Aubrey 2. The Queen was entertained on the downs above Bishop's Cannings (outside Devizes), of which George Ferebe was vicar.

30 From 'The Seven Wonders of England'.

31 From *Poly-Olbion*, Song III, 53–64.

32 Stanzas 1–5 and 12–16 of 'Guilt and Sorrow'.

33 From *The Angel in the House*, Canto VIII, 'Sarum Plain', section 5.

35 From *The Angel in the House*, Canto I, 'The Cathedral Close'.

37 From 'London and Bristol Delineated'.

38 *Les Poésies de A. D. Barnabooth*. Valery Larbaud's pseudonym was a combination of Barnes where he stayed, and Boots (the chemists).

41 William Diaper was curate of Brent *c*. 1710–12.

42 Edwin Henry Burrington's *Serio-Comic History of Bridgwater* (1866).

43 A fragment from Wordsworth's Alfoxden Notebook (*William Wordsworth: The Poems*, ed. J. O. Hayden, 1977).

44 (i) The opening lines of 'This Lime Tree Bower My Prison'. (ii) From 'Fears in Solitude', 203–32.

47 Thomas Bastard the epigrammatist was vicar of Bere Regis, near Dorchester.

53 Of these 'Wessex' heights Inkpen Beacon is in Wiltshire, Wills Neck in Somerset, and Bulbarrow and Pilsdon Pen are in Dorset. The 'great grey Plain' is Salisbury Plain. Yell'ham Bottom is Yellowham Bottom, near Dorchester. Froom is Hardy's spelling of the Frome.

55 From *Britannia's Pastorals*, Book I, Song 5, 471–8.

56 From *Britannia's Pastorals*, Book I, Song 2, 714–41. The great Benedictine Abbey of Tavistock was skirted by the Tavy.

57 Two out of eleven stanzas. *Collected Poems* (1834).

58 From 'Tamerton Church-Tower, or First Love'.

61 Richard Carew's *Survey of Cornwall* (1602).

66 From Chapter Four, 'Cornwall in Childhood', in *Summoned by Bells*.

69 George Wither was an undergraduate of Magdalen College, Oxford, from 1604 to 1606. His (at any rate early) motto was '*Nec habeo, nec careo, nec curo*', 'I neither have, nor lack, nor care.' I suppose he would have repudiated this poem of an undergraduate outing and that motto in the subsequent solemnity of his Puritan days. Medley Weir is up-river from Oxford, Port Meadow on one side, Binsey on the other.

70 Binsey parish is up-river from Oxford, opposite the great Thames-side extent of Port Meadow.

71 John Crowe Ransom from Tennessee was a Rhodes Scholar at Christ Church, Oxford, in 1913, and made his pilgrimage to the classic wood for hearing nightingales.

72 The opening stanzas of 'The Scholar-Gipsy', Arnold's Berkshire, Oxfordshire and Thames poem. Arnold was born and is buried (see

No. 74) at Laleham, on the Thames. He spent much of his childhood there; and was later at Balliol College.

73 The opening stanzas of 'Thyrsis', the companion poem to 'The Scholar-Gipsy'.

74 The closing lines.

76 Untitled fragment of a poem to be called 'Cheery Beggar', Hopkins having given some pence to a cheerful beggar by Magdalen Bridge.

77 Another untitled fragment.

80 Untitled by Morris.

82 Olney, Buckinghamshire, along the banks of the Ouse (cf. Hopkins on the felling of the poplars at Binsey, on the Thames, No. 70).

83 In south-west Oxfordshire, 2 miles from Burford.

84 Written by Ivor Gurney from his asylum.

87 From manuscript.

89 From manuscript, untitled fragments.

92 From *Poly-Olbion*. The Thirteenth Song, 13–40.

95 From *Poly-Olbion*. The Sixe and Twentieth Song, 107–36.

96 From *Sir Gawain and the Green Knight, c.* 1375, 2160–230. The trysting place of Sir Gawayn and the Green Knight has been plausibly identified as Ludchurch, a deep ferny cleft in the Staffordshire moors near Gradbach Glen, not far from Leek. There are steps into the cleft, and an invisible underground waterfall can be heard there in a cave. It is conjectured that the poet was a monk in the Cistercian house of Dieulacres, a few miles south on the outskirts of Leek.

98 From 'The Shepheards Sirena', 165–249, 301–34 (three stanzas omitted).

99 From *Poly-Olbion*. The Sixe and Twentieth Song, 187–220.

104 Twicknam Garden, i.e. Twickenham Park (then, of course, well out of London), the home of Lucy, Countess of Bedford, to whom Donne wrote several of his poems.

108 From 'A Rhapsody ... written upon a meeting with some of his friends at the Globe Tavern'. Cymbeline and Lud were two of the statues of England's mythical kings which stood on the Ludgate.

109 From 'Of Solitude'.

110 From *Trivia or, The Art of Walking the Streets of London*, (i) Book I, 151–74 (ii) Book III, 9–58.

111 From *The Rape of the Lock*.

112 From *Retirement*, 480–500.

114 From *The Prelude* (1805 text), Book VII, 119–228.

116 The opening of Wordsworth's 'Extempore upon the Death of James Hogg'.

127 See note on No. 38. The modest adornment of a little moss that he wants for his grave at All Saints' contrasts with the chrysanthemums which are loaded on French graves on that day.

130 The record of a bright rainbow which Hopkins saw at Havering atte Bower, in Essex, not far from his early home at Stratford, which now forms part of West Ham.

131   From Clare's fragmentary 'Child Harold', written while Clare was in a private asylum at High Beech, in Epping Forest.

132   See note on No. 131.

134   From 'The Apollyonists', stanza 40. Phineas Fletcher was a graduate of King's College, Cambridge.

135   From *The Prelude* (1805 text), (i) Book III, 1–61 (ii) Book III, 246–95.

136   From *In Memoriam*. Tennyson goes to the rooms of his dead friend Hallam at Trinity College, where they had both been undergraduates.

139   From John Clare's 'Child Harold'.

140   From *The Fleece*, Book II.

141   Bodleian Library. MS. Rawl. Poet. 219.

142   From *The Ancient Mansion*, 72–99.

143   From *Delay has Danger*, 715–24. A favourite passage with Tennyson.

144   From *The Borough*, Letter XXII.

145   From *The Borough*, Letter XXIII.

146   Descriptive of some point along the Suffolk shore between Dunwich and Covehithe; probably Easton Broad and Easton Wood. See note on No. 148.

147   'By the North Sea', Part VI. See note on No. 148. A ruined church still stood on the receding cliff top in Swinburne's time, as in Charles Keene's celebrated etching 'A last item of Dunwich'.

148   'By the North Sea', the first six stanzas of Part III. The low Suffolk coast between Covehithe, Southwold and Dunwich. Swinburne stayed at Wangford near Southwold in 1875. The wood by the North Sea at Easton Broad seemed to him lonely enough to be, in winter, Dante's wood of suicides.

149   Norfolk, near Hickling Broad.

150   *The Sad Shepherd*, II, vii, 13–27.

151   From *Poly-Olbion*, Song XXV, 139–48.

152   From *Poly-Olbion*, Song XXV, 85–112.

154   In 1875 and into 1876, after his release from prison in Brussels, Verlaine taught at a school at Stickney, in the Fens (where, *inter alia*, he read Tennyson's poems). After leaving Stickney he lived for a while in 1876 at the Whale Inn at Boston.

156   (ii) From 'The Palace of Art'. (iii) From 'The Last Tournament'.

157   From *In Memoriam*. Tennyson was born in the rectory at Somersby, which the family and himself left in 1837, when he was still writing *In Memoriam*.

158   From *In Memoriam*. Tennyson mourns his friend Hallam, whose body (hence the last two lines of this Lincolnshire piece) was coming home by sea from Trieste.

159   From *The Prelude* (1805 text), Book VII, 1–65.

160   The most luxuriant large primroses grow all the way up the hill path to the ruins of Montgomery Castle.

161   The Priory Groves, as they are now called, are close to the cathedral at Brecon. They were the grounds of Vaughan's friend, Colonel Herbert Price.

162 Vaughan's 'drowsy lake' is unquestionably Llangorse Lake near his home and birthplace at Newton, in Llansantffraed-juxta-Usk, Breconshire. Drowsy exactly describes a lake which often has a misty and curiously vague look.

163 In the first line the accepted texts follow what is likely to have been a misreading by the London printer of *Silex Scintillans*, Vaughan's second book, in which the poem appeared (1650): 'use' makes poor sense, 'Usk' makes good sense and clarifies the fourth line. Vaughan compares his blood with the Usk which flows down through a red sandstone soil, and turns red in spate.

165 Thomas Vaughan, clergyman, mystical and alchemical writer, and twin brother of Henry Vaughan, inserted his poem on the Usk, the river the twins loved so much, in his *Anima Magica Abscondita or, A Discourse of the Universal Spirit of Nature* (1650), with these prefatory words: 'Sometimes thou mayst walk in groves, which being full of majesty will much advance the soul; sometimes by clear, active rivers, for by such—say the mystic poets—Apollo contemplated.

> *All things which Phœbus in his musing spake*
> *The bless'd Eurotas heard.'*

And he went on with the sentence I have put above his poem as a title: 'So have I spent on the banks of Ysca many a serious hour.'

166 Probably Vaughan had in mind the Ffrwdgrech Falls on the Llwch, near Brecon, by a lane which clambers up towards the Brecon Beacons. In line 33 Vaughan's 'loud brook' is a more or less apt translation of 'Ffrwdgrech', which means bubbling or noisy stream.

167 The opening lines of the poem 'Looking Back'.

169 From 'Ambarvalia'.

172 A fragment untitled by Hopkins about either the Raven Falls or Rhaiadr Ddu, near Maentwrog in North Wales.

173 Maenefa, i.e. Moel Maenefa (949 ft) above St Beuno's College, east of St Asaph, where Hopkins studied with the Jesuits. It looks down on the Vale of Clwyd.

174 In the Vale of Clwyd. Hopkins to Robert Bridges, 1 Sept. 1877: 'The Hurrahing Sonnet was the outcome of half an hour of extreme enthusiasm as I walked home'—i.e. to St Beuno's College—'alone one day from fishing in the Elwy.'

177 From *In Memoriam*. 'The Danube to the Severn...'—Hallam died at Vienna, and was buried at Clevedon, above the mouth of the Severn. Tennyson wrote this section of his memorial sequence at Tintern Abbey, on the Wye. He had observed, in his words, how 'the rapids of the Wye are stilled by the incoming sea', that is to say by the high tide pushing up from the Severn.

179 The opening lines of *The Vision Concerning Piers Plowman*. It is supposed that Langland had in mind the stream at Colwall below the Herefordshire Beacon, which has its source in the Pewtress Well.

180 Two extracts from the First Book of *Aurora Leigh* (1857). Elizabeth Barrett lived as a child at Hope End, Colwall, and though the poem

speaks of Shropshire, it is the Herefordshire scenery she is describing.

182 Untitled by Housman.

184 It seems that Lord de Tabley was picturing the churchyard of Shotwick on the Dee, and that the poem commemorates his mother, who died in 1869. But she was buried in Berkshire, not at Shotwick.

186 A weak second stanza omitted. T. E. Brown grew up in Kirk Braddan Vicarage, outside Douglas in the Isle of Man. From Slieau Whallian, according to tradition, Manx witches were rolled to death in spiked barrels.

187 From *The Prelude* (1805 text), Book I, 301–50. The raven's nest was on Yewdale Crags.

188 From *The Prelude* (1805 text), Book I, 442–89.

189 Wordsworth's note: 'This poem was suggested on the banks of the brook that runs through Easedale, which is, in some parts of its course, as wild and beautiful as brook can be. I have composed thousands of verses by the side of it.'

190 From *The Prelude* (1805 text), Book II, 143–80.

191 From *The Prelude* (1805 text), Book I, 357–427.

193 A fragment, published in *William Wordsworth: The Poems*, ed. J. O. Hayden (1977).

194 From *The Prelude* (1805 text), Book VII, 1–61.

195 From 'Hyperion' ii, 34–40. Keats visited the stone circle of The Carles, under Blencathra, near Keswick, on 28 June 1818.

196 From 'A Vision of Judgement'.

199 The first fifty-eight lines.

200 From 'Memorial Verses'. Wordsworth's grave is in the churchyard at Grasmere, beside the Rothay, in a family corner.

201 The opening stanzas of 'The Hayswater Boat', which the young Arnold included in his first miscellaneous collection in 1849, and never reprinted; no doubt because the poem went on to speak of little people out of the fells boarding the mysterious lonely boat. Hayeswater is a high tarn north-east of Ambleside. Its beck runs down into Patterdale.

202 From 'Upon Appleton House', stanzas 76–81.

204 'Haworth Churchyard', less the opening fifty-four lines, and the epilogue which Arnold added thirty years later.

206 The version printed by F. W. Moorman in his *Yorkshire Dialect Poems* (1917).

208 John Bell, *Rhymes of the Northern Bards* (1812).

209 George Chatt, *Miscellaneous Poems* (Hexham, 1866). See note on No. 210.

210 Freda Downie, *Man Dancing with the Moon* (Mandeville Press, 1979). Elsdon is a lonely, rather peculiar village in Northumberland curlew country, near Rothbury. The three skulls preserved in the church are horse skulls.

211 Robert Chambers, *Popular Rhymes of Scotland* (1826).

212 From *The Lay of the Last Minstrel*, Canto VI, ii.

13   Kenneth Jackson, *Early Celtic Nature Poetry* (1935). A poem from the *Agallamh na senorach*, *c.* 1200.

14   Ardrossan looks across the Firth of Clyde to Arran (see No. 213).

16   From *Marmion*, Canto IV, XXX.

17   From *The Lay of the Last Minstrel*, Canto II.

20   From *Marmion*, the opening thirty-six lines of the Introduction to Canto I.

21   There is no village of Balmaquhapple; which is not to say that James Hogg was not thinking of a real village in Selkirkshire or Perthshire.

26   From *The Bothie of Tober-na-Vuolich*, III, 19–57.

27   The burn is the brief Arklet Water running down from Loch Arklet to Inversnaid, and so into Loch Lomond, on the eastern shore.

32   From *Mully of Mountown* (1702). Mountown was a house and estate on the edge of Dublin.

34   I take the 'airy mountain' to be Slieveleague, which drops from a ridge to the sea on one side and to a dark lake on the other side. Allingham grew up in Ballyshannon which looks across Donegal Bay to Slieveleague.

55   From *Of the Day Estivall*. Though he became a severe Puritan, Alexander Hume went to Paris as a young man to study law. During his four years in France he must have visited, I would say on the evidence of this poem, the neighbourhood of Bordeaux, and then have written this wine-country piece—perhaps about the country where the Dordogne flows into the Gironde—amazed by a Midsummer Day's heat so different from that of his Scotch summers. Scotch commentators like to deny that he is picturing a French scene, but what about the salads with olive oil, the wine in *caves*, the peaches, and the honey plums, i.e. *reines claudes* or greengages, which reached the British Isles only in 1724?

256   Racan's *cabane*, his *séjour de l'innocence*, was the very considerable Château de la Roche-Racan, in Indre-et-Loire, which he built for himself. In his village of St-Paterne-Racan they preserve a chasuble which Mme de Racan worked deliciously in coloured silks. Cotton's 'The Retirement' (No. 100) owes something to this famous poem.

257   The child is Wordsworth's, by the French girl Annette Vallon.

258   A fragment.

259   In 1843, the year of this poem, Mont-St-Michel (which is visible across the bay from Avranches) was still a prison.

260   The opening of a long poem. Lebrun grew up in the *château* at Tancarville; and returned in the year of his fame as a dramatist. It was in 1825, the same year, that he visited Scott at Abbotsford. Scott, who liked him, could not get his name right, and was always addressing him as M. Lenoir. Petrol, not moss and leaves and the tidal Seine, is the modern smell at Tancarville, from the barges which go up and down under the great modern suspension bridge.

261   Bray-sur-Marne does not exist, but Victor Hugo obviously was thinking of a real Champagne village and villagers he didn't wish to

upset—perhaps Chelles (now a small town), a few miles east of Par
on the north bank of the Marne. Another of his poems is about Chell
by name ('J'aime Chelles et ses cressonières ...'). The opening
Hugo's *Les Misérables* (1862), with the child Cosette, is imagined
Chelles.

262 From the section 'La Mer de Bretagne', in *Les Trophées*. The paint
was Heredia's friend Emmanuel Lansyer.

265 The first six of sixteen stanzas.

269 From 'Présentation de la Beauce à Notre-Dame de Chartres'. Claud
was a native of the great plain of the Beauce, born at Orléans.

272 From *Paradise Lost*, Book I, 300–4.

274 One of Chénier's many fragments. He had visited Italy.

275 From *Childe Harold's Pilgrimage*, the opening stanzas of Canto IV.

276 *Ruines of Rome*, sonnets 3, 27 and 28. Spenser was an undergraduate
Cambridge when he made his versions of du Bellay's *Les Antiquitez d*
Rome. Du Bellay had been four years in Rome.

277 From *Childe Harold's Pilgrimage*, Canto IV, stanzas CIII–CVII.

278 From *Adonais*, stanzas XLIX–LIII.

279 The opening lines of Shelley's 'Ode to Naples'.

280 From 'The Englishman in Italy', 13–228.

281 From 'De Gustibus', 14–47.

282 From *Amours de Voyage*, Introduction to Canto III.

283 From *Aurora Leigh*, Seventh Book.

285 From *Amours de Voyage*, Canto I, 13–27, 35–50. Written in 1849, th
year of Garibaldi's defence of Rome and its reoccupation by th
French.

286 From *Amours de Voyage*, Canto III, 214–39.

Index of First Lines

o.		page
˙58	A low-set island this September	101
˙57	A mist that from the moor arose	100
˙60	A mon émotion je sens que j'en approche	325
˙29	A plenteous place is Ireland	286
˙01	A region desolate and wild	258
˙56(ii)	A still salt pool, locked in	206
˙32	A traveller on the skirt of Sarum's Plain	66
˙81	Acton Beauchamp, the poorest place	236
˙22	Ah, London! London! our delight	169
˙25	Ah! vraiment c'est triste	172
˙44	Alas! for Peter not a helping hand	191
˙10	All day the irises have draped blue velvets	270
˙24	An omnibus across the bridge	171
˙16	And now the trembling light	49
˙23	«Angels»! seul coin luisant dans ce Londres du soir	170
˙54	Antres, et vous fontaines	312
˙28	Après avoir aimé des yeux dans Burlington Arcade	175
˙71	Around the quays, kicked off in twos	340
˙13	Arran of the many stags	271
˙36	As I roved out on a summer's morning	293
˙19	As I went down to Dymchurch Wall	56
˙56(iii)	As the crest of some slow-arching wave	206
˙55	As when some wayfaring man passing a wood	88
˙18	At five this morn, when Phoebus raised his head	51
˙74	Beside the broad, gray Thames one lies	115
˙76	Beyond Magdalen and by the Bridge	117
˙04	Blasted with sighs, and surrounded with tears	154
˙19	Blows the wind to-day, and the sun and the rain are flying	277
˙23	Blyth Aberdeane, thow beriall of all tounis	281
˙44(ii)	But now the gentle dew-fall sends abroad	79
˙33	By the great stones we chose our ground	68
˙34	By yellow Chame, where all the Muses reign	180
˙58	Calm is the morn without a sound	207
˙03	Calm was the day, and through the trembling air	149

175	Can I forget the sweet days that have been	22
135(ii)	Caverns there were within my mind	18
119	Ce fut à Londres, ville où l'Anglaise domine	16
26	Ces rocs de l'océan ont tout, terreur et grâce	6
111	Close by those meads, for ever crowned with flowers	15
9	Come on, sir; here's the place	4
94	Coming up England by a different line	13
54	Dean-bourn, farewell; I never look to see	8
147	Death, and change, and darkness everlasting	19
249	Des-Autels, qui redore	30
258	Des vallons de Bourgogne	32
31	Dull heap, that thus thy head	6
221	D'ye ken the big village of Balmaquhapple	27
115	Earth has not anything to show more fair	16
269(i)	Étoile de la mer voici la lourde nappe	33
289	Even iron can put forth	36
80	Fair is the world, now autumn's wearing	11
187	Fair seed-time had my soul	24
167	Fair, shining mountains of my pilgrimage	21
263	Far on its rocky knoll descried	32
143	Far to the left he saw the huts of men	19
100	Farewell, thou busy world, and may	14
176	Five years have past; five summers	22
222	Flow gently, sweet Afton, among thy green braes	28
106	From the dull confines of the drooping West	15
96	Gawayn spurred on	13
72	Go, for they call you, shepherd, from the hill	10
278	Go thou to Rome,—at once the Paradise	34
244	Grey brick upon brick	30
284	Had I but plenty of money, money enough and to spare	35
209	Hae ye ivver been at Elsdon	26
161	Hail sacred shades! cool, leavy house!	21
41	Happy are you, whom Quantock over looks	7
17	Hark! from yon high grey Downs	5
272	He stood and called	34
7	Heavens! what a goodly prospect spreads around	4
152	Here in my vaster pools, as white as snow	19
224	Here lies the body of Elizabeth Charlotte	28
156(i)	Here often, when a child, I lay reclined	20
228	Here the crow starves, here the patient stag	28
63	Hereto I come to view a voiceless ghost	9
248	Heureux qui, comme Ulysse	30
131	How beautiful this hill of fern swells on	17
73	How changed is here each spot man makes or fills	11
202	How safe, methinks, and strong, behind	25
142	How stately stand yon pines upon the hill	19
173	I awoke in the Midsummer not-to-call night	22

33(i)	I felt the wind soft from the land of souls	354
33(ii)	I found a house at Florence	355
30(ii)	I had a little chamber in the house	234
38	I heard the sighing of the reeds	296
59	I loved a lass, a fair one	103
36	I past beside the reverend walls	183
59	I reach the marble-streeted town	92
63	I see the Usk, and know my blood	213
05	I send, I send here my supremest kiss	154
75	I stood in Venice, on the Bridge of Sighs	342
79	I stood within the City disinterred	347
98	I thought of Thee, my partner and my guide	256
13	I wander thro' each charter'd street	161
92	I wandered lonely as a cloud	250
43	I was born in Belfast	299
07	I was thy neighbour once, thou rugged Pile	254
40	I will arise and go now	298
36	I wonder if in that far isle	241
17	If thou would'st view fair Melrose aright	276
52	Il a compris la race antique aux yeux pensifs	327
21	In a coign of a cliff between lowland and highland	57
30	In a quiet-water'd land, a land of roses	286
79	In a somer season, whan softe was the sonne	233
02	In London there I was bent	145
59	In one of these excursions, travelling then	209
46	In Sligo the country was soft	303
90	In summertime on Bredon	128
41	In the wracks of Walsingham	189
17	In this lone, open glade I lie	165
57	Is she not beautiful? reposing there	89
48	It faces west, and round the back and sides	83
62	It happened once, before the duller	95
57	It is a beauteous evening, calm and free	323
35(i)	It was a dreary morning when the Chaise	180
72	It was a hard thing to undo this knot	224
89	It was an April morning: fresh and clear	246
46	It was between the night and day	193
24	Jersey dort dans les flots	60
37	Just now the lilac is in bloom	184
00	Keep fresh the grass upon his grave	258
50	Know ye the witch's dell	198
61	La Champagne est fort laide où je suis	325
46	La mer est plus belle	82
59	La nuit morne tombait	324
38	La pluie tombera tout le jour	71
91	Larches are most fitting to small red hills	129
70	Last autumn, as we sat, ere fall of night	223

154	L'échelonnement des haies	20
45	Le long bois de sapins se tord	8
268	Le long du coteau courbe et des nobles vallées	33
126	Let others chaunt a country praise	17
77	Like shuttles fleet the clouds	11
121	L'immensité de l'humanité	16
101	London, thou art of townes A *per se*	14
89(i)	Long shines the line of wet lamps	12
127	Lorsque je serais mort depuis plusieurs années	17
148	Miles, and miles, and miles of desolation	19
232	Mountown! thou sweet retreat	28
92	Muse, first of Arden tell	13
70	My aspens dear, whose airy cages quelled	10
225	My heart's in the Highlands	28
184	My love lies in the gates of foam	23
98	Near to the silver Trent	13
30	Near Wilton sweet huge heaps of stone are found	6
75(i)	New-dated from the terms that reappear	11
203	No, not tonight	26
188	Nor was this fellowship vouchsaf'd to me	24
8(i)	Not yet enslaved, not wholly vile	4
269(ii)	Nous arrivons vers vous de l'autre Notre Dame	33
20	November dawns and dewy-glooming downs	5
220	November's sky is chill and drear	27
15	Now are our labours crowned with their reward	4
178	Now as I was young and easy under the apple boughs	23
255(ii)	Now noone is went, gaine is mid-day	31
212	O Caledonia! stern and wild	27
95	O Charnwood, be thou called	13
25	O flower of all wind-flowers and sea-flowers	6
250	O fontaine Bellerie	30
185	O Mary, go and call the cattle home	24
8(ii)	O native Britain! O my Mother Isle	4
155	Oh, Boston, Boston, thou hast nought to boast on	20
66(i)	Oh what a host of questions in me rose	98
114	Oh wond'rous power of words, how sweet they are	16
214	On to the beach the quiet waters crept	272
35	Once more I came to Sarum Close	6
191	One evening (surely I was led by her)	24
58	One morn I watch'd the rain subside	8
88	Only the wanderer	127
116	Our haughty life is crowned with darkness	16
65	Out of the night of the sea	97
79	Over, the four long years! And now there rings	118
265	Paris dort: avez-vous, nocturne sentinelle	33
290	Peace is written on the doorstep	36
277	Perchance she died in age—surviving all	344

274	Près des bords où Venise	342
71	Procne, Philomela, and Itylus	106
64	Queer are the ways of a man I know	96
251	Quiconque aura premier la main embesongnée	309
215	Quhy will ye, merchantis of renoun	273
199	Raised are the dripping oars	256
52	Reticulations creep upon the slack stream's face	85
60	Revisiting your marble-paved sea-perfumed town	93
56	Right so this river storms	88
3	Rivers arise; whether thou be the son	41
285(i)	Rome disappoints me much	361
285(ii)	Rome disappoints me still	361
266	Roule, roule ton flot indolent, morne Seine	331
273	Row us out from Desenzano	341
253	Saincte Gastine, ô douce secretaire	311
85	Sand has the ants, clay ferny weeds for play	126
211	Says Tweed to Till	270
195	Scarce images of life, one here, one there	253
130	See on one hand	177
29	Shine, O thou sacred Shepherds' star	64
22	Should all our churchmen foam in spite	59
108	Should we go now a-wand'ring, we should meet	156
168	Silent nymph, with curious eye	219
5	So, in the midst of Neptune's angry tide	41
270	Sous le pont Mirabeau coule la Seine	339
216	Still on the spot Lord Marmion stay'd	275
242	Still south I went and west and south again	298
112	Suburban villas, highway-side retreats	160
174	Summer ends now; now, barbarous in beauty	225
87	Terribly for mystery or glory my dawns have arisen	127
171	That first September day was blue and warm	224
66(ii)	The afternoons	99
233	The Boy from his bedroom-window	288
132	The brakes, like young stag's horns	178
81	The curfew tolls the knell of parting day	120
177	The Danube to the Severn gave	230
40	The darkness like a guillotine	72
283(iii)	The days went by. I took up the old days	356
23	The downs and tender-tinted cliffs	60
6	The fresh green lap of fair King Richard's land	42
255(i)	The golden globe incontinent	315
133	The green roads that end in the forest	179
267	The grey-green stretch of sandy grass	334
235	The Groves of Blarney	290
84	The high hills have a bitterness	125
139	The lake that held a mirror to the sun	188
129	The noises round my house. On cobbles bounding	176

153	The old mayor climbed the belfry tower	200
34	The painted autumn overwhelms	69
39	The place where soon I think to lie	72
82	The poplars are fell'd, farewell to the shade	124
1	The properte of every shire	35
49	The Roman Road runs straight and bare	84
10	The sea is calm to-night	44
110(i)	The seasons operate on ev'ry breast	157
93	The Severn sweeping smooth and broad	130
231	The splendour falls on castle walls	287
50	The spray sprang up across the cusps of the moon	84
138	The summer's morning sun creeps up the blue	188
218	The sun upon the Weirdlaw Hill	276
51	The swallows flew in the curves of an eight	85
151	The toiling fisher here is tewing of his net	199
237	The town of Passage	294
239	The trees are in their autumn beauty	297
183	The vane on Hughley steeple	237
89(ii)	The white faces are lit below the high bank	128
180(i)	Then, land!—then, England!	234
2	Then was there heard a most celestial sound	36
14	There are men in the village of Erith	48
53	There are some heights in Wessex	86
226	There is a stream, I name not its name	284
36	These people have not heard your name	70
43	These populous slopes	78
145	They feel the calm delight, and thus proceed	192
28	Thinking of those who walked here long ago	64
11	This blue-washed, old, thatched summerhouse	45
227	This darksome burn, horseback brown	285
4	This royal throne of kings, this sceptered isle	41
97	This while we are abroad	135
13	Thou art not, Penshurst, built to envious show	46
276	Thou stranger, which for Rome in Rome here seekest	343
109	Thou the faint beams of reason's scattered light	157
75(ii)	Thus, I come underneath this chapel-side	116
286	Tibur is beautiful, too	362
280	Time for rain! for your long hot dry Autumn	348
256	Tircis, il faut penser à faire la retraite	321
165	'Tis day, my crystal Usk	216
182	'Tis time, I think, by Wenlock town	236
78	Towery city and branchy between towers	117
264	Trou de flibustiers, vieux nid	329
287	Tuscan cypresses	363
196	'Twas at that sober hour when the light of day	253
162	'Twas so, I saw thy birth: that drowsy lake	213
120	Un dimanche d'été, quand le soleil s'en mêle	167

27	Un journal! Donnez-moi du papier	63
157	Unwatched, the garden bough shall sway	206
234	Up the airy mountain	289
190	Upon the Eastern Shore of Windermere	248
42	Upon the soft brown pillow of thy shore	77
160	Upon this primrose hill	211
252	Ville de Blois, naissance de ma Dame	311
245	'We are the dead,' we shouted up in fun	302
241	We heard the thrushes by the shore and sea	298
247	We Irish pride ourselves as patriots	304
44(i)	Well, they are gone, and here must I remain	78
288	Wet almond-trees, in the rain	365
37	What friendship can'st thou boast	71
281	What I love best in all the world	353
207	What if outside the dying pine trees	265
99	What should I care at all from what my name I take	139
194	What sounds are those, Helvellyn, which are heard	251
205	Wheear' as tha been sin' ah saw thee	262
164	When Daphne's lover here first wore the bays	214
206	When I were at home wi' my fayther	264
118	When men were all asleep the snow	166
107	When Neptune from his billows London spied	156
110(ii)	When night first bids the twinkling stars appear	158
169	When soft September brings again	223
61	When sun the earth least shadow spares	94
149	When the sea comes in at Horsey Gap	198
83	When Westwell Downs I gan to tread	124
204	Where, behind Keighley, the road	260
208	Where hast 'te been, ma canny hinny	267
166	With what deep murmurs through time's silent stealth	218
47	Wotton, my little Bere dwells on a hill	82
86	Yes. I remember Adlestrop	126
140	Yet much may be performed, to check the force	188
193	Yet once again do I behold the forms	251
282	Yet to the wondrous St Peter's	354
12	You came, and looked and loved the view	46